slow cooker
COOKBOOK

REIMAN MEDIA GROUP, INC.
GREENDALE, WI

Taste of Home · Reader's Digest

A TASTE OF HOME/READER'S DIGEST BOOK
© 2013 Reiman Media Group, Inc.
5400 S. 60th St., Greendale WI 53129

EDITORIAL

Editor-in-Chief: **CATHERINE CASSIDY**
Creative Director: **HOWARD GREENBERG**
Editorial Operations Director: **KERRI BALLIET**

Managing Editor, Print and Digital Books: **MARK HAGEN**
Associate Creative Director: **EDWIN ROBLES JR.**

Editor: **CHRISTINE RUKAVENA**
Art Director: **JESSIE SHARON**
Layout Designers: **NANCY NOVAK, CATHERINE FLETCHER**
Editorial Production Manager: **DENA AHLERS**
Copy Chief: **DEB WARLAUMONT MULVEY**
Copy Editor: **MARY C. HANSON**
Content Operations Manager: **COLLEEN KING**
Executive Assistant: **MARIE BRANNON**

Chief Food Editor: **KAREN BERNER**
Food Editors: **JAMES SCHEND; PEGGY WOODWARD, RD**
Associate Food Editor: **KRISTA LANPHIER**
Associate Editor/Food Content: **ANNIE RUNDLE**
Recipe Editors: **MARY KING; JENNI SHARP, RD; IRENE YEH**

Test Kitchen and Food Styling Manager: **SARAH THOMPSON**
Test Cooks: **MATTHEW HASS, LAUREN KNOELKE**
Food Stylists: **KATHRYN CONRAD (SENIOR), SHANNON ROUM, LEAH REKAU**
Prep Cooks: **MEGUMI GARCIA, NICOLE SPOHRLEDER, BETH VANOPDORP**

Photographers: **DAN ROBERTS, JIM WIELAND**
Photographer/Set Stylist: **GRACE NATOLI SHELDON**
Set Styling Manager: **STEPHANIE MARCHESE**
Set Stylists: **MELISSA HABERMAN, DEE DEE JACQ**

Business Analyst: **KRISTY MARTIN**
Billing Specialist: **MARY ANN KOEBERNIK**

BUSINESS

Vice President, Publisher: **JAN STUDIN, JAN_STUDIN@RD.COM**

General Manager, Taste of Home Cooking Schools: **ERIN PUARIEA**

Vice President, Brand Marketing: **JENNIFER SMITH**
Vice President, Circulation and Continuity Marketing: **DAVE FIEGEL**

READER'S DIGEST NORTH AMERICA

Vice President, Business Development: **JONATHAN BIGHAM**
President, Books and Home Entertaining: **HAROLD CLARKE**
Chief Financial Officer: **HOWARD HALLIGAN**
VP, General Manager, Reader's Digest Media: **MARILYNN JACOBS**
Chief Marketing Officer: **RENEE JORDAN**
Vice President, Chief Sales Officer: **MARK JOSEPHSON**
Vice President, General Manager, Milwaukee: **FRANK QUIGLEY**
Vice President, Chief Content Officer: **LIZ VACCARIELLO**

THE READER'S DIGEST ASSOCIATION, INC.

President and Chief Executive Officer: **ROBERT E. GUTH**

For other **TASTE OF HOME BOOKS** and products,
visit us at **TASTEOFHOME.COM.**

For more **READER'S DIGEST** products and information, visit
RD.COM (in the United States) or see **RD.CA** (in Canada).

International Standard Book Number: **978-1-61765-217-2**
Library of Congress Control Number: **2013931311**

COVER PHOTOGRAPHY

Photographer: **MARK DERSE**
Food Stylist: **KATHRYN CONRAD**
Set Stylist: **PAM STASNEY**

PICTURED ON FRONT COVER:
Beer-Braised Stew, page 52; Potluck Macaroni and Cheese, page 205; Country-Style Pork Loin, page 33; Mexican Taco Filling, page 72.

PICTURED ON BACK COVER:
Italian Chicken and Peppers, page 157; Enchilada Pie, page 19; Blueberry Grunt, page 225.

PICTURED ON SPINE:
Strawberry Rhubarb Sauce, page 241.

PRINTED IN CHINA.
3 5 7 9 10 8 6 4 2

MAY 2014

Contents

Come Home To Dinner!

Nothing beats coming home to a good hot meal already waiting for you. The slow cooker makes it easy and economical to enjoy home-cooked meals on your schedule. This collection of taste-tempting recipes from real home cooks contains 431 delicious creations for your slow cooker!

28

it would cost roughly 21 cents to operate a slow cooker for a total of 10 hours. If you roast a pork roast for only 2 hours in the oven instead of using the slow cooker for 10 hours, you would spend $2.51 to operate an electric oven or $1.49 to operate a gas oven. Also, slow cookers do not heat up the kitchen as ovens do, which saves on summertime home-cooling costs.

Purchasing a Slow Cooker

Slow cookers range in price from $20 to more than $200 and are available in sizes from 1½ to 7 quarts. Decide on a price range that fits your budget and choose a size appropriate for your family (see chart below).

Most slow cooker inserts are ceramic, but some pricier models have aluminum inserts that let you brown meats in them before slow cooking. For convenience, look for inserts that are dishwasher-safe.

Slow cookers are available in round and oval shapes. If you plan to prepare roasts in the slow cooker, you may wish to consider an oval shape. If stews and soups are your forte, then a round slow cooker is perfect for your cooking needs.

Cooking Basics

While slow cooker models vary, they usually have at least two settings, low (about 180°) and high (about 280°). Some models also have a keep-warm setting.

Advantages of Slow Cooking

CONVENIENCE. Slow cookers provide people with the convenience of safely preparing meals while being away from home. The appliances are readily available and budget-friendly.

HEALTH. As more people make better food choices to improve their health, slow cooking has gained popularity. Low-temperature cooking retains more vitamins in the foods, and leaner cuts of meat will become tender in the slow cooker without added fats. Many slow cooker recipes call for condensed soups, but lower-sodium and lower-fat versions can also be used. And, for many busy folks, knowing that a healthy meal is waiting at home helps them avoid the temptation of the drive-thru after work.

FINANCIAL SAVINGS. A slow cooker uses very little electricity because of its low wattage. For instance,

Slow Cooker Sizes	
HOUSEHOLD SIZE	**SLOW COOKER CAPACITY**
1 to 2 people	2 to 3½ quarts
3 to 4 people	3½ to 4½ quarts
4 to 5 people	4½ to 5 quarts
6 or more people	5 to 7 quarts

The keep-warm setting is useful if you plan to use the slow cooker to serve hot foods while entertaining. Some slow cookers will automatically switch to a keep-warm setting after cooking. This provides added convenience and helps you avoid overcooking the food while you're away from home.

A range in cooking time is provided to account for variables such as thickness of meat, the fullness of the slow cooker and desired finished temperature of the food being cooked. As you grow familiar with your slow cooker, you'll be able to judge which end of the range to use.

New slow cookers tend to heat up more quickly than older ones. If you have an older model and your recipe directs to cook on low, you may wish to cook on high for the first hour to ensure food safety.

Old slow cookers can lose their efficiency and may not achieve proper cooking temperatures. To confirm safe cooking temperatures, review the steps of "Slow Cooker Temperature Check" below.

To learn more about specific models, check online or in reputable consumer magazines for product reviews.

Slow Cooker Temperature Check

To be considered safe, a slow cooker must be able to cook slowly enough that it can be left unattended, yet it must be fast enough to keep the food at a proper temperature. Here's how to check your slow cooker:

1. Fill the slow cooker ½ to ⅔ full with room-temperature water.

2. Cover and heat on low for 8 hours.

3. Using a thermometer, check the temperature of the water quickly since the temperature can drop once the lid is removed.

4. The temperature should be at least 185°. If it's too hot, a meal cooked for 8 hours would likely be overdone. If the temperature is below 185°, the slow cooker is not safe to use and should be discarded.

Tips for Tasty Outcomes

- Be sure the lid is well-placed over the ceramic insert, not tilted or askew. The steam during cooking creates a seal.

- No peeking! Refrain from lifting the lid while food cooks in the slow cooker, unless you're instructed in a recipe to stir or add ingredients. The loss of steam can mean an extra 20 to 30 minutes of cooking time each time you lift the lid.

- Slow cooking may take longer at higher altitudes.

- When food is finished cooking, remove it from the slow cooker within 1 hour and promptly refrigerate any leftovers.

- Use a slow cooker on a buffet table to keep soup, stew, savory dips or mashed potatoes hot.

- Don't forget your slow cooker when you go camping, if electricity is available. When space is limited and you want "set-it-and-forget-it" meals, it's a handy appliance.

- Reheating food in a slow cooker is not recommended. Cooked food can be heated on the stovetop or in the microwave and then put into a slow cooker to keep hot for serving.

103

151

Preparing Foods for the Slow Cooker

BEANS. Dried beans can be tricky to cook in a slow cooker. Minerals in the water and variations in voltage affect various type of beans in different ways. Always soak dried beans prior to cooking. Soak them overnight or place them in a Dutch oven and add enough water to cover by 2 inches. Bring to a boil and boil for 2 minutes. Remove from the heat, cover and let stand for 1 to 4 hours or until softened. Drain and rinse beans, discarding liquid. Sugar, salt and acidic ingredients, such as vinegar, interfere with the beans' ability to cook and become tender. Add these ingredients only after the beans are fully cooked. Lentils and split peas do not need soaking.

DAIRY. Milk-based products tend to break down during slow cooking. Items like milk, cream, sour cream or cream cheese are best added during the last hour of cooking. Cheeses don't generally hold up during the slow cooker's extended cooking time and should be added near the end of cooking. Condensed cream soups generally hold up well in the slow cooker.

FISH & SEAFOOD. Fish and seafood cook quickly and can break down if cooked too long. They are generally added to the slow cooker toward the end of the cooking time to keep them at optimal quality.

MEAT. Meat may be browned before adding to the slow cooker. While browning is not necessary, it adds to the flavor and appearance of the meat and allows you to drain off the fat. Cut roasts over 3 pounds in half before placing in the slow cooker to ensure even cooking. Trim off any excess fat. Fat retains heat, and large amounts of fat could raise the temperature of the cooking liquid, causing the meat to overcook.

OATS. Quick-cooking and old-fashioned oats are often interchangeable in recipes. However, old-fashioned oats hold up better in the slow cooker.

PASTA. If added to a slow cooker when dry, pasta tends to become very sticky. It is better to cook it according to the package directions and stir it into the slow cooker just before serving. Small pastas, such as orzo and ditalini, may be cooked in the slow cooker. To keep them from becoming mushy, add during the last hour of cooking.

COUSCOUS. Couscous is best cooked on the stovetop rather than in the slow cooker.

RICE. Converted rice is ideal for all-day cooking. If using instant rice, add it during the last 30 minutes of cooking.

VEGETABLES. Firm vegetables like potatoes and carrots tend to cook more slowly than meat. Cut these foods into uniform pieces and place on the bottom and around the sides of the slow cooker. Place the meat over the vegetables. Add tender vegetables, like peas and zucchini, or ones you'd prefer to be crisp-tender, during the last 15 to 60 minutes of cooking.

Cleaning Tips

- Removable inserts make cleanup a breeze. Be sure to cool the insert before rinsing or cleaning with water to avoid cracking or warping. Do not immerse the metal base in water. Clean it with a damp sponge.

- If dishwasher-safe, place the insert in the dishwasher. Otherwise, wash in warm soapy water. Avoid using abrasive cleansers, since they may scratch the surface.

- To remove mineral stains on a ceramic insert, fill the cooker with hot water and 1 cup of white vinegar; cover. Turn the heat to high for 2 hours, then empty. When cool, wash with hot soapy water and a cloth or sponge. Rinse well and dry with a towel.

- To remove water marks from a highly glazed ceramic insert, rub the surface with canola oil and allow to stand for 2 hours before washing with hot soapy water.

Converting Recipes for the Slow Cooker

Almost any recipe that bakes in the oven or simmers on the stovetop can be converted for the slow cooker. Here are some guidelines:

Select recipes that simmer for at least 45 minutes. Good choices to start with are soups, stews, pot roasts, chili and one-dish meals.

Cooking Times

CONVENTIONAL TIME	SLOW COOKER
45 minutes	**LOW:** 6 to 8 hours **HIGH:** 3 to 4 hours
50 minutes or longer	**LOW:** 8 to 10 hours **HIGH:** 4 to 5 hours

Refer to your slow cooker's guidelines or recipe booklet or this cookbook. Look for a recipe that is similar to the one you want to convert for guidance. Note the quantity and size of the meat and vegetables, heat setting, cooking time and amount of liquid.

Since there is no evaporation, you will probably need to reduce the amount of liquid the recipe calls for. If a recipe calls for 6 to 8 cups of water, start with 5 cups. All slow cooker recipes should call for some liquid. If the recipe does not call for any, add about ½ cup of water, broth or juice.

Thickening Stews, Sauces & Gravies

Quick-cooking tapioca can be used as a thickener for stews. Add it along with other ingredients at the beginning of cooking.

To thicken juices at the end of cooking, use flour or cornstarch. Mix flour or cornstarch with some cold water until smooth. Stir into the slow cooker. Cover and cook on high for 30 minutes or until the cooking juices are thickened.

Or, strain cooking juices and place in a saucepan. Mix flour or cornstarch with some cold water until smooth. Stir into juices. Bring to a boil; cook and stir for 2 minutes or until thickened.

Useful Handles for Lifting Food

Layered dishes or meat loaves are easier to get out of the slow cooker using foil handles. Here's how:

1. For a 3-qt. slow cooker, cut three 20x3-in. strips of heavy-duty foil (or 25x3-in. for larger slow cookers). Or cut 6-inch-wide strips from regular foil and fold in half lengthwise. Crisscross the strips so they resemble the spokes of a wheel.

2. Place strips on the bottom and up the sides of the slow cooker insert. Let strips hang over the edge of the slow cooker. Coat strips with cooking spray.

3. Place food in the center of the strips and lower until the food rest on the bottom of the slow cooker.

4. After cooking, grasp the foil strips and carefully lift food up. Remove food from foil strips and serve.

Power Outage

If you are cooking in a slow cooker and the power goes out, the USDA recommends the following:

- Fully cooked foods are safe at room temperature for up to 2 hours. If they have sat longer than 2 hours, or if the time is uncertain, they should be discarded.

- If the food is not fully cooked and you're home when the power goes out, immediately finish cooking the food by another method, such as a gas stove or grill.

18

19

31

Lightened Up

Lentil & Chicken Sausage Stew

This hearty and healthy stew will warm your family right down to their toes! It's packed with veggies and warm tastes of autumn. Serve it with corn bread or rolls to soak up every last morsel.

—JAN VALDEZ CHICAGO, ILLINOIS

PREP: 15 MIN. **COOK:** 8 HOURS **MAKES:** 6 SERVINGS

- 1 carton (32 ounces) reduced-sodium chicken broth
- 1 can (28 ounces) diced tomatoes, undrained
- 3 fully cooked spicy chicken sausage links (3 ounces each), cut into ½-inch slices
- 1 cup dried lentils, rinsed
- 1 medium onion, chopped
- 1 medium carrot, chopped
- 1 celery rib, chopped
- 2 garlic cloves, minced
- ½ teaspoon dried thyme

In a 4- or 5-qt. slow cooker, combine all ingredients. Cover and cook on low for 8-10 hours or until lentils are tender.

Nutrition Facts: *1½ cups equals 231 calories, 4 g fat (1 g saturated fat), 33 mg cholesterol, 803 mg sodium, 31 g carbohydrate, 13 g fiber, 19 g protein.* **Diabetic Exchanges:** *2 lean meat, 2 vegetable, 1 starch.*

Italian Pulled Pork Sandwiches

Enjoy all the flavors of classic Italian sausage sandwiches with a healthier alternative that uses pulled pork instead.

—DELLARIO LIA MIDDLEPORT, NEW YORK

PREP: 20 MIN. **COOK:** 7 HOURS **MAKES:** 12 SERVINGS

- 1 boneless pork shoulder butt roast (3 pounds)
- 1 tablespoon fennel seed, crushed
- 1 tablespoon steak seasoning
- 1 teaspoon cayenne pepper, optional
- 1 tablespoon olive oil
- 2 medium green or sweet red peppers, thinly sliced
- 2 medium onions, thinly sliced
- 1 can (14½ ounces) diced tomatoes, undrained
- 12 whole wheat hamburger buns, split

1. Cut roast in half. Combine the fennel seed, steak seasoning and cayenne if desired; rub over roast. In a large skillet, brown roast in oil on all sides. Place in a 4- or 5-qt slow cooker. Add the peppers, onions and tomatoes; cover and cook on low for 7-9 hours or until meat is tender.

2. Remove roast; cool slightly. Skim fat from cooking juices. Shred pork with two forks and return to slow cooker; heat through. Using a slotted spoon, place ½ cup meat mixture on each bun.

Editor's Note: *This recipe was tested with McCormick's Montreal Steak Seasoning. Look for it in the spice aisle.*

Nutrition Facts: *1 sandwich equals 288 calories, 8 g fat (2 g saturated fat), 56 mg cholesterol, 454 mg sodium, 27 g carbohydrate, 5 g fiber, 26 g protein.* **Diabetic Exchanges:** *3 lean meat, 2 starch.*

Chinese Pork Chops

These delicious pork chops are so saucy and tender! I got the recipe years ago, and it's been a family favorite ever since.

—SHARON CRIDER
JUNCTION CITY, KANSAS

PREP: 15 MIN. **COOK:** 3 HOURS
MAKES: 6 SERVINGS

- 6 boneless pork loin chops (4 ounces each)
- 1 small onion, finely chopped
- ⅓ cup ketchup
- 3 tablespoons brown sugar
- 3 tablespoons water
- 3 tablespoons reduced-sodium soy sauce
- 1 garlic clove, minced
- 1 teaspoon ground ginger
- 3 cups hot cooked rice

Place pork chops in a 3-qt. slow cooker coated with cooking spray. In a small bowl, combine the onion, ketchup, brown sugar, water, soy sauce, garlic and ginger. Pour over chops. Cover and cook on low for 3-4 hours or until meat is tender. Serve with rice and cooking juices.

Nutrition Facts: *1 pork chop with ½ cup rice and 3 tablespoons juices equals 305 calories, 7 g fat (2 g saturated fat), 55 mg cholesterol, 496 mg sodium, 34 g carbohydrate, 1 g fiber, 25 g protein.* **Diabetic Exchanges:** *3 lean meat, 2 starch.*

KETCHUP

Ketchup is a versatile base for many sauces because it already contains sweet, sour and salty flavors. Brown sugar and soy sauce, plus the traditional Chinese flavorings of garlic and ginger, dress up ketchup in this recipe to make a surprisingly delicious sauce.

FAST FIX ▶ Corn and Broccoli in Cheese Sauce

This popular dish is a standby at our house. My daughter likes to add leftover ham to it. No one will ever guess it's lightened up!

—JOYCE JOHNSON
UNIONTOWN, OHIO

PREP: 10 MIN. **COOK:** 3 HOURS
MAKES: 8 SERVINGS

- 1 package (16 ounces) frozen corn, thawed
- 1 package (16 ounces) frozen broccoli florets, thawed
- 4 ounces reduced-fat process cheese (Velveeta), cubed
- ½ cup shredded cheddar cheese
- 1 can (10¼ ounces) reduced-fat reduced-sodium condensed cream of chicken soup, undiluted
- ¼ cup fat-free milk

In a 4-qt. slow cooker, combine the corn, broccoli and cheeses. In a small bowl, combine soup and milk; pour over vegetable mixture. Cover and cook on low for 3-4 hours or until heated through. Stir before serving.

Nutrition Facts: *¾ cup equals 148 calories, 5 g fat (3 g saturated fat), 16 mg cholesterol, 409 mg sodium, 21 g carbohydrate, 3 g fiber, 8 g protein.* **Diabetic Exchanges:** *1 starch, 1 medium-fat meat.*

Slow Cooker Beef au Jus

It's easy to fix this roast, which has lots of onion flavor. Sometimes I also add cubed potatoes and baby carrots to the slow cooker to make a terrific meal with plenty of leftovers.

—CAROL HILLE
GRAND JUNCTION, COLORADO

PREP: 20 MIN.
COOK: 6 HOURS + STANDING
MAKES: 10 SERVINGS

- 1 **beef rump roast or bottom round roast (3 pounds)**
- 1 **large onion, sliced**
- ¾ **cup reduced-sodium beef broth**
- 1 **envelope (1 ounce) au jus gravy mix**
- 2 **garlic cloves, halved**
- ¼ **teaspoon pepper**

1. Cut roast in half. In a large nonstick skillet coated with cooking spray, brown meat on all sides over medium-high heat.
2. Place onion in a 5-qt. slow cooker. Top with meat. Combine the broth, gravy mix, garlic and pepper; pour over meat. Cover and cook on low for 6-7 hours or until meat is tender.
3. Remove meat to a cutting board. Let stand for 10 minutes. Thinly slice meat and return to the slow cooker; serve with cooking juices and onion.

Nutrition Facts: *3 ounces cooked beef with ¼ cup cooking juices equals 188 calories, 7 g fat (2 g saturated fat), 82 mg cholesterol, 471 mg sodium, 3 g carbohydrate, trace fiber, 28 g protein.* **Diabetic Exchange:** *3 lean meat.*

Slow-Cooked Pork Tacos

Sometimes I'll substitute Bibb lettuce leaves for the tortillas to make crunchy lettuce wraps instead of tacos.

—KATHLEEN WOLF
NAPERVILLE, ILLINOIS

PREP: 20 MIN.   **COOK:** 4 HOURS
MAKES: 10 TACOS

- 1 **boneless pork sirloin roast (2 pounds), cut into 1-inch pieces**
- 1½ **cups salsa verde**
- 1 **medium sweet red pepper, chopped**
- 1 **medium onion, chopped**
- ¼ **cup chopped dried apricots**
- 2 **tablespoons lime juice**
- 2 **garlic cloves, minced**
- 1 **teaspoon ground cumin**
- ½ **teaspoon salt**
- ¼ **teaspoon white pepper**

Dash hot pepper sauce
- 10 **flour tortillas (8 inches), warmed**
  Reduced-fat sour cream, thinly sliced green onions, cubed avocado, shredded reduced-fat cheddar cheese and chopped tomato, optional

1. In a 3-qt. slow cooker, combine the first 11 ingredients. Cover and cook on high for 4-5 hours or until meat is tender.
2. Shred pork with two forks. Place about ½ cup pork mixture down the center of each tortilla. Serve with toppings if desired.

Nutrition Facts: *1 taco (calculated without optional toppings) equals 301 calories, 8 g fat (2 g saturated fat), 54 mg cholesterol, 616 mg sodium, 32 g carbohydrate, 1 g fiber, 24 g protein.* **Diabetic Exchanges:** *3 lean meat, 2 starch.*

Zippy Bean Stew

Bean stew is a staple for both my co-workers and me once the weather turns cool. Although this is a low-fat dish, it definitely doesn't taste like it!

—DEBBIE MATTHEWS
BLUEFIELD, WEST VIRGINIA

PREP: 10 MIN. **COOK:** 4 HOURS
MAKES: 6 SERVINGS

- 1 can (16 ounces) kidney beans, rinsed and drained
- 1 can (15 ounces) pinto beans, rinsed and drained
- 1 can (14½ ounces) diced tomatoes and green chilies
- 1 can (14½ ounces) vegetable broth or reduced-sodium chicken broth
- 2 cups frozen corn, thawed
- 1 can (4 ounces) chopped green chilies, undrained
- 3 cups water
- 2 medium carrots, sliced
- 1 large onion, chopped
- 2 garlic cloves, minced
- 2 teaspoons chili powder

In a 3-qt. slow cooker, combine the beans, tomatoes, broth, corn and chilies. Stir in water, carrots, onion, garlic and chili powder. Cover and cook on high 4-5 hours or until vegetables are tender.

Nutrition Facts: *1½ cups equals 218 calories, 1 g fat (trace saturated fat), 0 cholesterol, 964 mg sodium, 44 g carbohydrate, 10 g fiber, 11 g protein.* **Diabetic Exchanges:** *2 starch, 2 vegetable, 1 lean meat.*

BEANS

||||||||||||||||||||||||||||||||||||||||||||||||||||||||||||||||

Beans pack a nutritional one-two punch of protein and fiber, making them an excellent choice for people watching their weight. Bean recipes satisfy vegetarians and meat-eaters alike.

Slow Cooker Beef Brisket

This brisket is really easy to prepare and has been a family favorite for years. I added the fresh mushrooms to give it even more flavor.

—MARY ANN LEE
CLIFTON PARK, NEW YORK

PREP: 20 MIN. **COOK:** 6 HOURS
MAKES: 6-8 SERVINGS

- 1 fresh beef brisket (3 to 4 pounds)
- ½ pound sliced fresh mushrooms
- 2 bay leaves
- 2 cups crushed tomatoes
- 1 cup chopped onion
- ½ cup packed brown sugar
- ½ cup balsamic vinegar
- ½ cup ketchup
- ¼ cup cornstarch
- ¼ cup cold water

1. Cut brisket in half; place in a 5-qt. slow cooker. Add mushrooms and bay leaves. Combine the tomatoes, onion, brown sugar, vinegar and ketchup; pour over beef. Cover and cook on low for 6-7 hours or until meat is tender.

2. Remove beef and keep warm. Discard bay leaves. In a large saucepan, combine cornstarch and cold water until smooth. Gradually stir in cooking liquid. Bring to a boil; cook and stir for 2 minutes or until thickened. Slice meat across the grain; serve with gravy.

Editor's Note: *This is a fresh beef brisket, not corned beef.*

Nutrition Facts: *5 ounces cooked meat with ½ cup gravy equals 341 calories, 8 g fat (3 g saturated fat), 72 mg cholesterol, 339 mg sodium, 31 g carbohydrate, 2 g fiber, 37 g protein.* **Diabetic Exchanges:** *5 lean meat, 2 starch.*

Coconut Curry Chicken

My husband and I love this yummy dish! It's a breeze to prepare in the slow cooker, and it tastes just like a meal you'd have at your favorite Indian or Thai restaurant.
—**ANDI KAUFFMAN** BEAVERCREEK, OREGON

PREP: 20 MIN. **COOK:** 5 HOURS **MAKES:** 4 SERVINGS

- 2 **medium potatoes, peeled and cubed**
- 1 **small onion, chopped**
- 4 **boneless skinless chicken breast halves (4 ounces each)**
- 1 **cup light coconut milk**
- 4 **teaspoons curry powder**
- 1 **garlic clove, minced**
- 1 **teaspoon reduced-sodium chicken bouillon granules**
- ¼ **teaspoon salt**
- ¼ **teaspoon pepper**
- 2 **cups hot cooked rice**
- ¼ **cup thinly sliced green onions**
  Raisins, flaked coconut and chopped unsalted peanuts, optional

1. Place potatoes and onion in a 3- or 4-qt. slow cooker. In a large nonstick skillet coated with cooking spray, brown chicken on both sides.
2. Transfer to slow cooker. In a small bowl, combine the coconut milk, curry, garlic, bouillon, salt and pepper; pour over chicken. Cover and cook on low for 5-6 hours or until meat is tender.
3. Serve chicken and sauce with rice; sprinkle with green onions. Garnish with raisins, coconut and peanuts if desired.

Nutrition Facts: *1 serving (calculated without optional ingredients) equals 396 calories, 11 g fat (7 g saturated fat), 63 mg cholesterol, 309 mg sodium, 43 g carbohydrate, 3 g fiber, 27 g protein.* **Diabetic Exchanges:** *3 lean meat, 2½ starch, 2 fat.*

Asian Pork Roast

Slow-cooked dishes are a favorite in our home, and tender pork seasoned with honey, soy and spices is perfect for chilly evenings. The aroma fills the house with a scent that cries out, "Welcome home!"

—SHEREE SHOWN JUNCTION CITY, OREGON

PREP: 25 MIN. **COOK:** 4 HOURS **MAKES:** 12 SERVINGS

- 2 **large onions, thinly sliced**
- 3 **garlic cloves, minced**
- ½ **teaspoon salt**
- ½ **teaspoon pepper**
- 1 **boneless pork loin roast (3 pounds)**
- 1 **tablespoon canola oil**
- 3 **bay leaves**
- ¼ **cup hot water**
- ¼ **cup honey**
- ¼ **cup reduced-sodium soy sauce**
- 2 **tablespoons rice vinegar**
- 1 **teaspoon ground ginger**
- ½ **teaspoon ground cloves**
- 3 **tablespoons cornstarch**
- ¼ **cup cold water**
- 2 **tablespoons sesame seeds, toasted**

Hot cooked rice and sliced green onion tops, optional

1. Place onions in a 5-qt. slow cooker. In a small bowl, combine the garlic, salt and pepper. Cut roast in half; rub with garlic mixture. In a large nonstick skillet coated with cooking spray, brown pork in oil on all sides. Transfer to slow cooker; add bay leaves.

2. In a small bowl, combine hot water and honey; stir in the soy sauce, vinegar, ginger and cloves. Pour over pork. Cover and cook on low for 4-5 hours or until meat is tender.

3. Remove meat and onions from slow cooker; keep warm. Discard bay leaves. Combine the cornstarch and cold water until smooth; gradually stir into the slow cooker.

4. Cover and cook on high for 30 minutes or until thickened, stirring twice. Slice pork; top with sauce and sprinkle with sesame seeds. Serve with rice and garnish with green onion tops if desired..

Nutrition Facts: *3 ounces cooked pork with 3 tablespoons each onions and sauce (calculated without optional ingredients) equals 203 calories, 7 g fat (2 g saturated fat), 56 mg cholesterol, 342 mg sodium, 11 g carbohydrate, 1 g fiber, 23 g protein.* **Diabetic Exchanges:** *3 lean meat, 1 starch.*

Spicy Kielbasa Soup

Should you have any left over, this soup is great reheated—after the flavors have had time to blend. I like to serve steaming bowls of it with crusty rye bread.

—CAROL CUSTER
CLIFTON PARK, NEW YORK

PREP: 15 MIN. **COOK:** 8 HOURS
MAKES: 5 SERVINGS

- ½ pound reduced-fat smoked turkey kielbasa, sliced
- 1 medium onion, chopped
- 1 medium green pepper, chopped
- 1 celery rib with leaves, thinly sliced
- 4 garlic cloves, minced
- 2 cans (14½ ounces each) reduced-sodium chicken broth
- 1 can (15½ ounces) great northern beans, rinsed and drained
- 1 can (14½ ounces) stewed tomatoes, cut up
- 1 small zucchini, sliced
- 1 medium carrot, shredded
- 1 tablespoon dried parsley flakes
- ¼ teaspoon crushed red pepper flakes
- ¼ teaspoon pepper

1. In a large nonstick skillet, cook kielbasa over medium heat until lightly browned. Add the onion, green pepper and celery; cook and stir for 3 minutes. Add garlic; cook 1 minute longer.

2. Transfer to a 5-qt. slow cooker. Stir in remaining ingredients. Cover and cook on low 8-9 hours or until vegetables are tender.

Nutrition Facts: *1½ cups equals 194 calories, 2 g fat (trace saturated fat), 16 mg cholesterol, 1,187 mg sodium, 32 g carbohydrate, 7 g fiber, 14 g protein.* **Diabetic Exchanges:** *3 vegetable, 2 lean meat, 1 starch.*

Slow Cooker Fajitas

I love fajitas like those that are served in Mexican restaurants, but when I prepared them at home, the meat was always chewy. Then I tried this recipe in my slow cooker, and my husband and I savored every last tender bite!

—KATIE URSO SENECA, ILLINOIS

PREP: 25 MIN. **COOK:** 8 HOURS
MAKES: 8 SERVINGS

- 1 each medium green, sweet red and yellow peppers, cut into ½-inch strips
- 1 sweet onion, cut into ½-inch strips
- 2 pounds beef top sirloin steaks, cut into thin strips
- ¾ cup water
- 2 tablespoons red wine vinegar
- 1 tablespoon lime juice
- 1 teaspoon ground cumin
- 1 teaspoon chili powder
- ½ teaspoon salt
- ½ teaspoon garlic powder
- ½ teaspoon pepper
- ½ teaspoon cayenne pepper
- 8 flour tortillas (8 inches), warmed
- ½ cup salsa
- ½ cup shredded reduced-fat cheddar cheese
- 8 teaspoons minced fresh cilantro

1. Place peppers and onion in a 5-qt. slow cooker. Top with beef. Combine the water, vinegar, lime juice and seasonings; pour over meat. Cover and cook on low for 8-10 hours or until meat is tender.

2. Using a slotted spoon, place about ¾ cup meat mixture down the center of each tortilla. Top with salsa, cheese and cilantro; roll up.

Nutrition Facts: *1 fajita equals 335 calories, 10 g fat (3 g saturated fat), 69 mg cholesterol, 564 mg sodium, 32 g carbohydrate, 2 g fiber, 29 g protein.* **Diabetic Exchanges:** *3 lean meat, 2 starch, 1 vegetable.*

Ground Beef Stew

I created this chunky soup one night when looking for something inexpensive and easy to make. Every bowl is chock-full of ground beef, potatoes and baby carrots.

—**SANDRA CASTILLO**
JANESVILLE, WISCONSIN

PREP: 20 MIN.   **COOK:** 5 HOURS
MAKES: 12 SERVINGS (3 QUARTS)

- 1 **pound ground beef**
- 6 **medium potatoes, peeled and cubed**
- 1 **package (16 ounces) baby carrots**
- 3 **cups water**
- 2 **tablespoons Lipton beefy onion soup mix**
- 1 **garlic clove, minced**
- 1 **teaspoon Italian seasoning**
- 1 **to 1½ teaspoons salt**
- ¼ **teaspoon garlic powder**
- ¼ **teaspoon pepper**
- 1 **can (10¾ ounces) condensed tomato soup, undiluted**
- 1 **can (6 ounces) Italian tomato paste**

1. In a large skillet, cook the beef over medium heat until no longer pink; drain.
2. In a 5-qt. slow cooker, combine the next nine ingredients. Stir in the beef. Cover and cook on high for 4-5 hours.
3. Stir in soup and tomato paste; cover and cook 1 hour longer or until heated through.

Nutrition Facts: *1 cup equals 180 calories, 4 g fat (2 g saturated fat), 14 mg cholesterol, 434 mg sodium, 26 g carbohydrate, 3 g fiber, 10 g protein.* **Diabetic Exchanges:** *1½ starch, 1 lean meat, 1 vegetable.*

Garden Chicken Cacciatore

Here's the perfect Italian meal to serve company. It frees you up to visit with your guests and always receives rave reviews. I like to serve it with hot cooked pasta, a green salad and a dry red wine. Mangia!

—**MARTHA SCHIRMACHER** STERLING HEIGHTS, MICHIGAN

PREP: 15 MIN.   **COOK:** 8½ HOURS
MAKES: 12 SERVINGS

- 12 **boneless skinless chicken thighs (about 3 pounds)**
- 2 **medium green peppers, chopped**
- 1 **can (14½ ounces) diced tomatoes with basil, oregano and garlic, undrained**
- 1 **can (6 ounces) tomato paste**
- 1 **medium onion, sliced**
- ½ **cup reduced-sodium chicken broth**
- ¼ **cup dry red wine or additional reduced-sodium chicken broth**
- 3 **garlic cloves, minced**
- ¾ **teaspoon salt**
- ⅛ **teaspoon pepper**
- 2 **tablespoons cornstarch**
- 2 **tablespoons cold water**

1. Place chicken in a 4-qt. slow cooker. In a small bowl, combine the green peppers, tomatoes, tomato paste, onion, broth, wine, garlic, salt and pepper. Cover and cook on low for 8-10 hours or until chicken is tender.
2. Combine cornstarch and water until smooth; gradually stir into slow cooker. Cover and cook on high 30 minutes longer or until sauce is thickened.

Nutrition Facts: *1 chicken thigh with scant ½ cup of sauce equals 207 calories, 9 g fat (2 g saturated fat), 76 mg cholesterol, 410 mg sodium, 8 g carbohydrate, 1 g fiber, 23 g protein.* **Diabetic Exchanges:** *3 lean meat, 1 vegetable, ½ fat.*

Chili Cheese Dip

After trying to create a Mexican soup, I ended up with an outstanding dip that eats like a meal! My husband and children love it. It's also popular for football game days and family gatherings.

—SANDRA FICK LINCOLN, NEBRASKA

PREP: 20 MIN. **COOK:** 4½ HOURS
MAKES: 8 CUPS

- 1 **pound lean ground beef (90% lean)**
- 1 **cup chopped onion**
- 1 **can (16 ounces) kidney beans, rinsed and drained**
- 1 **can (15 ounces) black beans, rinsed and drained**
- 1 **can (14½ ounces) diced tomatoes in sauce**
- 1 **cup frozen corn**
- ¾ **cup water**
- 1 **can (2¼ ounces) sliced ripe olives, drained**
- 3 **teaspoons chili powder**
- ½ **teaspoon dried oregano**
- ¼ **teaspoon garlic powder**
- ¼ **teaspoon ground cumin**
- ½ **teaspoon chipotle hot pepper sauce**
- 1 **package (16 ounces) reduced-fat process cheese (Velveeta), cubed**
  Corn chips

1. In a large skillet, cook beef and onion until no longer pink; drain. Transfer to a 5-qt. slow cooker. Stir in beans, tomatoes, corn, water, olives, seasonings and hot sauce.
2. Cover and cook on low for 4-5 hours or until heated through; stir in cheese. Cover and cook for 30 minutes or until cheese is melted. Serve with corn chips.

Nutrition Facts: *¼ cup (calculated without chips) equals 87 calories, 3 g fat (1 g saturated fat), 12 mg cholesterol, 330 mg sodium, 9 g carbohydrate, 2 g fiber, 7 g protein.* **Diabetic Exchanges:** *1 lean meat, ½ starch.*

Stuffing from the Slow Cooker

If you're hosting a big Thanksgiving dinner, a simple slow-cooked stuffing can really simplify entertaining. This recipe comes in handy when you run out of oven space at large family gatherings. I use it often.

—DONALD SEILER
MACON, MISSISSIPPI

PREP: 30 MIN. **COOK:** 3 HOURS
MAKES: 12 SERVINGS

- 1 **cup chopped onion**
- 1 **cup chopped celery**
- ¼ **cup butter**
- 6 **cups cubed day-old white bread**
- 6 **cups cubed day-old whole wheat bread**
- 1 **teaspoon salt**
- 1 **teaspoon poultry seasoning**
- 1 **teaspoon rubbed sage**
- ½ **teaspoon pepper**
- 1 **can (14½ ounces) reduced-sodium chicken broth or vegetable broth**
- ½ **cup egg substitute**

1. In a small nonstick skillet over medium heat, cook onion and celery in butter until tender.
2. In a large bowl, combine the bread cubes, salt, poultry seasoning, sage and pepper. Stir in onion mixture. Combine broth and egg substitute; add to bread mixture and toss to coat.
3. Transfer to a 3-qt. slow cooker coated with cooking spray. Cover and cook on low for 3-4 hours or until heated through.

Nutrition Facts: *⅔ cup equals 141 calories, 5 g fat (3 g saturated fat), 10 mg cholesterol, 548 mg sodium, 19 g carbohydrate, 2 g fiber, 5 g protein.* **Diabetic Exchanges:** *1½ starch, ½ fat.*

Flavorful Beef Stew

This tasty and rich beef stew creates a thick sauce that goes great with bread. I find it much easier to prepare in the slow cooker than on the stove or in the oven.

—JACKITT
TASTE OF HOME ONLINE COMMUNITY

PREP: 25 MIN.   **COOK:** 6 HOURS
MAKES: 6 SERVINGS

- ½ **pound medium fresh mushrooms, quartered**
- 2 **medium red potatoes, cubed**
- 3 **medium carrots, sliced**
- 1 **medium onion, chopped**
- 1 **celery rib, thinly sliced**
- ¼ **cup all-purpose flour**
- 1 **tablespoon paprika**
- ¾ **teaspoon salt**
- ¼ **teaspoon pepper**
- 1 **pound beef stew meat, cut into 1-inch cubes**
- 1 **can (14½ ounces) beef broth**
- 4½ **teaspoons reduced-sodium teriyaki sauce**
- 2 **garlic cloves, minced**
- 1 **bay leaf**

1. In a 3-qt. slow cooker, combine the mushrooms, potatoes, carrots, onion and celery.
2. In a large resealable plastic bag, combine the flour, paprika, salt and pepper. Add beef, a few pieces at a time, and shake to coat. Place over vegetable mixture.
3. Combine the broth, teriyaki sauce, garlic and bay leaf; pour over beef.
4. Cover and cook on low for 6-8 hours or until meat and vegetables are tender. Discard bay leaf.

Nutrition Facts: *1 cup equals 202 calories, 6 g fat (2 g saturated fat), 47 mg cholesterol, 745 mg sodium, 19 g carbohydrate, 3 g fiber, 19 g protein.* **Diabetic Exchanges:** *2 lean meat, 1 starch, 1 vegetable.*

Chicken Thighs with Sausage

Whether you're serving your family or special guests, here's a delicious entree that hits the spot on cold winter nights.

—JOANNA IOVINO
KINGS PARK, NEW YORK

PREP: 25 MIN.   **COOK:** 6 HOURS
MAKES: 8 SERVINGS

- 2 **medium carrots, chopped**
- 2 **celery ribs, chopped**
- 1 **large onion, finely chopped**
- 8 **bone-in chicken thighs (about 3 pounds), skin removed**
- 1 **package (14 ounces) smoked turkey sausage, cut into ½-inch slices**
- ¼ **cup ketchup**
- 6 **garlic cloves, minced**
- 1 **tablespoon Louisiana-style hot sauce**
- 1 **teaspoon dried basil**
- 1 **teaspoon paprika**
- 1 **teaspoon dried thyme**
- ½ **teaspoon dried oregano**
- ½ **teaspoon pepper**
- ¼ **teaspoon ground allspice**
- 1 **teaspoon browning sauce, optional**

1. In a 4- or 5-qt. slow cooker, combine the carrots, celery and onion. Top with chicken and sausage.
2. In a small bowl, combine the ketchup, garlic, hot sauce, seasonings and, if desired, browning sauce. Spoon over meats. Cover and cook on low for 6-8 hours or until the chicken is tender.

Nutrition Facts: *1 chicken thigh with ⅓ cup sausage mixture equals 280 calories, 12 g fat (4 g saturated fat), 118 mg cholesterol, 675 mg sodium, 8 g carbohydrate, 1 g fiber, 33 g protein.* **Diabetic Exchanges:** *5 lean meat, ½ starch.*

Enchilada Pie

What an impressive, hearty dish—and it will satisfy both vegetarians and meat eaters alike!

—**JACQUELINE CORREA** LANDING, NEW JERSEY

PREP: 40 MIN. **COOK:** 4 HOURS **MAKES:** 8 SERVINGS

- 1 **package (12 ounces) frozen vegetarian meat crumbles**
- 1 **cup chopped onion**
- ½ **cup chopped green pepper**
- 2 **teaspoons canola oil**
- 1 **can (16 ounces) kidney beans, rinsed and drained**
- 1 **can (15 ounces) black beans, rinsed and drained**
- 1 **can (10 ounces) diced tomatoes and green chilies, undrained**
- ½ **cup water**
- 1½ **teaspoons chili powder**
- ½ **teaspoon ground cumin**
- ¼ **teaspoon pepper**
- 6 **whole wheat tortillas (8 inches)**
- 2 **cups (8 ounces) shredded reduced-fat cheddar cheese**

1. Cut three 25-in. x 3-in. strips of heavy-duty foil; crisscross so they resemble spokes of a wheel. Place strips on the bottom and up the sides of a 5-qt. slow cooker. Coat strips with cooking spray.

2. In a large saucepan, cook the meat crumbles, onion and green pepper in oil until vegetables are tender. Stir in both cans of beans, tomatoes, water, chili powder, cumin and pepper. Bring to a boil. Reduce heat; simmer, uncovered, for 10 minutes.

3. In prepared slow cooker, layer about a cup of bean mixture, one tortilla and ⅓ cup cheese. Repeat layers five times. Cover and cook on low for 4-5 hours or until heated through and cheese is melted.

4. Using foil strips as handles, remove the pie to a platter.

Editor's Note: *Vegetarian meat crumbles are a nutritious protein source made from soy. Look for them in the natural foods freezer section.*

Nutrition Facts: *1 piece equals 367 calories, 11 g fat (4 g saturated fat), 20 mg cholesterol, 818 mg sodium, 41 g carbohydrate, 9 g fiber, 25 g protein.* **Diabetic Exchanges:** *3 starch, 2 lean meat, 1 fat.*

Top-Rated Italian Pot Roast

I'm always collecting recipes from newspapers and magazines, and this one just sounded too good not to try! You'll love the blend of wholesome ingredients and aromatic spices.

—**KAREN BURDELL** LAFAYETTE, COLORADO

PREP: 30 MIN. **COOK:** 6 HOURS **MAKES:** 8 SERVINGS

- 6 **whole peppercorns**
- 4 **whole cloves**
- 3 **whole allspice**
- 1 **cinnamon stick (3 inches)**
- 1 **boneless beef chuck roast (2 pounds)**
- 2 **teaspoons olive oil**
- 2 **celery ribs, sliced**
- 2 **medium carrots, sliced**
- 1 **large onion, chopped**
- 4 **garlic cloves, minced**
- 1 **cup sherry or reduced-sodium beef broth**
- 1 **can (28 ounces) crushed tomatoes**
- ¼ **teaspoon salt**
  Hot cooked egg noodles, optional

1. Place the peppercorns, cloves, allspice and cinnamon stick on a double thickness of cheesecloth; bring up corners of cloth and tie with string to form a bag. Set aside.

2. In a large skillet, brown meat in oil on all sides; transfer to a 4-qt. slow cooker. Top with celery, carrots and spice bag.

3. In the same pan, saute onion in drippings until tender. Add garlic; cook 1 minute longer. Add sherry, stirring to loosen browned bits from pan. Bring to a boil; cook and stir until liquid is reduced to ⅔ cup. Stir in tomatoes and salt; pour over vegetables.

4. Cover and cook on low for 6-7 hours or until meat and vegetables are tender. Remove meat to a serving platter; keep warm. Discard spice bag. Skim fat from the vegetable mixture; serve with beef and egg noodles if desired.

Nutrition Facts: *3 ounces cooked meat with ⅔ cup vegetable mixture (calculated without noodles) equals 251 calories, 12 g fat (4 g saturated fat), 74 mg cholesterol, 271 mg sodium, 11 g carbohydrate, 3 g fiber, 24 g protein.* **Diabetic Exchanges:** *3 lean meat, 2 vegetable, ½ fat.*

Sweet 'n' Sour Sausage

Serve this tasty combination of slow-cooked veggies, pineapple and smoked sausage over rice or chow mein noodles—stir-fry style.

—BARBARA SCHUTZ PANDORA, OHIO

PREP: 15 MIN. **COOK:** 4½ HOURS
MAKES: 6 SERVINGS

- 1 pound smoked kielbasa or Polish sausage, sliced
- 1 can (20 ounces) unsweetened pineapple chunks, undrained
- 1½ cups fresh baby carrots, quartered lengthwise
- 1 large green pepper, cut into 1-inch pieces
- 1 medium onion, cut into chunks
- ⅓ cup packed brown sugar
- 1 tablespoon reduced-sodium soy sauce
- ½ teaspoon chicken bouillon granules
- ¼ teaspoon garlic powder
- ¼ teaspoon ground ginger
- 2 tablespoons cornstarch
- ¼ cup cold water
    Hot cooked rice or chow mein noodles

1. In a 3-qt. slow cooker, combine the first 10 ingredients. Cover and cook on low for 4-5 hours or until vegetables are tender.

2. Mix cornstarch and water until smooth; stir into sausage mixture. Cover and cook on high for 30 minutes or until thickened. Serve with rice.

Nutrition Facts: *1 cup (prepared with turkey sausage; calculated without rice) equals 250 calories, 4 g fat (1 g saturated fat), 34 mg cholesterol, 869 mg sodium, 43 g carbohydrate, 1 g fiber, 10 g protein.*
Diabetic Exchanges: *2 fruit, 1 lean meat, 1 vegetable, ½ starch.*

Makeover Creamy Artichoke Dip

Folks are sure to gather around this ooey-gooey dip whenever it's placed on the buffet table. It's a lightened-up take on a treasured family favorite.

—MARY SPENCER
GREENDALE, WISCONSIN

PREP: 20 MIN. **COOK:** 1 HOUR
MAKES: 5 CUPS

- 2 cans (14 ounces each) water-packed artichoke hearts, rinsed, drained and chopped
- 1 package (8 ounces) reduced-fat cream cheese, cubed
- ¾ cup (6 ounces) plain yogurt
- 1 cup (4 ounces) shredded part-skim mozzarella cheese
- 1 cup reduced-fat ricotta cheese
- ¾ cup shredded Parmesan cheese, divided
- ½ cup shredded reduced-fat Swiss cheese
- ¼ cup reduced-fat mayonnaise
- 2 tablespoons lemon juice
- 1 tablespoon chopped seeded jalapeno pepper
- 1 teaspoon garlic powder
- 1 teaspoon seasoned salt
    Tortilla chips

1. In a 3-qt. slow cooker, combine the artichokes, cream cheese, yogurt, mozzarella cheese, ricotta cheese, ½ cup Parmesan cheese, Swiss cheese, mayonnaise, lemon juice, jalapeno, garlic powder and seasoned salt.

2. Cover and cook on low for 1 hour or until heated through.

3. Sprinkle with remaining Parmesan cheese. Serve with tortilla chips.

Editor's Note: *Wear disposable gloves when cutting hot peppers; the oils can burn skin. Avoid touching your face.*

Nutrition Facts: *¼ cup (calculated without chips) equals 104 calories, 6 g fat (3 g saturated fat), 20 mg cholesterol, 348 mg sodium, 5 g carbohydrate, trace fiber, 7 g protein.* **Diabetic Exchanges:** *1 fat, ½ starch.*

Mushroom-Beef Spaghetti Sauce

I got the recipe for this sauce in a recipe exchange and wish I could credit the person who gave it to me. My children just love it! I added mushrooms, but if you'd like it even chunkier, add bell pepper and other veggies, too.

—MEG FISHER MARIETTA, GEORGIA

PREP: 20 MIN. **COOK:** 6 HOURS
MAKES: 12 SERVINGS (1½ QUARTS)

- 1 **pound lean ground beef (90% lean)**
- ½ **pound sliced fresh mushrooms**
- 1 **small onion, chopped**
- 2 **cans (14½ ounces each) diced tomatoes, undrained**
- 1 **can (12 ounces) tomato paste**
- 1 **can (8 ounces) tomato sauce**
- 1 **cup reduced-sodium beef broth**
- 2 **tablespoons dried parsley flakes**
- 1 **tablespoon brown sugar**
- 1 **teaspoon dried basil**
- 1 **teaspoon dried oregano**
- 1 **teaspoon salt**
- ¼ **teaspoon pepper**
  Hot cooked spaghetti

1. In a large nonstick skillet, cook the beef, mushrooms and onion over medium heat until meat is no longer pink; drain. Transfer to a 3-qt. slow cooker.
2. Stir in the tomatoes, tomato paste, tomato sauce, broth, parsley, brown sugar, basil, oregano, salt and pepper. Cover and cook on low for 6-8 hours. Serve with spaghetti.

Nutrition Facts: *½ cup (calculated without spaghetti) equals 115 calories, 3 g fat (1 g saturated fat), 19 mg cholesterol, 493 mg sodium, 12 g carbohydrate, 3 g fiber, 10 g protein.*
Diabetic Exchanges: *2 vegetable, 1 lean meat.*

Slow-Cooked Moroccan Chicken

Spices really work their magic on plain chicken in this exciting dish. Dried fruit and couscous add an exotic touch.

—KATHY MORGAN
RIDGEFIELD, WASHINGTON

PREP: 20 MIN. **COOK:** 6 HOURS
MAKES: 4 SERVINGS

- 4 **medium carrots, sliced**
- 2 **large onions, halved and sliced**
- 1 **broiler/fryer chicken (3 to 4 pounds), cut up, skin removed**
- ½ **teaspoon salt**
- ½ **cup chopped dried apricots**
- ½ **cup raisins**
- 2 **tablespoons all-purpose flour**
- 1 **can (14½ ounces) reduced-sodium chicken broth**
- ¼ **cup tomato paste**
- 2 **tablespoons lemon juice**
- 2 **garlic cloves, minced**
- 1½ **teaspoons ground ginger**
- 1½ **teaspoons ground cumin**
- 1 **teaspoon ground cinnamon**
- ¾ **teaspoon pepper**
  Hot cooked couscous

1. Place carrots and onions in a greased 5-qt. slow cooker. Sprinkle chicken with salt; add to slow cooker. Top with apricots and raisins. In a small bowl, combine flour and broth until smooth; whisk in the tomato paste, lemon juice, garlic, ginger, cumin, cinnamon and pepper. Pour over chicken.
2. Cover and cook on low for 6 to 7 hours or until chicken is tender. Serve with couscous.

Nutrition Facts: *1 serving (calculated without couscous) equals 435 calories, 9 g fat (3 g saturated fat), 110 mg cholesterol, 755 mg sodium, 47 g carbohydrate, 6 g fiber, 42 g protein.*

Tuscan Pork Stew

Tender chunks of pork slowly cook in a nicely seasoned, wine-infused broth. Add some crushed red pepper flakes for a little added kick.

—PENNY HAWKINS MEBANE, NORTH CAROLINA

PREP: 15 MIN. **COOK:** 8½ HOURS **MAKES:** 8 SERVINGS

- 1½ **pounds boneless pork loin roast , cut into 1-inch cubes**
- 2 **tablespoons olive oil**
- 2 **cans (14½ ounces each) Italian diced tomatoes, undrained**
- 2 **cups reduced-sodium chicken broth**
- 2 **cups frozen pepper stir-fry vegetable blend, thawed**
- ½ **cup dry red wine or additional reduced-sodium chicken broth**
- ¼ **cup orange marmalade**
- 2 **garlic cloves, minced**
- 1 **teaspoon dried oregano**
- ½ **teaspoon fennel seed**
- ½ **teaspoon pepper**
- ⅛ **teaspoon crushed red pepper flakes, optional**
- 2 **tablespoons cornstarch**
- 2 **tablespoons cold water**
  Hot cooked fettuccine, optional

1. In a large skillet, brown pork in oil; drain. Transfer to a 5-qt. slow cooker.

2. Stir in the tomatoes, broth, vegetable blend, wine, marmalade, garlic, oregano, fennel seed, pepper and pepper flakes if desired. Cover and cook on low for 8-10 hours or until meat is tender.

3. Combine cornstarch and water until smooth; gradually stir into stew. Cover and cook on high for 30 minutes or until thickened. Serve stew with fettuccine if desired.

Nutrition Facts: *1 cup (calculated without fettuccine) equals 232 calories, 7 g fat (2 g saturated fat), 42 mg cholesterol, 614 mg sodium, 19 g carbohydrate, 1 g fiber, 19 g protein.* **Diabetic Exchanges:** *2 lean meat, 1 starch, 1 vegetable, ½ fat.*

Hearty Beef Vegetable Stew

I can thank a co-worker for this wonderful recipe. It's awesome! A hit with everyone, including our two young kids, it's good for you, too.

—ANGELA NELSON
RUTHER GLEN, VIRGINIA

PREP: 20 MIN. **COOK:** 5 HOURS
MAKES: 6 SERVINGS

- 1½ pounds boneless beef chuck roast, cut into 1-inch cubes
- 2 teaspoons canola oil
- 1½ pounds red potatoes, cut into 1-inch cubes
- 3 medium carrots, cut into 1-inch lengths
- 1 medium onion, chopped
- ½ cup chopped celery
- 1 can (28 ounces) crushed tomatoes, undrained
- 3 tablespoons quick-cooking tapioca
- 2 tablespoons dried basil
- 1 tablespoon sugar
- ½ teaspoon salt
- ⅛ teaspoon pepper

1. In a large nonstick skillet, brown meat in oil over medium heat. Meanwhile, place the potatoes, carrots, onion and celery in a 5-qt. slow cooker.

2. Drain meat; add to slow cooker. Combine the tomatoes, tapioca, basil, sugar, salt and pepper; pour over the top.

3. Cover and cook on high for 5-6 hours or until meat and vegetables are tender.

Nutrition Facts: *1⅓ cups equals 380 calories, 8 g fat (3 g saturated fat), 78 mg cholesterol, 458 mg sodium, 46 g carbohydrate, 7 g fiber, 31 g protein.* **Diabetic Exchanges:** *3 lean meat, 2 starch, 2 vegetable.*

Cranberry Turkey Breast with Gravy

Here's a convenient way to serve your next holiday meal. The turkey turns out tender and moist—and you can use extra slow cookers to prepare side dishes such as homemade stuffing.

—SHIRLEY WELCH
TULSA, OKLAHOMA

PREP: 15 MIN. **COOK:** 5 HOURS
MAKES: 12 SERVINGS (3 CUPS GRAVY)

- 1 bone-in turkey breast (5 to 6 pounds)
- 1 can (14 ounces) whole-berry cranberry sauce
- ¼ cup orange juice
- 1 envelope onion soup mix
- ¼ teaspoon salt
- ¼ teaspoon pepper
- 3 to 4 teaspoons cornstarch
- 1 tablespoon water

1. Place turkey in a 5-qt. slow cooker. In a small bowl, combine the cranberry sauce, orange juice, onion soup mix, salt and pepper; pour over turkey. Cover and cook on low for 5-6 hours or until turkey is tender.

2. Remove turkey to a serving platter; keep warm. Skim fat from cooking juices; transfer to a small saucepan. Bring to a boil. Combine cornstarch and water until smooth. Gradually stir into the pan. Bring to a boil; cook and stir for 2 minutes or until thickened. Serve with turkey.

Nutrition Facts: *5 ounces cooked turkey with ¼ cup gravy equals 318 calories, 10 g fat (3 g saturated fat), 102 mg cholesterol, 346 mg sodium, 15 g carbohydrate, 1 g fiber, 40 g protein.* **Diabetic Exchanges:** *5 lean meat, 1 starch.*

Ham Tetrazzini

After modifying this recipe that came with my slow cooker to reduce the fat but not sacrifice flavor, I've served it at parties, family dinners and potlucks. Everyone is pleasantly surprised to find they're eating healthy!

—SUSAN BLAIR STERLING, MICHIGAN

PREP: 15 MIN. **COOK:** 4 HOURS
MAKES: 5 SERVINGS

- 1 can (10¾ ounces) reduced-sodium condensed cream of mushroom soup, undiluted
- 1 cup sliced fresh mushrooms
- 1 cup cubed fully cooked ham
- ½ cup fat-free evaporated milk
- 2 tablespoons white wine or water
- 1 teaspoon prepared horseradish
- 1 package (7 ounces) spaghetti
- ½ cup shredded Parmesan cheese

1. In a 3-qt. slow cooker, combine the soup, mushrooms, ham, milk, wine and horseradish. Cover and cook on low for 4 hours.

2. Cook spaghetti according to package directions; drain. Add the spaghetti and cheese to slow cooker; toss to coat.

Nutrition Facts: *1 cup equals 290 calories, 6 g fat (3 g saturated fat), 24 mg cholesterol, 759 mg sodium, 39 g carbohydrate, 2 g fiber, 16 g protein.* **Diabetic Exchanges:** *2½ starch, 1 lean meat, ½ fat.*

Easy Minestrone

I have three small boys who are not big fans of vegetables, but they always enjoy my hearty soup. It's a terrific recipe to put together in the morning and forget about the rest of the day.

—YVONNE ANDRUS HIGHLAND, UTAH

PREP: 20 MIN. **COOK:** 6 HOURS
MAKES: 10 SERVINGS (ABOUT 3¼ QUARTS)

- 4 medium tomatoes, chopped
- 2 medium carrots, chopped
- 2 celery ribs, chopped
- 1 medium zucchini, halved and sliced
- 1½ cups shredded cabbage
- 1 can (16 ounces) kidney beans, rinsed and drained
- 1 can (15 ounces) garbanzo beans or chickpeas, rinsed and drained
- 6 cups reduced-sodium chicken broth or vegetable broth
- 1¼ teaspoons Italian seasoning
- 1 teaspoon salt
- ¼ teaspoon pepper
- 2 cups cooked elbow macaroni
- 5 tablespoons shredded Parmesan cheese

1. In a 5-qt. slow cooker, combine the first 11 ingredients. Cover and cook on low for 6-8 hours or until vegetables are tender.

2. Just before serving, stir in macaroni and heat through. Serve with cheese.

Nutrition Facts: *1⅓ cups with 1½ teaspoons cheese equals 149 calories, 2 g fat (1 g saturated fat), 2 mg cholesterol, 798 mg sodium, 25 g carbohydrate, 6 g fiber, 9 g protein.* **Diabetic Exchanges:** *1 starch, 1 lean meat, 1 vegetable.*

Slow-Cooked Bread Pudding

This warm and hearty dessert is the perfect chill-chaser. And the slow cooker fills your kitchen with an amazing aroma. My stomach is growling just thinking about it!

—MAIAH MILLER
CARLSBAD, CALIFORNIA

PREP: 15 MIN. **COOK:** 3 HOURS
MAKES: 8 SERVINGS

- 4   whole wheat bagels, split and cut into ¾-inch pieces
- 1   large tart apple, peeled and chopped
- ½   cup dried cranberries
- ¼   cup golden raisins
- 2   cups fat-free milk
- 1   cup egg substitute
- ½   cup sugar
- 2   tablespoons butter, melted
- 1   teaspoon ground cinnamon
- 1   teaspoon vanilla extract

1. In a 3-qt. slow cooker coated with cooking spray, combine the bagels, apple, cranberries and raisins. In a large bowl, whisk the milk, egg substitute, sugar, butter, cinnamon and vanilla. Pour over bagel mixture and stir to combine; gently press bagels down into the milk mixture.

2. Cover and cook on low for 3-4 hours or until a knife inserted near the center comes out clean.

Nutrition Facts: *1 serving equals 231 calories, 3 g fat (2 g saturated fat), 9 mg cholesterol, 257 mg sodium, 45 g carbohydrate, 4 g fiber, 8 g protein.*

Pork and Bean Burritos

I have been making this recipe for 20 years, changing it here and there until I created the perfect version. It's a favorite of company and family alike.

—SHARON BELMONT
LINCOLN, NEBRASKA

PREP: 20 MIN. **COOK:** 8 HOURS
MAKES: 14 SERVINGS

- 1   boneless pork sirloin roast (3 pounds)
- ¼   cup reduced-sodium chicken broth
- 1   envelope reduced-sodium taco seasoning
- 1   tablespoon dried parsley flakes
- 2   garlic cloves, minced
- ½   teaspoon pepper
- ¼   teaspoon salt
- 1   can (16 ounces) refried beans
- 1   can (4 ounces) chopped green chilies
- 14   flour tortillas (8 inches), warmed
    Optional toppings: shredded lettuce, chopped tomatoes, chopped green pepper, guacamole, reduced-fat sour cream and shredded reduced-fat cheddar cheese

1. Cut roast in half; place in a 4- or 5-qt. slow cooker. In a small bowl, combine the broth, taco seasoning, parsley, garlic, pepper and salt. Pour over roast. Cover and cook on low for 8-10 hours or until meat is very tender.

2. Remove pork from the slow cooker; cool slightly. Shred with two forks; set aside. Skim fat from the liquid; stir in beans and chilies. Return pork to the slow cooker; heat through.

3. Spoon ½ cup pork mixture down the center of each tortilla; add toppings of your choice. Fold sides and ends over filling and roll up.

To freeze burritos: *Roll up burritos without toppings. Wrap individually in paper towels, then foil. Transfer to a resealable plastic bag. May be frozen for up to 2 months. To use frozen burritos, unwrap foil. Place paper towel-wrapped burritos on a microwave-safe plate. Microwave on high for 3-4 minutes or until heated through. Serve with toppings of your choice.*

Nutrition Facts: *1 burrito (calculated without toppings) equals 320 calories, 9 g fat (3 g saturated fat), 61 mg cholesterol, 606 mg sodium, 33 g carbohydrate, 2 g fiber, 26 g protein.* **Diabetic Exchanges:** *2 starch, 2 lean meat, 1 fat.*

EGGS

If you prefer, use four beaten eggs in this recipe instead of egg substitute. Real eggs will add 23 calories per serving.

Southwestern Beef Stew

A zippy beef stew seasoned with picante sauce is great on cold winter nights. It's ready in minutes after you come home from a long day at work.

—**REGINA STOCK** TOPEKA, KANSAS

PREP: 30 MIN. **COOK:** 8¼ HOURS
MAKES: 7 SERVINGS

- 2 **pounds beef stew meat, cut into 1-inch cubes**
- 1 **jar (16 ounces) picante sauce**
- 2 **medium potatoes, peeled and cut into ½-inch cubes**
- 4 **medium carrots, cut into ½-inch slices**
- 1 **large onion, chopped**
- 1 **teaspoon chili powder**
- ¼ **teaspoon salt**
- ¼ **teaspoon ground cumin**
- 1 **tablespoon cornstarch**
- ¼ **cup cold water**

1. In a large nonstick skillet, brown beef on all sides; drain. Transfer to a 3-qt. slow cooker. Stir in the picante sauce, potatoes, carrots, onion, chili powder, salt and cumin.

2. Cover and cook on low for 8-9 hours or until meat and vegetables are tender.

3. In a small bowl, combine the cornstarch and water until smooth; stir into stew. Cover and cook on high for 15 minutes or until thickened.

Nutrition Facts: *1 cup equals 266 calories, 9 g fat (3 g saturated fat), 81 mg cholesterol, 436 mg sodium, 18 g carbohydrate, 2 g fiber, 26 g protein.* **Diabetic Exchanges:** *3 lean meat, 2 vegetable, ½ starch.*

Spicy Goulash

Ground cumin, chili powder and a can of Mexican diced tomatoes jazz up my goulash recipe. Even the macaroni is prepared in the slow cooker.

—**MELISSA POLK**
WEST LAFAYETTE, INDIANA

PREP: 25 MIN. **COOK:** 5½ HOURS
MAKES: 12 SERVINGS

- 1 **pound lean ground beef (90% lean)**
- 4 **cans (14½ ounces each) Mexican diced tomatoes, undrained**
- 2 **cans (16 ounces each) kidney beans, rinsed and drained**
- 2 **cups water**
- 1 **medium onion, chopped**
- 1 **medium green pepper, chopped**
- ¼ **cup red wine vinegar**
- 2 **tablespoons chili powder**
- 1 **tablespoon Worcestershire sauce**
- 2 **teaspoons beef bouillon granules**
- 1 **teaspoon dried basil**
- 1 **teaspoon dried parsley flakes**
- 1 **teaspoon ground cumin**
- ¼ **teaspoon pepper**
- 2 **cups uncooked elbow macaroni**

1. In a large skillet, cook beef over medium heat until no longer pink; drain. Transfer to a 5-qt. slow cooker. Stir in the tomatoes, beans, water, onion, green pepper, vinegar, chili powder, Worcestershire sauce, bouillon and seasonings. Cover and cook on low for 5-6 hours or until heated through.

2. Stir in macaroni; cover and cook 30 minutes longer or until macaroni is tender.

Nutrition Facts: *1 cup equals 213 calories, 4 g fat (1 g saturated fat), 24 mg cholesterol, 585 mg sodium, 30 g carbohydrate, 6 g fiber, 15 g protein.* **Diabetic Exchanges:** *2 lean meat, 1½ starch, 1 vegetable.*

Turkey Meatballs and Sauce

My sweetie and I have been fighting the battle of the bulge forever. This is my less-fattening take on meatballs. They're slow-cooker easy and so flavorful!

—**JANE MCMILLAN** DANIA BEACH, FLORIDA

PREP: 30 MIN. **COOK:** 6 HOURS **MAKES:** 8 SERVINGS

¼ cup egg substitute
½ cup seasoned bread crumbs
⅓ cup chopped onion
½ teaspoon pepper
¼ teaspoon salt-free seasoning blend
1½ pounds lean ground turkey
SAUCE
1 can (15 ounces) tomato sauce
1 can (14½ ounces) diced tomatoes, undrained
1 small zucchini, chopped
1 medium green pepper, chopped
1 medium onion, chopped
1 can (6 ounces) tomato paste
2 bay leaves
2 garlic cloves, minced
1 teaspoon dried oregano
1 teaspoon dried basil
1 teaspoon dried parsley flakes
¼ teaspoon crushed red pepper flakes
¼ teaspoon pepper
1 package (16 ounces) whole wheat spaghetti

1. In a large bowl, combine the egg substitute, bread crumbs, onion, pepper and seasoning blend. Crumble turkey over mixture and mix well. Shape into 1-in. balls; place on a rack coated with cooking spray in a shallow baking pan. Bake, uncovered, at 400° for 15 minutes or until no longer pink.

2. Meanwhile, in a 4- or 5-qt. slow cooker, combine the tomato sauce, tomatoes, zucchini, green pepper, onion, tomato paste, bay leaves, garlic and seasonings. Stir in meatballs. Cover and cook on low for 6 hours. Cook spaghetti according to package directions; serve with meatballs and sauce.

Nutrition Facts: *4 meatballs with ¾ cup sauce and 1 cup spaghetti equals 416 calories, 8 g fat (2 g saturated fat), 67 mg cholesterol, 533 mg sodium, 61 g carbohydrate, 10 g fiber, 28 g protein.*

Shredded Beef Sandwiches

Cola is the secret ingredient in my delicious slow-cooked beef.

—MARIE ELAINE BASINGER
CONNELLSVILLE, PENNSYLVANIA

PREP: 30 MIN. **COOK:** 8¼ HOURS
MAKES: 8 SERVINGS

- ¾ cup cola
- ¼ cup Worcestershire sauce
- 2 garlic cloves, minced
- 1 tablespoon white vinegar
- 1 teaspoon reduced-sodium beef bouillon granules
- ½ teaspoon chili powder
- ½ teaspoon ground mustard
- ¼ teaspoon cayenne pepper
- 1 beef rump roast (2 pounds)
- 2 teaspoons canola oil
- 2 medium onions, chopped
- ½ cup ketchup
- 8 kaiser rolls

1. In a measuring cup, combine the cola, Worcestershire sauce, garlic, vinegar, bouillon and seasonings; set aside. Cut roast in half. In a nonstick skillet, brown meat in oil on all sides.

2. Place onions in a 3-qt. slow cooker. Top with meat. Pour half of cola mixture over meat. Cover and cook on low for 8-10 hours or until meat is tender. Cover and refrigerate remaining cola mixture.

3. Remove meat from cooking liquid and cool. Strain cooking liquid, reserving onions and discarding the liquid. When meat is cool enough to handle, shred with two forks. Return meat and onions to slow cooker.

4. Combine ketchup and reserved cola mixture; pour over meat and heat through. Serve on rolls.

Nutrition Facts: *1 sandwich equals 354 calories, 10 g fat (2 g saturated fat), 59 mg cholesterol, 714 mg sodium, 40 g carbohydrate, 2 g fiber, 26 g protein.* **Diabetic Exchanges:** *3 lean meat, 2½ starch.*

Turkey Sloppy Joes

These tangy sandwiches go over well at gatherings large and small. I frequently take them to potlucks, and I'm always asked for the recipe. People are surprised to learn that I use lean ground turkey.

—MARYLOU LARUE
FREELAND, MICHIGAN

PREP: 15 MIN. **COOK:** 4 HOURS
MAKES: 8 SERVINGS

- 1 pound lean ground turkey
- 1 small onion, chopped
- ½ cup chopped celery
- ¼ cup chopped green pepper
- 1 can (10¾ ounces) reduced-sodium condensed tomato soup, undiluted
- ½ cup ketchup
- 2 tablespoons prepared mustard
- 1 tablespoon brown sugar
- ¼ teaspoon pepper
- 8 hamburger buns, split

1. In a large skillet coated with cooking spray, cook the turkey, onion, celery and green pepper over medium heat until meat is no longer pink; drain. Stir in the soup, ketchup, mustard, brown sugar and pepper.

2. Transfer to a 3-qt. slow cooker. Cover and cook on low for 4 hours. Serve on buns.

Nutrition Facts: *1 sandwich equals 247 calories, 7 g fat (2 g saturated fat), 45 mg cholesterol, 553 mg sodium, 32 g carbohydrate, 2 g fiber, 14 g protein.* **Diabetic Exchanges:** *2 starch, 1½ lean meat.*

Round Steak Sauerbraten

My easy version of an Old World classic takes just minutes to prepare for the slow cooker. The flavorful beef is also great with white rice or dirty rice.

—**LINDA BLOOM** MCHENRY, ILLINOIS

PREP: 20 MIN. **COOK:** 7 HOURS
MAKES: 10 SERVINGS

- 1 envelope brown gravy mix
- 2 tablespoons plus 1½ teaspoons brown sugar
- 2½ cups cold water, divided
- 1 cup chopped onion
- 2 tablespoons white vinegar
- 2 teaspoons Worcestershire sauce
- 2 bay leaves
- 2½ pounds beef top round steak, cut into 3-inch x ½-inch strips
- 2 teaspoons salt
- 1 teaspoon pepper
- ¼ cup cornstarch
- 10 cups hot cooked egg noodles

1. In a 5-qt. slow cooker, combine the gravy mix, brown sugar, 2 cups water, onion, vinegar, Worcestershire sauce and bay leaves.
2. Sprinkle beef with salt and pepper; stir into gravy mixture. Cover and cook on low for 6-8 hours or until meat is tender.
3. Combine cornstarch and remaining water until smooth; stir into beef mixture. Cover and cook on high for 30 minutes or until thickened. Discard bay leaves. Serve with noodles.

Nutrition Facts: ¾ cup beef mixture with 1 cup noodles equals 331 calories, 6 g fat (2 g saturated fat), 96 mg cholesterol, 741 mg sodium, 37 g carbohydrate, 2 g fiber, 32 g protein. **Diabetic Exchanges:** 3 lean meat, 2½ starch.

Vegetarian Chili Ole!

I combine ingredients for this hearty chili the night before, start my trusty slow cooker in the morning and come home to a rich, spicy meal at night!

—**MARJORIE AU** HONOLULU, HAWAII

PREP: 35 MIN. **COOK:** 6 HOURS
MAKES: 7 SERVINGS

- 1 can (16 ounces) kidney beans, rinsed and drained
- 1 can (15 ounces) black beans, rinsed and drained
- 1 can (14½ ounces) diced tomatoes, undrained
- 1½ cups frozen corn
- 1 large onion, chopped
- 1 medium zucchini, chopped
- 1 medium sweet red pepper, chopped
- 1 can (4 ounces) chopped green chilies
- 1 ounce Mexican chocolate, chopped
- 1 cup water
- 1 can (6 ounces) tomato paste
- 1 tablespoon cornmeal
- 1 tablespoon chili powder
- ½ teaspoon salt
- ½ teaspoon dried oregano
- ½ teaspoon ground cumin
- ¼ teaspoon hot pepper sauce, optional
  Optional toppings: diced tomatoes, chopped green onions and queso fresco

1. In a 4-qt. slow cooker, combine the first nine ingredients. Combine the water, tomato paste, cornmeal, chili powder, salt, oregano, cumin and pepper sauce, if desired, until smooth; stir into slow cooker.
2. Cover and cook on low for 6-8 hours or until the vegetables are tender.
3. Serve chili with toppings of your choice.

Nutrition Facts: 1 cup (calculated without optional ingredients) equals 216 calories, 1 g fat (trace saturated fat), 0 cholesterol, 559 mg sodium, 43 g carbohydrate, 10 g fiber, 11 g protein. **Diabetic Exchanges:** 2½ starch, 1 lean meat.

FAST FIX ▶ Slow-Cooked Pork and Beans

I like to get this dish started before leaving for work in the morning. When I get home, my supper's ready! A generous helping of tender pork and beans is perfect alongside a slice of warm corn bread.

—PATRICIA HAGER
NICHOLASVILLE, KENTUCKY

PREP: 15 MIN. **COOK:** 6 HOURS
MAKES: 12 SERVINGS

- 1 **boneless pork loin roast (3 pounds)**
- 1 **medium onion, sliced**
- 3 **cans (15 ounces each) pork and beans**
- 1½ **cups barbecue sauce**
- ¼ **cup packed brown sugar**
- 1 **teaspoon garlic powder**

1. Cut roast in half; place in a 5-qt. slow cooker. Top with onion. In a large bowl, combine the beans, barbecue sauce, brown sugar and garlic powder; pour over meat. Cover and cook on low for 6-8 hours or until meat is tender.
2. Remove roast; shred with two forks. Return meat to slow cooker; heat through.

Nutrition Facts: *1 cup equals 217 calories, 6 g fat (2 g saturated fat), 56 mg cholesterol, 404 mg sodium, 16 g carbohydrate, 2 g fiber, 24 g protein.*

Mexican Chicken Soup

As a busy mom, I'm always looking for dinner recipes that can be prepared in the morning. My kids love the taco-like flavors of this soup.

—MARLENE KANE
LAINESBURG, MICHIGAN

PREP: 10 MIN. **COOK:** 3 HOURS
MAKES: 6 SERVINGS

- 1½ **pounds boneless skinless chicken breasts, cubed**
- 2 **teaspoons canola oil**
- ½ **cup water**
- 1 **envelope reduced-sodium taco seasoning**
- 1 **can (32 ounces) V8 juice**
- 1 **jar (16 ounces) salsa**
- 1 **can (15 ounces) black beans, rinsed and drained**
- 1 **package (10 ounces) frozen corn, thawed**
- 6 **tablespoons reduced-fat cheddar cheese**
- 6 **tablespoons reduced-fat sour cream**
- 2 **tablespoons minced fresh cilantro**

1. In a large nonstick skillet, saute chicken in oil until no longer pink. Add water and taco seasoning; simmer, uncovered, until chicken is well coated.
2. Transfer to a 5-qt. slow cooker. Stir in the V8 juice, salsa, beans and corn. Cover and cook on low for 3-4 hours or until heated through. Serve with cheese, sour cream and cilantro.

Nutrition Facts: *1½ cups with 1 tablespoon each of cheese and sour cream and 1 teaspoon cilantro equals 345 calories, 7 g fat (3 g saturated fat), 72 mg cholesterol, 1,315 mg sodium, 34 g carbohydrate, 7 g fiber, 31 g protein.* **Diabetic Exchanges:** *4 lean meat, 2 vegetable, 1½ starch, ½ fat.*

Coconut-Pecan Sweet Potatoes

These delicious sweet potatoes cook effortlessly in the slow cooker so you can tend to other things. Coconut gives this classic dish new, mouthwatering flavor.

—RAQUEL HAGGARD
EDMOND, OKLAHOMA

PREP: 15 MIN. **COOK:** 4 HOURS
MAKES: 12 SERVINGS

- 4 **pounds sweet potatoes, peeled and cut into chunks**
- ½ **cup chopped pecans**
- ½ **cup flaked coconut**
- ⅓ **cup sugar**
- ⅓ **cup packed brown sugar**
- ¼ **cup reduced-fat butter, melted**
- ½ **teaspoon ground cinnamon**
- ¼ **teaspoon salt**
- ½ **teaspoon coconut extract**
- ½ **teaspoon vanilla extract**

1. Place sweet potatoes in a 5-qt. slow cooker coated with cooking spray. Combine the pecans, coconut, sugar, brown sugar, butter, cinnamon and salt; sprinkle over potatoes.
2. Cover and cook on low for 4 hours or until potatoes are tender. Stir in extracts.

Editor's Note: *This recipe was tested with Land O'Lakes light stick butter.*

Nutrition Facts: *⅔ cup equals 211 calories, 7 g fat (3 g saturated fat), 5 mg cholesterol, 103 mg sodium, 37 g carbohydrate, 3 g fiber, 2 g protein.*

Slow-Cooker Berry Cobbler

Even during warm weather, you can enjoy the scrumptious taste of homemade cobbler without heating up the kitchen.

—KAREN JAROCKI YUMA, ARIZONA

PREP: 15 MIN. **COOK:** 2 HOURS
MAKES: 8 SERVINGS

- 1¼ **cups all-purpose flour, divided**
- 2 **tablespoons plus 1 cup sugar, divided**
- 1 **teaspoon baking powder**
- ¼ **teaspoon ground cinnamon**
- 1 **egg, lightly beaten**
- ¼ **cup fat-free milk**
- 2 **tablespoons canola oil**
- ⅛ **teaspoon salt**
- 2 **cups fresh or frozen raspberries, thawed**
- 2 **cups fresh or frozen blueberries, thawed**
  Low-fat vanilla frozen yogurt, optional

1. In a large bowl, combine 1 cup flour, 2 tablespoons sugar, baking powder and cinnamon. Combine the egg, milk and oil; stir into dry ingredients just until moistened (batter will be thick). Spread batter evenly into a 5-qt. slow cooker coated with cooking spray.
2. In a large bowl, combine the salt and remaining flour and sugar; add berries and toss to coat. Spread over batter.
3. Cover and cook on high for 2 to 2½ hours or until a toothpick inserted into cobbler comes out clean. Serve with frozen yogurt if desired.

Nutrition Facts: *1 serving (calculated without frozen yogurt) equals 250 calories, 4 g fat (trace saturated fat), 27 mg cholesterol, 142 mg sodium, 51 g carbohydrate, 4 g fiber, 3 g protein.*

Country-Style Pork Loin

Here's a pork roast so moist and tender, it melts in your mouth. My son puts it at the top of his list of favorite foods. My family really likes it with mashed potatoes.

—**CORINA FLANSBERG** CARSON CITY, NEVADA

PREP: 20 MIN. **COOK:** 5 HOURS + STANDING
MAKES: 8 SERVINGS

- 1 **boneless pork loin roast (3 pounds)**
- ½ **cup all-purpose flour**
- 1 **teaspoon onion powder**
- 1 **teaspoon ground mustard**
- 2 **tablespoons canola oil**
- 2 **cups reduced-sodium chicken broth**
- ¼ **cup cornstarch**
- ¼ **cup cold water**
  Hot mashed potatoes, optional

1. Cut roast in half. In a large resealable plastic bag, combine the flour, onion powder and mustard. Add pork, one portion at a time, and shake to coat. In a large skillet, brown pork in oil on all sides.
2. Transfer to a 5-qt. slow cooker. Pour broth over pork. Cover and cook on low for 5-6 hours or until tender. Remove pork and keep warm. Let pork stand for 10-15 minutes before slicing.
3. Strain cooking juices, reserving 2½ cups juices; skim fat from reserved juices. Transfer to a small saucepan. Bring liquid to a boil. Combine cornstarch and water until smooth; gradually stir into the pan. Bring to a boil; cook and stir for 2 minutes or until thickened. Serve pork and gravy with mashed potatoes if desired.

Nutrition Facts: *5 ounces cooked meat with ¼ cup gravy (calculated without potatoes) equals 291 calories, 11 g fat (3 g saturated fat), 85 mg cholesterol, 204 mg sodium, 10 g carbohydrate, trace fiber, 34 g protein.* **Diabetic Exchanges:** *5 lean meat, 1 fat, ½ starch.*

Slow-Cooked Pork Roast Dinner

This delicious recipe will give you the most tender pork you have ever tasted! You can cut it with a fork, and it's just as moist the next day...if there are any leftovers.
—**JANE MONTGOMERY** PIQUA, OHIO

PREP: 25 MIN. **COOK:** 6 HOURS **MAKES:** 8 SERVINGS

- 1 **large onion, halved and sliced**
- 1 **boneless pork loin roast (2½ pounds)**
- 4 **medium potatoes, peeled and cubed**
- 1 **package (16 ounces) frozen sliced carrots**
- 1 **cup hot water**
- ¼ **cup sugar**
- 3 **tablespoons cider vinegar**
- 2 **tablespoons reduced-sodium soy sauce**
- 1 **tablespoon ketchup**
- ½ **teaspoon salt**
- ½ **teaspoon pepper**
- ¼ **teaspoon garlic powder**
- ¼ **teaspoon chili powder**
- 2 **tablespoons cornstarch**
- 2 **tablespoons cold water**

1. Place onion in the bottom of a 5-qt. slow cooker. Add the pork, potatoes and carrots. Whisk the hot water, sugar, vinegar, soy sauce, ketchup, salt, pepper, garlic powder and chili powder; pour over pork and vegetables. Cover and cook on low for 6-8 hours or until meat is tender.

2. Remove pork and vegetables to a serving platter; keep warm. Skim fat from cooking juices; transfer to a small saucepan. Bring liquid to a boil. Combine cornstarch and water until smooth. Gradually stir into the pan. Bring to a boil; cook and stir for 2 minutes or until thickened. Serve with meat and vegetables.

Nutrition Facts: *4 ounces cooked pork with ⅔ cup vegetables and ⅓ cup gravy equals 304 calories, 7 g fat (2 g saturated fat), 70 mg cholesterol, 401 mg sodium, 30 g carbohydrate, 3 g fiber, 29 g protein.* **Diabetic Exchanges:** *4 lean meat, 1½ starch, 1 vegetable.*

Indonesian Peanut Chicken

Here's a great make-ahead recipe! I cut up fresh chicken, put it in a bag with the remaining slow-cooker ingredients and freeze. To cook, just remove the bag a day ahead to thaw in the fridge, then pour all the contents into the slow cooker.

—SARAH NEWMAN
MAHTOMEDI, MINNESOTA

PREP: 15 MIN. **COOK:** 4 HOURS
MAKES: 6 SERVINGS

- 1½ **pounds boneless skinless chicken breasts, cut into 1-inch cubes**
- ⅓ **cup chopped onion**
- ⅓ **cup water**
- ¼ **cup reduced-fat creamy peanut butter**
- 3 **tablespoons chili sauce**
- ¼ **teaspoon salt**
- ¼ **teaspoon cayenne pepper**
- ¼ **teaspoon pepper**
- 3 **cups hot cooked brown rice**
- 6 **tablespoons chopped salted peanuts**
- 6 **tablespoons chopped sweet red pepper**

1. Place chicken in a 4-qt. slow cooker. In a small bowl, combine the onion, water, peanut butter, chili sauce, salt, cayenne and pepper; pour over chicken. Cover and cook on low for 4-6 hours or until chicken is no longer pink.
2. Shred meat with two forks and return to slow cooker; heat through. Serve with rice. Sprinkle with peanuts and red pepper.

Nutrition Facts: *½ cup chicken mixture with ½ cup rice and 1 tablespoon each peanuts and red pepper equals 353 calories, 12 g fat (2 g saturated fat), 63 mg cholesterol, 370 mg sodium, 31 g carbohydrate, 3 g fiber, 31 g protein.* **Diabetic Exchanges:** *3 lean meat, 2 starch, 2 fat.*

Slow-Cooked Steak Fajitas

We all enjoy the flavors of Mexican food, so I was glad when I spotted a recipe that's loaded with vegetables. The beef always comes out nice and tender.

—TWILA BURKHOLDER
MIDDLEBURG, PENNSYLVANIA

PREP: 10 MIN. **COOK:** 8½ HOURS
MAKES: 12 SERVINGS

- 1 **beef flank steak (1½ pounds)**
- 1 **can (14½ ounces) diced tomatoes with garlic and onion, undrained**
- 1 **jalapeno pepper, seeded and chopped**
- 2 **garlic cloves, minced**
- 1 **teaspoon ground coriander**
- 1 **teaspoon ground cumin**
- 1 **teaspoon chili powder**
- ½ **teaspoon salt**
- 1 **medium onion, sliced**
- 1 **medium green pepper, julienned**
- 1 **medium sweet red pepper, julienned**
- 1 **tablespoon minced fresh cilantro**
- 2 **teaspoons cornstarch**
- 1 **tablespoon water**
- 12 **flour tortillas (6 inches), warmed**
- ¾ **cup fat-free sour cream**
- ¾ **cup salsa**

1. Thinly slice steak across the grain into strips; place in a 5-qt. slow cooker. Add the tomatoes, jalapeno, garlic, coriander, cumin, chili powder and salt. Cover and cook on low for 7 hours.
2. Add the onion, peppers and cilantro. Cover and cook 1-2 hours longer or until meat is tender.
3. Combine cornstarch and water until smooth; gradually stir into the slow cooker. Cover and cook on high for 30 minutes or until slightly thickened.
4. Using a slotted spoon, spoon about ½ cup meat mixture down the center of each tortilla. Fold bottom of tortilla over filling and roll up. Serve fajitas with sour cream and salsa.

Editor's Note: *Wear disposable gloves when cutting hot peppers; the oils can burn skin. Avoid touching your face.*

Nutrition Facts: *1 fajita equals 273 calories, 11 g fat (3 g saturated fat), 23 mg cholesterol, 494 mg sodium, 35 g carbohydrate, 2 g fiber, 21 g protein.* **Diabetic Exchanges:** *2 starch, 2 lean meat, 1 vegetable.*

Thai Chicken Thighs

Thanks to the slow cooker, this traditional Thai dish with peanut butter, jalapeno peppers and chili sauce is easy to make. If you want to crank up the spice a bit, use more jalapeno peppers.

—TASTE OF HOME TEST KITCHEN

PREP: 25 MIN. **COOK:** 5 HOURS
MAKES: 8 SERVINGS

- 8 **bone-in chicken thighs (about 3 pounds), skin removed**
- ½ **cup salsa**
- ¼ **cup creamy peanut butter**
- 2 **tablespoons lemon juice**
- 2 **tablespoons reduced-sodium soy sauce**
- 1 **tablespoon chopped seeded jalapeno pepper**
- 2 **teaspoons Thai chili sauce**
- 1 **garlic clove, minced**
- 1 **teaspoon minced fresh gingerroot**
- 2 **green onions, sliced**
- 2 **tablespoons sesame seeds, toasted**
  Hot cooked basmati rice, optional

1. Place chicken in a 3-qt. slow cooker. In a small bowl, combine the salsa, peanut butter, lemon juice, soy sauce, jalapeno, Thai chili sauce, garlic and ginger; pour over chicken.

2. Cover and cook on low for 5-6 hours or until chicken is tender. Sprinkle with green onions and sesame seeds. Serve chicken with rice if desired.

Editor's Note: *Wear disposable gloves when cutting hot peppers; the oils can burn skin. Avoid touching your face.*

Nutrition Facts: *1 chicken thigh with ¼ cup sauce (calculated without rice) equals 261 calories, 15 g fat (4 g saturated fat), 87 mg cholesterol, 350 mg sodium, 5 g carbohydrate, 1 g fiber, 27 g protein.* **Diabetic Exchanges:** *4 lean meat, 1 fat, ½ starch.*

Traditional Beef Stew

PREP: 15 MIN. **COOK:** 8 HOURS
MAKES: 4 SERVINGS

- 1 **pound beef stew meat, cut into 1-inch cubes**
- 1 **pound fresh baby carrots**
- 2 **medium potatoes, cut into chunks**
- 2 **medium onions, cut into wedges**
- 1 **cup drained diced tomatoes**
- 1 **cup beef broth**
- 1 **celery rib, cut into ½-inch pieces**
- 2 **tablespoons quick-cooking tapioca**
- 1 **teaspoon Worcestershire sauce**
- ¼ **teaspoon salt**
- ¼ **teaspoon pepper**

1. In a 3-qt. slow cooker, combine all ingredients.

2. Cover and cook on low for 8-10 hours or until meat and vegetables are tender.

Nutrition Facts: *1½ cups equals 334 calories, 8 g fat (3 g saturated fat), 70 mg cholesterol, 611 mg sodium, 39 g carbohydrate, 6 g fiber, 26 g protein.* **Diabetic Exchanges:** *3 lean meat, 2 starch, 2 vegetable.*

> ❝The aroma of this classic beef stew is irresistible, making it impossible not to dig in the moment you walk in the door!❞

—ROSANA PAPE HAMILTON, INDIANA

Meat Loaf from the Slow Cooker

This simple, easy-to-make meat loaf is one of my personal favorites. I'm often asked for the recipe.
—**LAURA BURGESS** MOUNT VERNON, SOUTH DAKOTA

PREP: 25 MIN. **COOK:** 3 HOURS **MAKES:** 8 SERVINGS

- ½ cup tomato sauce
- ½ cup egg substitute
- ¼ cup ketchup
- 1 teaspoon Worcestershire sauce
- 1 small onion, chopped
- ⅓ cup crushed saltines (about 10 crackers)
- ¾ teaspoon minced garlic
- ½ teaspoon seasoned salt
- ⅛ teaspoon seasoned pepper
- 1½ pounds lean ground beef (90% lean)
- ½ pound reduced-fat bulk pork sausage

SAUCE
- ½ cup ketchup
- 3 tablespoons brown sugar
- ¾ teaspoon ground mustard
- ¼ teaspoon ground nutmeg

1. Cut three 25-in. x 3-in. strips of heavy-duty foil; crisscross so they resemble spokes of a wheel. Place strips on the bottom and up the sides of a 4- or 5-qt. slow cooker. Coat strips with cooking spray.

2. In a large bowl, combine the first nine ingredients. Crumble beef and sausage over mixture and mix well (mixture will be moist). Shape into a loaf. Place meat loaf in the center of the strips.

3. In a small bowl, combine sauce ingredients. Spoon over meat loaf. Cover and cook on low 3-4 hours or until no pink remains and a thermometer reads 160°. Using foil strips as handles, remove the meat loaf to a platter.

Nutrition Facts: *1 slice equals 267 calories, 12 g fat (5 g saturated fat), 72 mg cholesterol, 740 mg sodium, 16 g carbohydrate, trace fiber, 23 g protein.* **Diabetic Exchanges:** *3 lean meat, 1 starch, ½ fat.*

50

77

70

Beef

FAST FIX ▶ Chipotle Beef Sandwiches

A jar of chipotle salsa makes it easy to spice up beef sirloin for mouthwatering sandwiches. Keep this no-stress recipe in mind the next time you have to feed a hungry crowd.

—JESSICA RING MADISON, WISCONSIN

PREP: 25 MIN. **COOK:** 7 HOURS **MAKES:** 10 SERVINGS

- 1 large sweet onion, halved and thinly sliced
- 1 beef sirloin tip roast (3 pounds)
- 1 jar (16 ounces) chipotle salsa
- ½ cup beer or nonalcoholic beer
- 1 envelope Lipton beefy onion soup mix
- 10 kaiser rolls, split

1. Place onion in a 5-qt. slow cooker. Cut roast in half; place over onion. Combine the salsa, beer and soup mix. Pour over top. Cover and cook on low for 7-8 hours or until meat is tender.
2. Remove roast. Shred meat with two forks and return to the slow cooker; heat through. Using a slotted spoon, spoon shredded meat onto rolls.

FAST FIX ▶ Chuck Roast Italiano

Moist, flavorful and a cinch to throw together, this roast creates a rich, glossy gravy that tastes wonderful over noodles or potatoes.

—JENNY BLOOMQUIST HELENA, MONTANA

PREP: 10 MIN. **COOK:** 8 HOURS **MAKES:** 10 SERVINGS

- 1 boneless beef chuck roast (4 pounds)
- 1 package Italian salad dressing mix
- 1 envelope au jus gravy mix
- 1 envelope brown gravy mix
- ½ cup water, divided

Cut roast in half. Place in a 4- or 5-qt. slow cooker. Combine the salad dressing mix, au jus mix and gravy mix with ¼ cup water; rub over roast. Pour remaining water around the roast. Cover and cook on low for 8-10 hours or until tender. Serve with gravy.

Tender Salsa Beef

This is my Mexican-style twist on comfort food. To keep it kid-friendly, use mild salsa.

—STACIE STAMPER
NORTH WILKESBORO, NORTH CAROLINA

PREP: 15 MIN. **COOK:** 8 HOURS **MAKES:** 8 SERVINGS

- 1½ pounds beef stew meat, cut into ¾-inch cubes
- 2 cups salsa
- 1 tablespoon brown sugar
- 1 tablespoon reduced-sodium soy sauce
- 1 garlic clove, minced
- 4 cups hot cooked brown rice

In a 3-qt. slow cooker, combine the beef, salsa, brown sugar, soy sauce and garlic. Cover and cook on low for 8-10 hours or until meat is tender. Using a slotted spoon, serve beef with rice.

Chicago-Style Beef Sandwiches

I'm originally from the Windy City, so I love Chicago-style beef. These tender sandwiches have an authentic flavor, and they're so simple to prepare using a slow cooker.

—**LOIS SZYDLOWSKI** TAMPA, FLORIDA

PREP: 30 MIN. **COOK:** 8 HOURS **MAKES:** 12 SERVINGS

- 1 boneless beef chuck roast (4 pounds)
- 1 teaspoon salt
- ¾ teaspoon pepper
- 2 tablespoons olive oil
- ½ pound fresh mushrooms
- 2 medium carrots, cut into chunks
- 1 medium onion, cut into wedges
- 6 garlic cloves, halved
- 2 teaspoons dried oregano
- 1 carton (32 ounces) beef broth
- 1 tablespoon beef base
- 12 Italian rolls, split
- 1 jar (16 ounces) giardiniera, drained

1. Cut roast in half; sprinkle with salt and pepper. In a large skillet, brown meat in oil on all sides. Transfer to a 5-qt. slow cooker.

2. In a food processor, combine the mushrooms, carrots, onion, garlic and oregano. Cover and process until finely chopped. Transfer to slow cooker. Combine beef broth and base; pour over top. Cover and cook on low for 8-10 hours or until tender.

3. Remove meat and shred with two forks. Skim fat from cooking juices. Return meat to slow cooker; heat through. Using a slotted spoon, serve beef on buns; top with giardiniera.

Editor's Note: *Look for beef base near the broth and bouillon in your grocery store.*

Brisket with Cranberry Gravy

Use any leftover meat and gravy to make delicious hot sandwiches the following day.

—NOELLE LABRECQUE
ROUND ROCK, TEXAS

PREP: 15 MIN. **COOK:** 5½ HOURS
MAKES: 12 SERVINGS

- 1 medium onion, sliced
- 1 fresh beef brisket (3 pounds), halved
- 1 can (14 ounces) jellied cranberry sauce
- ½ cup thawed cranberry juice concentrate
- 2 tablespoons cornstarch
- ¼ cup cold water

1. Place onion in a 5-qt. slow cooker; top with brisket. Combine cranberry sauce and juice concentrate; pour over beef. Cover and cook on low for 5½ to 6 hours or until meat is tender.

2. Remove brisket and keep warm. Strain cooking juices, discarding onion; skim fat. Place in a small saucepan and bring to a boil. Combine cornstarch and cold water until smooth; gradually stir into the pan. Cook and stir for 2 minutes or until thickened. Thinly slice brisket across the grain; serve with gravy.

Editor's Note: *This is a fresh beef brisket, not corned beef.*

Southwestern Beef Tortillas

Cooked to tender perfection in the slow cooker, the beef in this recipe is treated to an easy and delicious jalapeno-flavored sauce. It makes a savory and satisfying filling in tortillas.

—MARIE RIZZIO
INTERLOCHEN, MICHIGAN

PREP: 25 MIN. **COOK:** 8½ HOURS
MAKES: 8 SERVINGS

- 1 boneless beef chuck roast (2 pounds)
- ½ cup water
- 4 large tomatoes, peeled and chopped
- 1 large green pepper, thinly sliced
- 1 medium onion, chopped
- 1 garlic clove, minced
- 1 bay leaf
- 2 tablespoons canola oil
- ¾ cup ketchup
- ½ cup pickled jalapeno slices
- 1 tablespoon juice from pickled jalapeno slices
- 1 tablespoon cider vinegar
- 1 teaspoon salt
- ⅛ teaspoon garlic salt
- 8 flour tortillas (8 inches), warmed

1. Place roast and water in a 3-qt. slow cooker. Cover and cook on low for 8-9 hours or until the meat is tender.

2. Remove meat. When cool enough to handle, shred meat with two forks. Skim fat from cooking liquid; set aside ½ cup.

3. Meanwhile, in a large skillet, cook the tomatoes, green pepper, onion, garlic and bay leaf in oil over low heat for 15-20 minutes or until vegetables are softened.

4. Stir in the ketchup, jalapeno slices and juice, vinegar, salt, garlic salt and reserved cooking liquid. Bring to a boil. Stir in shredded beef; heat through. Discard bay leaf. Serve beef mixture on tortillas.

Beef Tips

This recipe was given to my mother when I was young, and the entire family loved it. Now I often make it for my own family.

—**DIANE BENSKIN** LEWISVILLE, TEXAS

PREP: 20 MIN. **COOK:** 6¼ HOURS
MAKES: 4 SERVINGS

- 1 **pound beef sirloin tips, cut into 1-inch cubes**
- 2 **medium carrots, chopped**
- 2 **medium celery ribs, chopped**
- 1 **cup chopped onion**
- 1 **can (10¾ ounces) condensed golden mushroom soup, undiluted**
- ⅔ **cup white wine or beef broth**
- 2 **teaspoons cornstarch**
- ¼ **cup cold water**
  Hot cooked egg noodles

1. In a 3-qt. slow cooker, combine the beef, carrots, celery, onion, soup and wine.
2. Cover and cook on low for 6-7 hours or until meat is tender.
3. Combine the cornstarch and cold water until smooth; gradually stir into the cooking juices. Cover and cook on high for 15 minutes or until mixture is thickened. Serve with noodles.

FAST FIX ▶ ## Sweet and Savory Brisket

It's wonderful to come home from work and have this mouthwatering brisket waiting for you. The beef doubles as a tasty sandwich filling, too. And the slow cooker makes it so convenient!

—**CHRIS SNYDER**
BOULDER, COLORADO

PREP: 10 MIN. **COOK:** 8 HOURS
MAKES: 8-10 SERVINGS

- 1 **beef brisket (3 to 3½ pounds), cut in half**

- 1 **cup ketchup**
- ¼ **cup grape jelly**
- 1 **envelope onion soup mix**
- ½ **teaspoon pepper**

1. Place half of the brisket in a 5-qt. slow cooker. In a small bowl, combine the ketchup, jelly, soup mix and pepper; spread half over meat. Top with the remaining meat and ketchup mixture.
2. Cover and cook on low for 8-10 hours or until meat is tender. Slice brisket; serve with cooking juice.
Editor's Note: *This is a fresh beef brisket, not corned beef.*

REFRESHED CELERY

Give limp celery a second chance to season entrees, soups and stews. Cut the ends from the limp celery stalks and place the stalks in a glass of cold water in the refrigerator for several hours or overnight. You'll be surprised how refreshed the celery will be.

Corned Beef & Cabbage for the Wine Lover

With its elegant flavor and lovely appearance, you'd never guess how easy it is to prepare this traditional St. Patrick's Day favorite. Thanks to the slow cooker, it comes together effortlessly.

—SUSAN CEPEDA
MIAMI LAKES, FLORIDA

PREP: 25 MIN. **COOK:** 9 HOURS
MAKES: 6 SERVINGS

- ¾ **pound fingerling potatoes, cut in half**
- 2 **cups fresh baby carrots**
- 2 **medium onions, cut into wedges**
- 4 **garlic cloves, minced**
- 1½ **cups white wine or beef broth**
- 1 **corned beef brisket with spice packet (3 to 3½ pounds)**
- ½ **cup stone-ground mustard**
- 1 **small head cabbage, cut into thin wedges**
- 1 **can (14 ounces) sauerkraut, rinsed and well drained**

1. In a 6- or 7-qt. slow cooker, combine the potatoes, carrots, onions and garlic. Pour wine over vegetables. Cut brisket in half. Spread with mustard; place over vegetables (discard spice packet from corned beef or save for another use).
2. Cover and cook on low for 8-10 hours or until meat and vegetables are tender, adding the cabbage and sauerkraut during the last hour of cooking. Serve beef with vegetables.

Asian-Style Round Steak

I have long relied on this hearty dish, chock-full of veggies, to satisfy my family at mealtime. My friend gave me the recipe more than two decades ago and all I added was a little extra meat, the celery and mushrooms.

—MARILYN WOLFE
DES MOINES, IOWA

PREP: 20 MIN. **COOK:** 7 HOURS
MAKES: 8 SERVINGS

- 2 **pounds beef top round steak, cut into 3-inch strips**
- 2 **tablespoons canola oil**
- 3 **celery ribs, chopped**
- 1 **cup chopped onion**
- ¼ **cup reduced-sodium soy sauce**
- 1 **teaspoon sugar**
- ½ **teaspoon salt**
- ½ **teaspoon minced garlic**
- ¼ **teaspoon ground ginger**
- ¼ **teaspoon pepper**
- 2 **medium green peppers, julienned**
- 1 **can (15 ounces) tomato sauce**
- 1 **can (14 ounces) bean sprouts, rinsed and drained**
- 1 **can (8 ounces) sliced water chestnuts, drained**
- 1 **jar (4½ ounces) sliced mushrooms, drained**
- 1 **tablespoon cornstarch**
- ½ **cup cold water**
  Hot cooked rice

1. In a large skillet, brown meat in oil on all sides. Transfer meat and drippings to a 5-qt. slow cooker. Combine the celery, onion, soy sauce, sugar, salt, garlic, ginger and pepper; pour over meat. Cover and cook on low for 5½ to 6 hours or until the meat is tender.
2. Add the green peppers, tomato sauce, bean sprouts, water chestnuts and mushrooms; cover and cook on low 1 hour longer.
3. Combine cornstarch and water until smooth; stir into beef mixture. Cover and cook on high for 30 minutes or until sauce is thickened. Serve with rice.

Pizza Casserole

A friend from church gave me the recipe for this tasty slow cooker casserole. It's always one of the first dishes emptied at potlucks, and it can easily be adapted to personal tastes. You will love it!

—JULIE STERCHI JACKSON, MISSOURI

PREP: 25 MIN. **COOK:** 4 HOURS
MAKES: 12 SERVINGS

- 3 **pounds ground beef**
- ½ **cup chopped onion**
- 1 **jar (28 ounces) spaghetti sauce**
- 2 **jars (4½ ounces each) sliced mushrooms, drained**
- 1 **teaspoon salt**
- ½ **teaspoon garlic powder**
- ½ **teaspoon dried oregano**
  Dash pepper
- 1 **package (16 ounces) wide egg noodles, cooked and drained**
- 2 **packages (3½ ounces each) sliced pepperoni**
- 2 **cups (8 ounces) shredded cheddar cheese**
- 2 **cups (8 ounces) shredded part-skim mozzarella cheese**

1. In a Dutch oven, brown beef and onion over medium heat until meat is no longer pink; drain. Add the spaghetti sauce, mushrooms, salt, garlic powder, oregano and pepper; heat through.
2. Spoon half of mixture into a 5-qt. slow cooker. Top with half of the noodles, pepperoni and cheeses. Repeat layers. Cover and cook on low for 4-5 hours or until cheese is melted.

FAST FIX ▶ Easy Roast Beef and Gravy

This is by far the simplest way to make roast beef and gravy. On busy days, I can put it in the slow cooker and completely forget about it. We like ours served with mashed potatoes and fruit salad.

—ABBY METZGER
LARCHWOOD, IOWA

PREP: 15 MIN. **COOK:** 8 HOURS
MAKES: 8-10 SERVINGS

- 1 **boneless beef chuck roast (3 pounds)**
- 2 **cans (10¾ ounces each) condensed cream of mushroom soup, undiluted**
- ⅓ **cup sherry or beef broth**
- 1 **envelope onion soup mix**

1. Cut roast in half; place in a 3-qt. slow cooker. In a large bowl, combine the remaining ingredients; pour over roast.
2. Cover and cook on low for 8-10 hours or until meat is tender.

FAST FIX ▶ Round Steak Supper

Here's a hearty stick-to-your-ribs dinner that will also help you stick to your budget!

—SANDRA CASTILLO
JANESVILLE, WISCONSIN

PREP: 10 MIN. **COOK:** 6 HOURS
MAKES: 4 SERVINGS

- 4 **large potatoes, peeled and cubed**
- 1½ **pounds beef top round steak**
- 1 **can (10¾ ounces) condensed cream of mushroom soup, undiluted**
- ½ **cup water**
- 1 **envelope onion soup mix**
  Pepper and garlic powder to taste

1. Place potatoes in a 3-qt. slow cooker. Cut beef into four pieces; place over potatoes. Combine the soup, water, soup mix, pepper and garlic powder. Pour over the beef.
2. Cover and cook on low for 6-8 hours or until meat and potatoes are tender.

Flank Steak Roll-Up

As the working mother of five hungry boys, I've come to rely on my slow cooker to give me a head start on meals. For a special dinner, I roll a mushroom-flavored stuffing into flank steak and simmer it in a dressed-up gravy mix. This one's great for company!

—SHERYL JOHNSON
LAS VEGAS, NEVADA

PREP: 15 MIN. **COOK:** 8 HOURS
MAKES: 6 SERVINGS

- 1 can (4 ounces) mushroom stems and pieces, undrained
- 2 tablespoons butter, melted
- 1 package (6 ounces) seasoned stuffing mix
- 1 beef flank steak (1¾ pounds)
- 1 envelope brown gravy mix
- ¼ cup chopped green onions
- ¼ cup dry red wine or beef broth

1. In bowl, toss the mushrooms, butter and dry stuffing mix. Spread over steak to within 1 in. of edges. Roll up jelly-roll style, starting with a long side; tie with kitchen string. Place in a 3-qt. slow cooker.

2. Prepare gravy mix according to package directions; add onions and wine. Pour over meat. Cover and cook on low for 8-10 hours. Remove meat to a serving platter and keep warm. Strain cooking juices and thicken if desired. Remove string from roll-up; slice beef and serve with gravy.

WINE OR BROTH

If you don't want to open up fresh wine or broth for the flank steak recipe, just use ¼ cup water mixed with ¼ teaspoon bouillon granules instead. The gravy will still have plenty of flavor.

Swiss Steak Supper

Here's a satisfying slow-cooked dinner that's loaded with veggies. To save a step, you can season the steak with peppered seasoned salt instead of using both seasoned salt and pepper.

—KATHLEEN ROMANIUK
CHOMEDEY, QUEBEC

PREP: 20 MIN. **COOK:** 5 HOURS
MAKES: 6 SERVINGS

- 1½ pounds beef top round steak
- ½ teaspoon seasoned salt
- ¼ teaspoon coarsely ground pepper
- 1 tablespoon canola oil
- 3 medium potatoes
- 1½ cups fresh baby carrots
- 1 medium onion, sliced
- 1 can (14½ ounces) Italian diced tomatoes
- 1 jar (12 ounces) home-style beef gravy
- 1 tablespoon minced fresh parsley

1. Cut steak into six serving-size pieces; flatten to ¼-in. thickness. Rub with seasoned salt and pepper. In a large skillet, brown beef in oil on both sides; drain.

2. Cut each potato into eight wedges. In a 5-qt. slow cooker, layer the potatoes, carrots, beef and onion. Combine tomatoes and gravy; pour over the top.

3. Cover and cook on low for 5-6 hours or until meat and vegetables are tender. Sprinkle with parsley.

Cajun-Style Pot Roast

I often make this well-seasoned beef roast when expecting dinner guests. It gives me time to visit, and everyone always enjoys it—even my friend who's a chef.

—GINGER MENZIES
OAK CREEK, COLORADO

PREP: 15 MIN. **COOK:** 6 HOURS
MAKES: 6 SERVINGS

- 1 **boneless beef chuck roast (2 to 3 pounds)**
- 2 **tablespoons Cajun seasoning**
- 1 **tablespoon olive oil**
- 2 **cans (10 ounces each) diced tomatoes and green chilies**
- 1 **medium sweet red pepper, chopped**
- 1½ **cups chopped celery**
- ¾ **cup chopped onion**
- ¼ **cup quick-cooking tapioca**
- 1½ **teaspoons minced garlic**
- 1 **teaspoon salt**
  Hot cooked rice

1. Cut roast in half; sprinkle with Cajun seasoning. In a large skillet, brown roast in oil on all sides. Transfer to a 5-qt. slow cooker. Combine the tomatoes, red pepper, celery, onion, tapioca, garlic and salt; pour over roast.
2. Cover and cook on low for 6-8 hours or until meat is tender. Serve with rice.

Brisket 'n' Bean Burritos

Smoky bacon and tender beef make this easy recipe a real winner.

—RUTH WEATHERFORD
HUNTINGTON BEACH, CALIFORNIA

PREP: 20 MIN. **COOK:** 4½ HOURS
MAKES: 10 SERVINGS

- 2 **pounds fresh beef brisket**
- 1 **cup chopped onion**
- 3 **bacon strips, diced**
- 1 **can (8 ounces) tomato sauce**
- ¾ **teaspoon pepper**
- ¼ **teaspoon salt**
- 1 **can (16 ounces) refried beans**
- ½ **cup salsa**
- 1 **can (4 ounces) chopped green chilies**
- 1½ **cups (6 ounces) shredded Monterey Jack cheese**
- 10 **flour tortillas (10 inches), warmed**

1. Place brisket in a 5-qt. slow cooker; top with onion and bacon. Combine the tomato sauce, pepper and salt; pour over meat. Cover and cook on low for 4½ to 5 hours or until meat is tender.
2. In a microwave-safe bowl, combine the refried beans, salsa and chilies. Cover and microwave on high for 2-3 minutes or until heated through. Remove meat from the slow cooker; shred with two forks.
3. Layer the bean mixture, meat and cheese off-center on each tortilla. Fold sides and ends over filling and roll up.
4. Serve immediately or wrap individually in paper towels, then foil. Transfer to a resealable plastic bag. May be frozen for up to 2 months.
To use frozen burritos: *Unwrap foil. Place paper towel-wrapped burritos on a microwave-safe plate. Microwave on high for 3-4 minutes or until heated through.*
Editor's Note: *This is a fresh beef brisket, not corned beef.*

Burgundy Beef

On chilly days, it's a pleasure coming home to this savory pot roast bubbling in the slow cooker. The tender beef and vegetables in a rich gravy are scrumptious over a bed of noodles.

—**LORA SNYDER** COLUMBUS, MASSACHUSETTS

PREP: 20 MIN.   **COOK:** 8 HOURS   **MAKES:** 6 SERVINGS

- ½ **pound sliced fresh mushrooms**
- ½ **pound fresh baby carrots**
- 1 **medium green pepper, julienned**
- 1 **boneless beef chuck roast (2½ pounds)**
- 1 **can (10¾ ounces) condensed golden mushroom soup, undiluted**
- ¼ **cup Burgundy wine or beef broth**
- 1 **tablespoon Worcestershire sauce**
- 1 **envelope onion soup mix**
- ¼ **teaspoon pepper**
- 2 **to 3 tablespoons cornstarch**
- 2 **tablespoons cold water**
- **Hot cooked wide egg noodles**

1. In a 5-qt. slow cooker, combine the mushrooms, carrots and green pepper; place roast on top. In a small bowl, combine the soup, wine, Worcestershire sauce, soup mix and pepper; pour over roast. Cover and cook on low for 8-9 hours or until meat is tender.

2. Transfer roast and vegetables to a serving platter; keep warm. Strain cooking juices and skim fat; place in a large saucepan.

3. Combine cornstarch and cold water until smooth; gradually stir into cooking juices. Bring to a boil; cook and stir for 2 minutes or until thickened. Serve with the beef, vegetables and noodles.

No-Fuss Swiss Steak

PREP: 10 MIN. **COOK:** 6 HOURS
MAKES: 8-10 SERVINGS

- 3 pounds beef top round steak, cut into serving-size pieces
- 2 tablespoons canola oil
- 2 medium carrots, sliced
- 2 celery ribs, sliced
- 1¾ cups water
- 1 can (11 ounces) condensed tomato rice soup, undiluted
- 1 can (10½ ounces) condensed French onion soup, undiluted
- ½ teaspoon pepper
- 1 bay leaf

1. In a large skillet, brown the beef in oil over medium-high heat; drain. Transfer to a 5-qt. slow cooker. Add carrots and celery. Combine the water, soups, pepper and bay leaf; pour over the meat and vegetables.
2. Cover and cook on low for 6-8 hours or until meat is tender. Discard bay leaf. Thicken cooking juices if desired.

> ❝I make this dish regularly because my kids love the savory steak, tangy gravy and fork-tender veggies.❞
> —SHARON MORRELL
> PARKER, SOUTH DAKOTA

Italian Pot Roast

Pot roast is a favorite of my husband's. You'll love the tender beef seasoned with Italian herbs. I'm always asked for the recipe.

—**DEBBIE DALY** BUCKINGHAM, ILLINOIS

PREP: 20 MIN. **COOK:** 5 HOURS
MAKES: 8 SERVINGS

- 1 boneless beef chuck roast (3 to 4 pounds)
- 1 can (28 ounces) diced tomatoes, drained
- ¾ cup chopped onion
- ¾ cup Burgundy wine or beef broth
- 1½ teaspoons salt
- 1 teaspoon dried basil
- ½ teaspoon dried oregano
- 1 garlic clove, minced
- ¼ teaspoon pepper
- ¼ cup cornstarch
- ½ cup cold water

1. Cut roast in half. Place in a 5-qt. slow cooker. Add the tomatoes, onion, wine, salt, basil, oregano, garlic and pepper. Cover and cook on low for 5-6 hours or until meat is tender.
2. Remove meat to a serving platter; keep warm. Skim fat from cooking juices; transfer to a small saucepan. Combine cornstarch and water until smooth, then gradually stir into pan. Bring to a boil; cook and stir for 2 minutes or until thickened. Serve with meat.

Beef Roast Dinner

Since the beef is slow cooked, you can use less expensive roasts and have the same mouthwatering results you would get with more costly cuts. Change up the veggies for variety, nutrition or to suit your tastes!

—SANDRA DUDLEY
BEMIDJI, MINNESOTA

PREP: 20 MIN. **COOK:** 8 HOURS
MAKES: 10 SERVINGS

- 1 **pound red potatoes (about 4 medium), cubed**
- ¼ **pound small fresh mushrooms**
- 1½ **cups fresh baby carrots**
- 1 **medium green pepper, chopped**
- 1 **medium parsnip, chopped**
- 1 **small red onion, chopped**
- 1 **beef rump roast or bottom round roast (3 pounds)**
- 1 **can (14½ ounces) beef broth**
- ¾ **teaspoon salt**
- ¾ **teaspoon dried oregano**
- ¼ **teaspoon pepper**
- 3 **tablespoons cornstarch**
- ¼ **cup cold water**

1. Place vegetables in a 5-qt. slow cooker. Cut roast in half; place in slow cooker. Combine the broth, salt, oregano and pepper; pour over meat. Cover and cook on low for 8 hours or until meat is tender.
2. Remove meat and vegetables to a serving platter; keep warm. Skim fat from cooking juices; transfer to a small saucepan. Bring liquid to a boil.
3. Combine cornstarch and water until smooth. Gradually stir into the pan. Bring to a boil; cook and stir for 2 minutes or until thickened. Serve gravy with meat and vegetables.

Artichoke Beef Stew

The recipe for this special stew was given to me by a dear friend before she moved to another state. She served it with homemade dumplings, but my husband prefers noodles.

—JANELL SCHMIDT
ATHELSTANE, WISCONSIN

PREP: 25 MIN. **COOK:** 7½ HOURS
MAKES: 6-8 SERVINGS

- ⅓ **cup all-purpose flour**
- 1 **teaspoon salt**
- ½ **teaspoon pepper**
- 2½ **pounds beef stew meat, cut into 1-inch cubes**
- 3 **tablespoons canola oil**
- 1 **can (10½ ounces) condensed beef consomme, undiluted**
- 2 **medium onions, halved and sliced**
- ½ **pound small fresh mushrooms, halved**
- 1 **cup red wine or beef broth**
- 1 **garlic clove, minced**
- ½ **teaspoon dill weed**
- 2 **jars (6½ ounces each) marinated artichoke hearts, drained and chopped**
   Hot cooked noodles

1. In a large resealable plastic bag, combine the flour, salt and pepper. Add beef, a few pieces at a time, and shake to coat. In a large skillet, brown beef in oil in batches.
2. Transfer to a 3- or 4-qt. slow cooker with a slotted spoon. Gradually add consomme to the pan, stirring to loosen browned bits. Stir in the onions, mushrooms, wine, garlic and dill. Pour over beef.
3. Cover and cook for low for 7-8 hours or until tender. Stir in the artichokes; cook 30 minutes longer or until heated through. Serve with noodles.

Garlic Beef Stroganoff

I'm a mom and work full time, so I try to use my slow cooker whenever possible. This Stroganoff is perfect because I can get it ready in the morning before the kids get up.

—ERIKA ANDERSON
WAUSAU, WISCONSIN

PREP: 20 MIN. **COOK:** 7 HOURS
MAKES: 6-8 SERVINGS

- 2 teaspoons beef bouillon granules
- 1 cup boiling water
- 1 can (10¾ ounces) condensed cream of mushroom soup, undiluted
- 2 jars (4½ ounces each) sliced mushrooms, drained
- 1 large onion, chopped
- 3 garlic cloves, minced
- 1 tablespoon Worcestershire sauce
- 1½ to 2 pounds beef top round steak, cut into thin strips
- 2 tablespoons canola oil
- 1 package (8 ounces) cream cheese, cubed
  Hot cooked noodles

1. In a 3-qt. slow cooker, dissolve bouillon in water. Add the soup, mushrooms, onion, garlic and Worcestershire sauce. In a skillet, brown beef in oil. Transfer to the slow cooker.
2. Cover and cook on low for 7-8 hours or until the meat is tender. Stir in cream cheese until smooth. Serve with noodles.

Spinach Alfredo Lasagna

With Alfredo and spaghetti sauce, plus ground beef, spinach and three kinds of cheese, this special lasagna is super-hearty and a true family-pleaser. When serving, be sure to scoop all the way down the slow cooker's ceramic insert to get some of each layer.

—DEBORAH BRUNO
MIRA LOMA, CALIFORNIA

PREP: 20 MIN. **COOK:** 4 HOURS
MAKES: 8 SERVINGS

- 1 pound ground beef
- 1 medium onion, chopped
- 2 garlic cloves, minced
- 1 jar (24 ounces) spaghetti sauce
- 1 package (8 ounces) no-cook lasagna noodles
- 1 carton (15 ounces) ricotta cheese
- ½ cup grated Parmesan cheese
- 2 tablespoons minced fresh parsley
- ½ teaspoon pepper
- 8 cups (32 ounces) shredded part-skim mozzarella cheese
- 1 package (10 ounces) frozen chopped spinach, thawed and squeezed dry
- 1 jar (15 ounces) Alfredo sauce

1. In a large skillet, cook the beef, onion and garlic over medium heat until meat is no longer pink; drain. Stir in spaghetti sauce.
2. Spread 1 cup meat mixture in an ungreased 5- or 6-qt. slow cooker. Arrange four noodles over sauce, breaking noodles to fit if necessary. In a small bowl, combine the ricotta cheese, Parmesan cheese, parsley and pepper; spread half over noodles. Layer with 2 cups mozzarella cheese and 1 cup meat mixture.
3. Top with four noodles, spinach, Alfredo sauce, 2 cups mozzarella cheese, four noodles and remaining ricotta mixture. Layer with 2 cups mozzarella cheese, 1 cup meat mixture and any remaining noodles, meat mixture and mozzarella cheese.
4. Cover and cook on low for 4-5 hours or until noodles are tender.

Steak and Mushroom Sauce

Here's a dinner that's light on ingredients but big on taste. It's our favorite easy recipe. All you need is a salad to make it a meal.

—LOIS HEDKE
SOUTH ROCKWOOD, MICHIGAN

PREP: 20 MIN. **COOK:** 6 HOURS
MAKES: 2 SERVINGS

- ½ medium green pepper, cut into ½-inch pieces
- ¼ cup sliced onion
- 1 beef top round steak (10 ounces), cut in half
- ⅔ cup condensed cream of mushroom soup, undiluted
- ⅓ cup water
- 1½ cups uncooked egg noodles

1. Place green pepper and onion in a 1½-qt. slow cooker; top with beef. In a small bowl, combine soup and water; pour over meat. Cover and cook on low for 6-7 hours or until meat is tender.

2. Cook noodles according to package directions; drain. Serve with round steak and gravy.

Sweet 'n' Tender Cabbage Rolls

I've used this recipe for more than 30 years, and the extra time it takes to assemble the rolls is well worth the effort. I always make two batches because they go so fast. You can make these the night before and cook them the next day.

—SONJA BENZ CARMEL, INDIANA

PREP: 40 MIN. **COOK:** 7 HOURS
MAKES: 7 SERVINGS

- 1 large head cabbage
- 2 eggs, lightly beaten
- ½ cup 2% milk
- 2 cups cooked long grain rice
- 2 jars (4½ ounces each) sliced mushrooms, well drained
- 1 small onion, chopped
- 2 teaspoons salt
- 1 teaspoon dried parsley flakes
- 1 teaspoon dried oregano
- 1 teaspoon dried basil
- ½ teaspoon pepper
- 2 pounds lean ground beef (90% lean)

SAUCE
- 2 cans (8 ounces each) tomato sauce
- ½ cup packed brown sugar
- 2 tablespoons lemon juice
- 2 teaspoons Worcestershire sauce

1. Cook cabbage in boiling water just until leaves fall off head. Set aside 14 large leaves for rolls. (Refrigerate remaining cabbage for another use.) Cut out thick vein from the bottom of each reserved leaf, making a V-shaped cut.

2. In a large bowl, combine the eggs, milk, rice, mushrooms, onion and seasonings. Crumble beef over mixture and mix well. Place about ½ cup on each cabbage leaf; overlap cut ends and fold in sides, beginning from the cut end. Roll up completely to enclose filling.

3. Place seven rolls, seam side down, in a 5-qt. slow cooker. Combine sauce ingredients; pour half over cabbage rolls. Top with remaining rolls and sauce. Cover and cook on low for 7-8 hours or until a thermometer reads 160°.

Beer-Braised Stew

Friends and family will never guess that the secret ingredient in this wonderful stew is beer! What a nice meal to come home to: Just cook the noodles, and dinner is ready.

GERI FAUSTICH APPLETON, WISCONSIN

PREP: 20 MIN. **COOK:** 6 HOURS **MAKES:** 8 SERVINGS

- 3 **bacon strips, diced**
- 2 **pounds beef stew meat, cut into 1-inch cubes**
- ½ **teaspoon pepper**
- ¼ **teaspoon salt**
- 2 **tablespoons canola oil**
- 2 **cups fresh baby carrots**
- 1 **medium onion, cut into wedges**
- 1 **teaspoon minced garlic**
- 1 **bay leaf**
- 1 **can (12 ounces) beer or nonalcoholic beer**
- 1 **tablespoon soy sauce**
- 1 **tablespoon Worcestershire sauce**
- 1 **teaspoon dried thyme**
- 2 **tablespoons all-purpose flour**
- ¼ **cup water**
  Hot cooked noodles

1. In a large skillet, cook bacon over medium heat until crisp. Remove to paper towels; drain, discarding drippings. Sprinkle beef with pepper and salt. In the same skillet, brown beef in oil in batches; drain.

2. Transfer to a 5-qt. slow cooker. Add the carrots, bacon, onion, garlic and bay leaf. In a small bowl, combine the beer, soy sauce, Worcestershire sauce and thyme. Pour over beef mixture.

3. Cover and cook on low for 5½ to 6 hours or until meat and vegetables are tender.

4. In a small bowl, combine flour and water until smooth. Gradually stir into slow cooker. Cover and cook on high for 30 minutes or until thickened. Discard bay leaf. Serve beef with noodles.

Toasty French Dip

This is one of my husband's very favorite meals. Served with a green salad, it makes a wonderful supper. It would also work great for sandwiches at a football game party!

—**DOROTHY CONNELLEY**
BELLE FOURCHE, SOUTH DAKOTA

PREP: 30 MIN. **COOK:** 6 HOURS
MAKES: 8 SERVINGS

- 1 **large onion, sliced**
- 1 **boneless beef rump roast (3 pounds)**
- 2 **cans (10½ ounces each) condensed French onion soup**
- 1 **loaf (1 pound) French bread, halved lengthwise**
- ¼ **cup butter, softened**
- 1 **tablespoon grated Parmesan cheese**
- ½ **teaspoon garlic salt**
- 8 **slices part-skim mozzarella cheese**

1. Place onion in a 5-qt. slow cooker. Cut roast in half; place over onion. Pour soup over beef. Cover and cook on low for 6-8 hours or until meat is tender.

2. Remove meat to a cutting board. Let stand for 10 minutes. Thinly slice meat across the grain and return to the slow cooker. Heat through.

3. Place bread on an ungreased baking sheet. Combine the butter, Parmesan cheese and garlic salt; spread over bread.

4. Bake at 400° for 10-12 minutes or until lightly browned. Layer bread bottom with mozzarella cheese, beef and onion. Replace bread top; cut into eight portions. Serve with cooking juices.

Slow-Cooked Taco Meat Loaf

Taco meat loaf is a hit with my family. My three sons eat two pieces each, which is incredible, considering that they are very picky toddlers. The Southwest-style meat loaf is topped with a sweet and tangy sauce.

—**LACEY KIRSCH**
THORNTON, COLORADO

PREP: 20 MIN.
COOK: 3 HOURS + STANDING
MAKES: 8 SERVINGS

- 2 **cups crushed tortilla chips**
- 1 **cup (4 ounces) shredded cheddar cheese**
- 1 **cup salsa**
- 2 **eggs, lightly beaten**
- ¼ **cup sliced ripe olives**
- 1 **envelope taco seasoning**
- 2 **pounds lean ground beef (90% lean)**
- ½ **cup ketchup**
- ¼ **cup packed brown sugar**
- 2 **tablespoons Louisiana-style hot sauce**

1. Cut four 20-in. x 3-in. strips of heavy-duty foil; crisscross so they resemble spokes of a wheel. Place strips on the bottom and up the sides of a 3-qt. slow cooker. Coat strips with cooking spray.

2. In a large bowl, combine the first six ingredients. Crumble beef over mixture and mix well. Shape into a round loaf. Place meat loaf in the center of the strips. Cover and cook on low for 3-4 hours or until no pink remains and a thermometer reads 160°.

3. Combine the ketchup, brown sugar and hot sauce; pour over meat loaf during the last hour of cooking. Let stand for 10 minutes. Using foil strips as handles, remove the meat loaf to a platter.

Confetti Casserole

To create this comforting casserole, I used a recipe from the cookbook that came with my first slow cooker, but I added more of the ingredients we love. I like to serve it with fresh bread from my bread maker.

—JOY VINCENT
NEWPORT, NORTH CAROLINA

PREP: 20 MIN. **COOK:** 8 HOURS
MAKES: 6 SERVINGS

- 1 **pound ground beef**
- 1 **medium onion, finely chopped**
- 1 **teaspoon garlic powder**
- 4 **medium potatoes, peeled and quartered**
- 3 **medium carrots, cut into 1-inch chunks**
- 1 **package (9 ounces) frozen cut green beans**
- 1 **package (10 ounces) frozen corn**
- 1 **can (14½ ounces) Italian diced tomatoes, undrained**

1. In a large skillet, cook the beef, onion and garlic powder over medium heat until meat is no longer pink; drain.
2. In a 3-qt. slow cooker, layer the potatoes, carrots, beans and corn. Top with beef mixture. Pour tomatoes over the top. Cover and cook on low for 8-10 hours or until potatoes are tender.

LAYERING MATTERS

Potatoes and other dense foods can take a long time to cook in the slow cooker. They are often layered in the bottom of the slow cooker, where they can be closer to the heat than an item that is layered on top. For best results, always follow any layering instructions that a recipe provides.

Flank Steak Tacos

Here's a fast and flavorful way to prepare steak filling for fajitas. The yummy flavor comes from aromatic ingredients like garlic and gingerroot. There's even a can of cola in the recipe.

—LAURIE SADOWSKI ST. CATHARINES, ONTARIO

PREP: 20 MIN. **COOK:** 6 HOURS
MAKES: 6 SERVINGS

- 1 **beef flank steak (1½ pounds)**
- 2 **teaspoons ground ginger**
- 2 **teaspoons crushed red pepper flakes**
- ¾ **teaspoon garlic powder**
- ¼ **teaspoon pepper**
- 1 **medium sweet red pepper, cut into strips**
- 1 **medium green pepper, cut into strips**
- 1 **can (12 ounces) cola**
- 5 **green onions, chopped**
- ⅓ **cup soy sauce**
- 2 **tablespoons minced fresh gingerroot**
- 2 **tablespoons tomato paste**
- 1 **garlic clove, minced**
- 6 **flour tortillas (8 inches), warmed**

1. Cut steak in half lengthwise. In a small bowl, combine the ground ginger, pepper flakes, garlic powder and pepper; rub over steak. Transfer to a 3-qt. slow cooker; add red and green peppers. Combine the cola, green onions, soy sauce, gingerroot, tomato paste and garlic; pour over the top.
2. Cover and cook on low for 6-7 hours or until meat is tender. Shred meat with two forks; return to the slow cooker and heat through. Spoon beef mixture onto tortillas with a slotted spoon.

Barbecued Beef Short Ribs

These tender slow-cooked ribs with a tangy sauce are a cinch to make. They're great for picnics and parties.

—ERIN GLASS
WHITE HALL, MARYLAND

PREP: 25 MIN. **COOK:** 4½ HOURS
MAKES: 8 SERVINGS

- 4 pounds bone-in beef short ribs, trimmed
- 2 tablespoons canola oil
- 1 large sweet onion, halved and sliced
- ½ cup water
- 1 bottle (12 ounces) chili sauce
- ¾ cup plum preserves or preserves of your choice
- 2 tablespoons brown sugar
- 2 tablespoons red wine vinegar
- 2 tablespoons Worcestershire sauce
- 2 tablespoons Dijon mustard
- ¼ teaspoon ground cloves

1. In a large skillet, brown ribs in oil in batches. Place onion and water in a 5-qt. slow cooker; add ribs. Cover and cook on low for 4 to 5 hours or until meat is tender.
2. In a small saucepan, combine the remaining ingredients; cook and stir until heated through.
3. Remove ribs from slow cooker. Discard cooking liquid. Return ribs to the slow cooker; pour sauce over ribs.
4. Cover and cook on high for 30 minutes or until the sauce is thickened.

Slow-Cooked Tender Beef Brisket

Brisket can be difficult to cook, but this recipe always turns out great. I live in the country and have a 60-mile commute to work each day, so I use the slow cooker often. After a long day, it's a great way to get a good meal on the table in a hurry for my family.

—JENNI ARNOLD
WOODBURY, TENNESSEE

PREP: 15 MIN. **COOK:** 8 HOURS
MAKES: 10 SERVINGS

- 1 fresh beef brisket (4 pounds)
- 1 can (15 ounces) tomato sauce
- 1 bottle (12 ounces) beer or nonalcoholic beer
- 1 cup chopped green pepper
- ⅔ cup chopped onion
- 2 tablespoons brown sugar
- 2 tablespoons balsamic vinegar
- 2 tablespoons Worcestershire sauce
- 2 teaspoons prepared mustard
- 1 teaspoon salt
- 1 teaspoon garlic powder
- ½ teaspoon pepper

1. Cut brisket into thirds; place in a 5-qt. slow cooker. In a large bowl, combine the remaining ingredients; pour over beef. Cover and cook on low for 8-9 hours or until meat is tender.
2. Thinly slice meat across the grain. If desired, thicken the cooking liquid.
Editor's Note: *This is a fresh beef brisket, not corned beef.*

Coffee Beef Roast

Day-old coffee is the key to this flavorful beef roast. It simmers in the slow cooker until it's fall-apart tender. Try it just once, and I'm sure you'll cook it again.

—CHARLES TRAHAN
SAN DIMAS, CALIFORNIA

PREP: 15 MIN. **COOK:** 8 HOURS
MAKES: 6 SERVINGS

- 1 **beef sirloin tip roast (2½ pounds), cut in half**
- 2 **teaspoons canola oil**
- 1½ **cups sliced fresh mushrooms**
- ⅓ **cup sliced green onions**
- 2 **garlic cloves, minced**
- 1½ **cups brewed coffee**
- 1 **teaspoon liquid smoke, optional**
- ½ **teaspoon salt**
- ½ **teaspoon chili powder**
- ¼ **teaspoon pepper**
- ¼ **cup cornstarch**
- ⅓ **cup cold water**

1. In a large nonstick skillet, brown roast on all sides in oil over medium-high heat. Place in a 5-qt. slow cooker. In the same skillet, saute mushrooms, onions and garlic until tender; stir in the coffee, liquid smoke if desired, salt, chili powder and pepper. Pour over roast.

2. Cover and cook on low for 8-10 hours or until meat is tender. Remove roast and keep warm. Pour cooking juices into a 2-cup measuring cup; skim fat.

3. In a small saucepan, combine cornstarch and water until smooth. Gradually stir in 2 cups cooking juices. Bring to a boil; cook and stir for 2 minutes or until thickened. Serve with beef.

FAST FIX ▶ Italian Beef Sandwiches

I often start these sandwiches before I leave for work, and supper is ready when I get home! This recipe is also good to take to a get-together.

—CAROL ALLEN
MCLEANSBORO, ILLINOIS

PREP: 15 MIN. **COOK:** 8 HOURS
MAKES: 10-12 SERVINGS

- 1 **boneless beef chuck roast (3 to 4 pounds)**
- 3 **tablespoons dried basil**
- 3 **tablespoons dried oregano**
- 1 **cup water**
- 1 **envelope onion soup mix**
- 10 **to 12 Italian rolls or sandwich buns**

1. Cut roast in half; place in a 5-qt. slow cooker. Combine the basil, oregano and water; pour over roast. Sprinkle with soup mix.

2. Cover and cook on low for 8-10 hours or until meat is tender. Remove meat; shred with two forks and keep warm. Strain broth and skim fat. Serve meat on rolls; use broth for dipping if desired.

FAST FIX ▶ Fruited Pot Roast

Here's a wonderful variation on classic pot roast. The fruit is a nice change from the vegetables that usually accompany this dish. My family really enjoys it.

—LINDA SOUTH
PINEVILLE, NORTH CAROLINA

PREP: 15 MIN. **COOK:** 6 HOURS
MAKES: 6 SERVINGS

- 1 **package (7 ounces) mixed dried fruit**
- 1 **large onion, cut into wedges**
- 1 **can (5½ ounces) unsweetened apple juice**
- 1 **boneless beef chuck roast (2 pounds)**
- ½ **teaspoon salt**
- ¼ **teaspoon ground allspice**
- ¼ **teaspoon pepper**

1. Place fruit and onion in a 3- or 4-qt. slow cooker; add apple juice. Top with roast; sprinkle with seasonings.

2. Cover and cook on low for 6-8 hours or until meat is tender. Serve beef with fruit mixture.

French Dip au Jus

I created this sandwich because so many French Dip recipes seem bland or rely on a mix. Mine is simple to make and tastes better than most restaurant versions!

—**LINDSAY EBERT** OREM, UTAH

PREP: 30 MIN. **COOK:** 8 HOURS
MAKES: 8 SERVINGS

- 1½ teaspoons beef base
- 1 teaspoon dried thyme
- 1 beef rump roast or bottom round roast (3 pounds), cut in half
- 1 medium onion, quartered
- ½ cup reduced-sodium soy sauce
- 2 garlic cloves, minced
- 1 bay leaf
- ½ teaspoon pepper
- 8 cups water
- 2 tablespoons Dijon mustard
- 2 loaves French bread (1 pound each), split and toasted
- 12 slices part-skim mozzarella cheese
- 1 jar (4½ ounces) sliced mushrooms, drained

1. Combine beef base and thyme; rub over roast. Place in a 5-qt. slow cooker. Combine the onion, soy sauce, garlic, bay leaf and pepper; pour over roast. Add water.

2. Cover and cook on low for 8-9 hours or until meat is tender. Remove roast to a cutting board; cool slightly. Strain cooking juices, reserving onion; skim fat from juices. Discard bay leaf. Thinly slice meat.

3. To assemble sandwiches, spread mustard over bread. Top each bottom with three slices cheese; layer with beef, remaining cheese, mushrooms and reserved onion. Replace tops. Cut each loaf into four slices; serve with reserved juices.

Editor's Note: *Look for beef base near the broth and bouillon.*

Fiesta Beef Bowls

My easy entree will knock your socks off! Zesty ingredients turn round steak into a phenomenal meal in one.

—**DEBORAH LINN** VALDEZ, ALASKA

PREP: 25 MIN. **COOK:** 8½ HOURS
MAKES: 6 SERVINGS

- 1½ pounds boneless beef top round steak
- 1 can (10 ounces) diced tomatoes and green chilies
- 1 medium onion, chopped
- 2 garlic cloves, minced
- 1 teaspoon dried oregano
- 1 teaspoon chili powder
- 1 teaspoon ground cumin
- ¼ teaspoon salt
- ¼ teaspoon pepper
- 2 cans (15 ounces each) pinto beans, rinsed and drained
- 3 cups hot cooked rice
- ½ cup shredded cheddar cheese
- 6 tablespoons sliced ripe olives
- 6 tablespoons thinly sliced green onions
- 6 tablespoons guacamole

1. Place round steak in a 3-qt. slow cooker. In a small bowl, combine the tomatoes, onion, garlic and seasonings; pour over steak. Cover and cook on low for 8-9 hours or until meat is tender.

2. Remove meat from slow cooker. Add beans to tomato mixture. Cover and cook on high for 30 minutes or until beans are heated through. When cool enough to handle, slice meat.

3. In individual bowls, layer the rice, meat and bean mixture. Top with the cheese, olives, onions and guacamole.

Special Slow-Cooked Beef

This hearty entree is easy to prepare for Sunday dinner. While the beef cooks, the chef has lots of time to attend to other things. With mashed potatoes on the side, it's comforting food for the cooler months.

—JULI GEORGE
GRANDVILLE, MICHIGAN

PREP: 35 MIN. **COOK:** 6 HOURS
MAKES: 8 SERVINGS

- 1 boneless beef chuck roast (3 pounds), cubed
- 1 tablespoon canola oil
- 1 tablespoon Italian seasoning
- 1 teaspoon salt
- 1 garlic clove, minced
- ½ cup sliced ripe olives, drained
- ⅓ cup oil-packed sun-dried tomatoes, drained and chopped
- 1 cup beef broth
- ½ cup fresh pearl onions, peeled
- 1 tablespoon cornstarch
- 2 tablespoons cold water

1. In a large skillet, brown meat in oil in batches; drain. Transfer to a 5-qt. slow cooker. Sprinkle with Italian seasoning, salt and garlic; top with olives and tomatoes. Add broth and onions. Cover and cook on low for 6-8 hours or until meat is tender.

2. With a slotted spoon, remove beef and onions to a serving platter and keep warm. Pour the cooking juices into a small saucepan; skim the fat.

3. Combine cornstarch and water until smooth; gradually stir into cooking juices. Bring to a boil; cook and stir for 2 minutes or until thickened. Spoon over the beef mixture.

Pot Roast with Gravy

My family loves this slow-cooked tangy roast with its rich onion and mushroom gravy. We even look forward to the leftovers.

—DEBORAH DAILEY
VANCOUVER, WASHINGTON

PREP: 30 MIN. **COOK:** 6½ HOURS
MAKES: 10 SERVINGS

- 1 beef rump roast or bottom round roast (5 pounds)
- 6 tablespoons balsamic vinegar, divided
- 1 teaspoon salt
- ½ teaspoon garlic powder
- ¼ teaspoon pepper
- 2 tablespoons canola oil
- 3 garlic cloves, minced
- 4 bay leaves
- 1 large onion, thinly sliced
- 3 teaspoons beef bouillon granules
- ½ cup boiling water
- 1 can (10¾ ounces) condensed cream of mushroom soup, undiluted
- 4 to 5 tablespoons cornstarch
- ¼ cup cold water

1. Cut roast in half; rub with 2 tablespoons vinegar. Combine the salt, garlic powder and pepper; rub over meat. In a large skillet, brown roast in oil on all sides. Transfer to a 5-qt. slow cooker.

2. Place the garlic, bay leaves and onion on roast. In a small bowl, dissolve bouillon in boiling water; stir in soup and remaining vinegar. Slowly pour over roast. Cover and cook on low for 6-8 hours or until meat is tender.

3. Remove roast; keep warm. Discard bay leaves. Whisk cornstarch and cold water until smooth; stir into cooking juices. Cover and cook on high for 30 minutes or until gravy is thickened. Slice roast; return to slow cooker and heat through.

Seasoned Short Ribs

These juicy barbecue-style short ribs are sure to be a hit with your family. Line the broiler pan with foil for easy cleanup.

—TASTE OF HOME TEST KITCHEN

PREP: 25 MIN. **COOK:** 6 HOURS
MAKES: 4 SERVINGS

- 1½ cups tomato juice
- ½ cup maple syrup
- ¼ cup chopped onion
- 3 tablespoons cider vinegar
- 1 tablespoon Worcestershire sauce
- 1 tablespoon Dijon mustard
- 2 teaspoons minced garlic
- ¼ teaspoon ground cinnamon
- ¼ teaspoon ground cloves
- 4 pounds bone-in beef short ribs
- 1 teaspoon pepper
- 1 tablespoon cornstarch
- 2 tablespoons cold water

1. In a small bowl, combine the first nine ingredients; set aside. Cut ribs into serving-size pieces; place on a broiler pan. Sprinkle with pepper.
2. Broil 4-6 in. from the heat for 3-5 minutes on each side or until browned; drain on paper towels. Place ribs in a 5-qt. slow cooker; top with tomato juice mixture.
3. Cover and cook on low for 6-7 hours or until meat is tender.
4. In a small bowl, combine cornstarch and cold water until smooth. Pour 1 cup cooking liquid into a small saucepan; skim off fat. Bring to a boil; stir in cornstarch mixture. Return to a boil; cook and stir for 2 minutes or until thickened. Serve over ribs.

Texas Beef Barbecue

Shredded beef sandwiches are a favorite in our family. The beef simmers for hours in a slightly sweet sauce with plenty of savory spices.

—JENNIFER BAUER
LANSING, MICHIGAN

PREP: 15 MIN. **COOK:** 8 HOURS
MAKES: 16 SERVINGS

- 1 beef sirloin tip roast (4 pounds)
- 1 can (5½ ounces) spicy hot V8 juice
- ½ cup water
- ¼ cup white vinegar
- ¼ cup ketchup
- 2 tablespoons Worcestershire sauce
- ½ cup packed brown sugar
- 1 teaspoon salt
- 1 teaspoon ground mustard
- 1 teaspoon paprika
- ¼ teaspoon chili powder
- ⅛ teaspoon pepper
- 16 kaiser rolls, split

1. Cut roast in half; place in a 5-qt. slow cooker. Combine the V8 juice, water, vinegar, ketchup, Worcestershire sauce, brown sugar and seasonings; pour over roast. Cover and cook on low for 8-10 hours or until meat is tender.
2. Remove meat and shred with two forks; return to slow cooker and heat through. Spoon ½ cup meat mixture onto each roll.

Bavarian Pot Roast

I grew up eating pot roast but disliked it until I came across this delightful version. I changed a few ingredients to suit my taste. My 7-year-old especially loves the seasoned apple gravy.

—PATRICIA GASMUND
ROCKFORD, ILLINOIS

PREP: 10 MIN. **COOK:** 7 HOURS
MAKES: 6 SERVINGS

- 1 beef top round roast (2 pounds)
- 1 cup unsweetened apple juice
- ½ cup tomato sauce
- 1 small onion, chopped
- 1 tablespoon white vinegar
- 1½ teaspoons minced fresh gingerroot
- 1 teaspoon salt
- 1 teaspoon ground cinnamon
- 2 tablespoons cornstarch
- ¼ cup water

1. In a large skillet coated with cooking spray, brown the beef roast on all sides. Transfer to a 3-qt. slow cooker.
2. In a small bowl, combine the juice, tomato sauce, onion, vinegar, ginger, salt and cinnamon; pour over roast. Cover and cook on low for 6 hours.
3. In a small bowl, combine cornstarch and water until smooth; stir into cooking juices until well combined.
4. Cover and cook 1 hour longer or until the meat is tender and gravy begins to thicken.

Picante Beef Roast

I created this recipe because I love the flavor of taco seasoning and don't think it should be reserved just for tacos! My recipe couldn't be easier, and it works great with a pork roast, too.

—MARGARET THIEL
LEVITTOWN, PENNSYLVANIA

PREP: 15 MIN. **COOK:** 8 HOURS
MAKES: 8 SERVINGS

- 1 beef rump roast or bottom round roast (3 pounds), trimmed
- 1 jar (16 ounces) picante sauce
- 15 ounces tomato sauce
- 1 envelope taco seasoning
- 3 tablespoons cornstarch
- ¼ cup cold water

1. Cut roast in half; place in a 5-qt. slow cooker. In a large bowl, combine the picante sauce, tomato sauce and taco seasoning; pour over roast. Cover and cook on low for 8-9 hours or until meat is tender.
2. Remove meat to a serving platter; keep warm. Skim fat from cooking juices; transfer 3 cups to a small saucepan. Bring liquid to a boil. Combine cornstarch and water until smooth. Gradually stir into the pan. Bring to a boil; cook and stir for 2 minutes or until thickened. Serve with roast.

SMART WAYS WITH PICANTE BEEF

If you don't have picante sauce on hand, you can use salsa instead. It's more chunky than picante sauce. Try serving the leftover beef wrapped up in tortillas with shredded cheese and refried beans.

Slow-Cooked Lasagna

My scrumptious take on lasagna is made super-easy in a slow cooker. The finished dish cuts really well! I also like that it makes a smaller batch than most lasagnas.

—REBECCA O'BRYAN ALVATON, KENTUCKY

PREP: 45 MIN. **COOK:** 4¼ HOURS + STANDING
MAKES: 6 SERVINGS

- 1 **pound ground beef**
- 1 **medium green pepper, chopped**
- 1 **medium onion, chopped**
- 1 **jar (24 ounces) herb and garlic pasta sauce**
- 4 **cups (16 ounces) shredded part-skim mozzarella cheese**
- 1 **carton (15 ounces) ricotta cheese**
- 1 **tablespoon Italian seasoning**
- ½ **teaspoon garlic powder**
- ½ **teaspoon salt**
- ¼ **teaspoon pepper**
- 4 **no-cook lasagna noodles**
- 2 **tablespoons shredded Parmesan cheese**

1. In a large skillet, cook the beef, green pepper and onion over medium heat until meat is no longer pink; drain. Stir in pasta sauce; heat through. In a large bowl, combine the mozzarella and ricotta cheeses, Italian seasoning, garlic powder, salt and pepper.
2. Spread 1 cup meat sauce in an oval 3-qt. slow cooker. Break one lasagna noodle into three pieces. Layer 1⅓ noodles over sauce, breaking noodles to fit as necessary. Top with ⅔ cup meat sauce and 1⅓ cups cheese mixture. Repeat layers twice. Top with remaining sauce.
3. Cover and cook on low for 4-5 hours or until noodles are tender. Sprinkle with Parmesan cheese. Cover and cook 15 minutes longer. Let stand for 10 minutes before cutting.

Steak Strips with Dumplings

Take in a parade on the Fourth of July or spend a day by the lake and come home to this delicious slow-cooked specialty! Homemade dumplings make it unique.

—JOHN SMALLDRIDGE
PRINCETON, IDAHO

PREP: 25 MIN. **COOK:** 5 HOURS
MAKES: 2 SERVINGS

- ¾ pound beef top round steak, cut into ½-inch strips
- ¼ teaspoon pepper
- 2 teaspoons canola oil
- ⅔ cup condensed cream of chicken soup, undiluted
- ½ cup beef broth
- 4 large fresh mushrooms, sliced
- ¼ cup each chopped onion, green pepper and celery

DUMPLINGS
- ½ cup all-purpose flour
- ¾ teaspoon baking powder
- ¼ teaspoon salt
- 2 tablespoons beaten egg
- 3 tablespoons 2% milk
- ½ teaspoon dried parsley flakes

1. Sprinkle steak with pepper. In a small skillet, brown steak in oil over medium-high heat. Transfer to a 1½-qt. slow cooker. Combine the soup, broth and vegetables; pour over steak. Cover and cook on low for 4-5 hours.
2. For dumplings, in a small bowl, combine the flour, baking powder and salt. Stir in egg and milk just until blended. Drop by tablespoonfuls onto meat mixture. Sprinkle with parsley.
3. Cover and cook on high for 1 hour or until a toothpick inserted in a dumpling comes out clean (do not lift cover while cooking).

Slow Cooker Sauerbraten

My family is of German Lutheran descent, and although we enjoy traditional sauerbraten, I never liked the amount of time and fuss it takes to make it. This recipe is so good and oh-so-easy. We enjoy it served with dumplings, spaetzle, veggies or a salad.

—NORMA ENGLISH
BADEN, PENNSYLVANIA

PREP: 20 MIN. **COOK:** 6 HOURS
MAKES: 10 SERVINGS

- 1 boneless beef chuck roast or rump roast (3 to 4 pounds)
- 4 cups water
- 1 bottle (14 ounces) ketchup
- 1 large onion, chopped
- ¾ cup packed brown sugar
- ¾ cup cider vinegar
- 1 tablespoon mixed pickling spices
- 3 bay leaves
- 1½ cups crushed gingersnap cookies (about 30 cookies)

GRAVY
- 2 tablespoons cornstarch
- ¼ cup cold water

1. Cut roast in half. Place in a 5-qt. slow cooker; add water. In a large bowl, combine the ketchup, onion, brown sugar and vinegar; pour over roast.
2. Place pickling spices and bay leaves on a double thickness of cheesecloth; bring up corners of cloth and tie with string to form a bag. Add spice bag and cookie crumbs to slow cooker.
3. Cover and cook on low for 6-8 hours or until meat is tender.
4. Remove roast and keep warm. Discard spice bag. Strain cooking juices; transfer 4 cups to a large saucepan. Combine cornstarch and water until smooth; stir into cooking juices. Bring to a boil; cook and stir for 2 minutes or until thickened. Serve with beef.

FAST FIX So-Easy Swiss Steak

Let your slow cooker simmer up this fuss-free and flavorful Swiss steak. It's perfect for busy days—the longer it cooks, the better it tastes!

—SARAH BURKS WATHENA, KANSAS

PREP: 10 MIN. **COOK:** 6 HOURS
MAKES: 2 SERVINGS

- 1 tablespoon all-purpose flour
- ¼ teaspoon salt
- ⅛ teaspoon pepper
- ¾ pound beef top round steak, cut in half
- ½ medium onion, cut into ¼-inch slices
- ⅓ cup chopped celery
- 1 can (8 ounces) tomato sauce

1. In a large resealable plastic bag, combine the flour, salt and pepper. Add beef; seal bag and shake to coat.

2. Place onion in a 3-qt. slow cooker coated with cooking spray. Layer with the beef, celery and tomato sauce. Cover and cook on low for 6-8 hours or until the meat is tender.

Italian Roast with Alfredo Potatoes

Surprise! This special meal is actually easy enough for any night of the week. Since the roast is made in the slow cooker, you'll have time to make the delicious homemade mashed potatoes.

—TASTE OF HOME TEST KITCHEN

PREP: 20 MIN. **COOK:** 7 HOURS
MAKES: 10 SERVINGS

- 1 boneless beef chuck roast (4 pounds), trimmed
- 1 envelope brown gravy mix
- 1 envelope Italian salad dressing mix
- ½ cup water
- 1 medium sweet red pepper, cut into 1-inch pieces
- 1 cup chopped green pepper
- ⅔ cup chopped onion
- 8 medium red potatoes, quartered
- 2 tablespoons cornstarch
- ¼ cup cold water
- ¾ cup refrigerated Alfredo sauce
- 2 tablespoons butter
- ¼ teaspoon pepper
- 1 tablespoon minced chives

1. Cut roast in half; place in a 5-qt. slow cooker. In a small bowl, combine the gravy mix, dressing mix and water; pour over roast. Top with peppers and onion. Cover and cook on low for 7-8 hours or until meat is tender.

2. Place potatoes in a large saucepan and cover with water. Bring to a boil. Reduce heat; cover and simmer for 15-20 minutes or until tender.

3. Remove beef and keep warm. Skim fat from cooking juices if necessary; pour into a large saucepan. Combine cornstarch and cold water until smooth; stir into cooking juices. Bring to a boil; cook and stir for 2 minutes or until thickened.

4. Drain potatoes; mash with Alfredo sauce, butter and pepper. Sprinkle with chives. Serve with beef and gravy.

Tangy Pot Roast

Catalina dressing gives this roast a special flavor. And the slow cooker takes the edge off those hectic days.

—PAULA BEACH MILTON, NEW YORK

PREP: 15 MIN. **COOK:** 7 HOURS
MAKES: 6 SERVINGS

- 3 medium potatoes, thinly sliced
- 1⅓ cups thinly sliced fresh carrots
- ⅔ cup sliced onion
- 1 boneless beef chuck roast (3 pounds)
- 1 teaspoon salt
- ½ teaspoon pepper
- ½ cup Catalina salad dressing
- ¼ cup dry red wine or beef broth

1. Place the potatoes, carrots and onion in a 5-qt. slow cooker. Cut roast in half; rub with salt and pepper. Place over vegetables. Combine salad dressing and wine; pour over roast.
2. Cover and cook on low for 7-8 hours or until tender. Skim fat from cooking juices; thicken juices if desired.

FAST FIX ▶ Flavorful Beef Roast

Convenient mixes help to create a delicious beef roast dinner!

—ARLENE BUTLER OGDEN, UTAH

PREP: 10 MIN. **COOK:** 7 HOURS
MAKES: 12-15 SERVINGS

- 2 boneless beef chuck roasts (2½ pounds each)
- 1 envelope ranch dressing mix
- 1 envelope Italian salad dressing mix
- 1 envelope brown gravy mix
- ½ cup water

Place beef in a 5-qt. slow cooker. Combine the salad dressings and gravy mix; stir in water. Pour over meat. Cover and cook on low for 7-8 hours or until tender. If desired, thicken cooking juices for gravy.

Special Pot Roast

I like to serve my fork-tender pot roast with sauteed tarragon carrots and rosemary-roasted red potatoes. This homey meal pleases all tastes—and the aroma as it cooks is an added bonus.

—VERA CARROLL
MEDFORD, MASSACHUSETTS

PREP: 10 MIN. **COOK:** 6½ HOURS
MAKES: 6 SERVINGS

- 1 large sweet onion, chopped
- 1 cup sliced baby portobello mushrooms
- 1 beef rump roast or bottom round roast (3 pounds)
- ½ teaspoon salt
- ¼ teaspoon pepper
- 1 cup dry red wine or beef broth
- 1 tablespoon brown sugar
- 1 tablespoon Dijon mustard
- 1 teaspoon Worcestershire sauce
- 2 tablespoons cornstarch
- 2 tablespoons cold water

1. Place onion and mushrooms in a 5-qt. slow cooker. Rub roast with salt and pepper; cut in half and place over onion mixture. In a small bowl, combine the wine, brown sugar, mustard and Worcestershire sauce; pour over roast. Cover and cook on low for 6-8 hours or until meat is tender.
2. Mix cornstarch and water until smooth; stir into cooking juices. Cover and cook on high for 30 minutes or until gravy is thickened.

Green Chili Beef Burritos

I get rave reviews every time I make this recipe. The shredded beef has a luscious slow-cooked flavor that you can't get anywhere else.

—JENNY FLAKE
NEWPORT BEACH, CALIFORNIA

PREP: 30 MIN. **COOK:** 9 HOURS
MAKES: 12 SERVINGS

- 1 boneless beef chuck roast (3 pounds)
- 1 can (14½ ounces) beef broth
- 2 cups green enchilada sauce
- 1 can (4 ounces) chopped green chilies
- ½ cup Mexican-style hot tomato sauce
- ½ teaspoon salt
- ½ teaspoon garlic powder
- ½ teaspoon pepper
- 12 flour tortillas (12 inches)
     Optional toppings: shredded lettuce, chopped tomatoes, shredded cheddar cheese and sour cream

1. Cut roast in half and place in a 3- or 4-qt. slow cooker. Add broth. Cover and cook on low for 8-9 hours or until meat is tender.
2. Remove beef. When cool enough to handle, shred meat with two forks. Skim fat from cooking liquid; reserve ½ cup liquid. Return shredded beef and reserved liquid to the slow cooker. Stir in the enchilada sauce, green chilies, tomato sauce, salt, garlic powder and pepper.
3. Cover and cook on low for 1 hour or until heated through. Serve beef on tortillas with the toppings of your choice.
Editor's Note: *This recipe was tested with El Pato brand Mexican-style hot tomato sauce. If you cannot find it, you may substitute ½ cup tomato sauce, 1 teaspoon hot pepper sauce, ⅛ teaspoon onion powder and ⅛ teaspoon chili powder.*

Hungarian Goulash

You will love how easily this slow-cooked version of a beloved ethnic dish comes together. My son shared the recipe with me many years ago.

—JACKIE KOHN DULUTH, MINNESOTA

PREP: 15 MIN. **COOK:** 8 HOURS
MAKES: 6-8 SERVINGS

- 2 pounds beef top round steak, cut into 1-inch cubes
- 1 cup chopped onion
- 2 tablespoons all-purpose flour
- 1½ teaspoons paprika
- 1 teaspoon garlic salt
- ½ teaspoon pepper
- 1 can (14½ ounces) diced tomatoes, undrained
- 1 bay leaf
- 1 cup (8 ounces) sour cream
    Hot cooked egg noodles

1. Place beef and onion in a 3-qt. slow cooker. Combine the flour, paprika, garlic salt and pepper; sprinkle over beef and stir to coat. Stir in tomatoes and bay leaf. Cover and cook on low for 8-10 hours or until meat is tender.
2. Discard bay leaf. Just before serving, stir in sour cream; heat through. Serve with noodles.

Mushroom Beef and Noodles

Here's a flavorful beef dish that's great for serving your family and friends. I've shared the recipe with many cooks over the years.

—VIRGIL KILLMAN
MASCOUTAH, ILLINOIS

PREP: 10 MIN. **COOK:** 8 HOURS
MAKES: 6-8 SERVINGS

- 1 can (10¾ ounces) condensed golden mushroom soup, undiluted
- 1 can (10¾ ounces) condensed beefy mushroom soup, undiluted
- 1 can (10¾ ounces) condensed French onion soup, undiluted
- ¼ cup seasoned bread crumbs
- 2 pounds beef stew meat, cut into ½-inch cubes
- 1 package (12 ounces) egg noodles

In a 3-qt. slow cooker, combine soups and bread crumbs. Stir in beef. Cover and cook on low for 8 hours or until tender. Cook noodles according to package directions; drain. Serve with beef.

Picadillo

Most traditional recipes out there have numerous variations. This is my take on a Cuban classic. For added convenience, I adapted it for the slow cooker.

—SANFORD BROWN COVINGTON, GEORGIA

PREP: 30 MIN. **COOK:** 4½ HOURS **MAKES:** 8 SERVINGS

- 2 large onions, chopped
- 2 tablespoons olive oil
- ¾ cup white wine or beef broth
- 2 pounds lean ground beef (90% lean)
- 1¼ cups crushed tomatoes
- 1 can (8 ounces) tomato sauce
- ⅓ cup tomato paste
- 4 garlic cloves, minced
- 2 teaspoons dried oregano
- ½ teaspoon salt
- ½ teaspoon ground cinnamon
- ½ teaspoon ground cloves
- ½ teaspoon pepper
- 1 cup raisins
- 1 medium green pepper, chopped
- ¾ cup pimiento-stuffed olives, coarsely chopped
- 2 tablespoons chopped seeded jalapeno pepper
  Hot cooked brown rice

1. In a large skillet, cook onions in oil over low heat for 15-20 minutes or until golden brown, stirring occasionally. Add wine; cook and stir 2 minutes longer. Transfer to a 3- or 4-qt. slow cooker.

2. In the same skillet, cook beef over medium heat until no longer pink. Add to slow cooker. Combine the tomatoes, tomato sauce, tomato paste, garlic and seasonings; pour over top. Cover and cook on low for 4-6 hours or until heated through.

3. Place raisins in a small bowl. Cover with boiling water; let stand for 5 minutes. Drain. Stir the green pepper, olives, jalapeno and raisins into the slow cooker. Cover and cook for 30 minutes. Serve with brown rice.

Editor's Note: *Wear disposable gloves when cutting hot peppers; the oils can burn skin. Avoid touching your face.*

Polynesian Roast Beef

This easy and delicious recipe from my sister has been a family favorite for years. Pineapple and peppers add a perfect contrast to the rich and savory beef.

—ANNETTE MOSBARGER
PEYTON, COLORADO

PREP: 15 MIN. **COOK:** 7 HOURS
MAKES: 10-11 SERVINGS

- 1 **beef top round roast (3¼ pounds)**
- 2 **tablespoons browning sauce, optional**
- ¼ **cup all-purpose flour**
- 1 **teaspoon salt**
- ¼ **teaspoon pepper**
- 1 **medium onion, sliced**
- 1 **can (8 ounces) unsweetened sliced pineapple**
- ¼ **cup packed brown sugar**
- 2 **tablespoons cornstarch**
- ¼ **teaspoon ground ginger**
- ½ **cup beef broth**
- ¼ **cup reduced-sodium soy sauce**
- ½ **teaspoon minced garlic**
- 1 **medium green pepper, sliced**

1. Cut roast in half; brush with browning sauce if desired. Combine flour, salt and pepper; rub over beef. Place onion in a 3-qt. slow cooker; top with beef.
2. Drain pineapple, reserving juice; refrigerate the pineapple. In a small bowl, combine the brown sugar, cornstarch and ginger; whisk in the broth, soy sauce, garlic and reserved pineapple juice until smooth. Pour over meat. Cover and cook on low for 6-8 hours.
3. Add pineapple and green pepper. Cook 1 hour longer or until meat is tender.

Cola Beef Brisket

Perfect for summer because the slow cooker helps keep your kitchen cool, this beef is also fork-tender!

—STEPHANIE STRONG
MT. JULIET, TENNESSEE

PREP: 10 MIN. **COOK:** 6 HOURS
MAKES: 7 SERVINGS (2 CUPS GRAVY)

- 1 **fresh beef brisket (3 pounds)**
- 1 **cup chili sauce**
- 1 **cup cola**
- 1 **envelope onion soup mix**
- 1 **tablespoon cornstarch**
- 1 **tablespoon cold water**

1. Cut brisket in half and place in a 5-qt. slow cooker. Combine the chili sauce, cola and soup mix; pour over brisket. Cover and cook on low for 6-7 hours or until meat is tender.
2. Remove meat to a serving platter and keep warm. Skim fat from cooking juices; transfer to a small saucepan. Bring liquid to a boil.
3. Combine cornstarch and water until smooth. Gradually stir into the pan. Bring to a boil; cook and stir for 2 minutes or until thickened. Thinly slice meat across the grain; serve with gravy.
Editor's Note: *This is a fresh beef brisket, not corned beef.*

Glazed Corned Beef Dinner

This recipe is so tasty, it's now the only way my family will eat corned beef. The glaze is the kicker!

—SHANNON STRATE
SALT LAKE CITY, UTAH

PREP: 20 MIN. **COOK:** 8¼ HOURS
MAKES: 8 SERVINGS

- 8 medium red potatoes, quartered
- 2 medium carrots, sliced
- 1 medium onion, sliced
- 1 corned beef brisket with spice packet (3 pounds)
- 1½ cups water
- 4 orange peel strips (3 inches)
- 3 tablespoons orange juice concentrate
- 3 tablespoons honey
- 1 tablespoon Dijon mustard

1. Place the potatoes, carrots and onion in a 5-qt. slow cooker. Cut brisket in half; place over vegetables. Add the water, orange peel and contents of spice packet.
2. Cover and cook on low for 8-9 hours or until meat and vegetables are tender.
3. Using a slotted spoon, transfer corned beef and vegetables to a 13-in. x 9-in. baking dish. Discard orange peel.
4. Combine the orange juice concentrate, honey and mustard; pour over meat. Bake, uncovered, at 375° for 15-20 minutes, basting meat occasionally.

Sweet-Sour Beef

I like to serve this sweet-and-sour dish over pasta shells and garnish each serving with fresh chives. Chock-full of tender beef, sliced carrots, green pepper and onion, it is so hearty and delicious.

—BETH HUSBAND
BILLINGS, MONTANA

PREP: 15 MIN. **COOK:** 7 HOURS
MAKES: 10-12 SERVINGS

- 2 pounds beef top round steak or boneless beef chuck roast, cut into 1-inch cubes
- 2 tablespoons canola oil
- 2 cans (8 ounces each) tomato sauce
- 2 cups sliced carrots
- 2 cups pearl onions or 2 small onions, cut into wedges
- 1 large green pepper, cut into 1-inch pieces
- ½ cup molasses
- ⅓ cup cider vinegar
- ¼ cup sugar
- 2 teaspoons chili powder
- 2 teaspoons paprika
- 1 teaspoon salt
  Hot cooked pasta

1. In a large skillet, brown steak in oil; transfer to a 5-qt. slow cooker. Add the next 10 ingredients; stir well.
2. Cover and cook on low for 7-8 hours or until meat is tender. Thicken cooking liquid if desired. Serve with pasta.

Beef Brisket in Beer

One bite of my tender brisket, and you'll be hooked! With its rich and satisfying gravy, it's perfect served with a side of mashed potatoes.
—**EUNICE STOEN** DECORAH, IOWA

PREP: 15 MIN. **COOK:** 8 HOURS
MAKES: 6 SERVINGS

- 1 fresh beef brisket (2½ to 3 pounds)
- 2 teaspoons liquid smoke, optional
- 1 teaspoon celery salt
- ½ teaspoon pepper
- ¼ teaspoon salt
- 1 large onion, sliced
- 1 can (12 ounces) beer or nonalcoholic beer
- 2 teaspoons Worcestershire sauce
- 2 tablespoons cornstarch
- ¼ cup cold water

1. Cut brisket in half; rub with liquid smoke if desired, celery salt, pepper and salt. Place in a 3-qt. slow cooker. Top with onion. Combine beer and Worcestershire sauce; pour over meat.
2. Cover and cook on low for 8-9 hours or until tender.
3. Remove brisket and keep warm. Strain cooking juices; transfer to a small saucepan. Combine cornstarch and water until smooth; stir into juices. Bring to a boil; cook and stir for 2 minutes or until thickened. Serve beef with gravy.

Editor's Note: *This is a fresh beef brisket, not corned beef.*

Steak Burritos

Slowly simmered all day, this beef is tender and a snap to shred. Just fill the flour tortillas and add your favorite toppings for a tasty meal.
—**VALERIE JONES** PORTLAND, MAINE

PREP: 15 MIN. **COOK:** 8 HOURS
MAKES: 10 SERVINGS

- 2 beef flank steaks (about 1 pound each)
- 2 envelopes taco seasoning
- 1 medium onion, chopped
- 1 can (4 ounces) chopped green chilies
- 1 tablespoon white vinegar
- 10 flour tortillas (8 inches), warmed
- 1½ cups (6 ounces) shredded Monterey Jack cheese
- 1½ cups chopped seeded plum tomatoes
- ¾ cup sour cream

1. Cut steaks in half; rub with taco seasoning. Place in a 3-qt. slow cooker coated with cooking spray. Top with onion, chilies and vinegar. Cover and cook on low for 8-9 hours or until meat is tender.
2. Remove meat and cool slightly; shred with two forks. Return to slow cooker; heat through.
3. Spoon about ½ cup of meat mixture near the center of each tortilla. Top with cheese, tomato and sour cream. Fold the bottom and sides of tortilla over filling and roll up.

German-Style Short Ribs

My whole family gets excited when I plug in the slow cooker to make these fall-off-the-bone beef ribs. We like them served with rice or buttery egg noodles.

—BREGITTE RUGMAN
SHANTY BAY, ONTARIO

PREP: 15 MIN. **COOK:** 8 HOURS
MAKES: 8 SERVINGS

- ¾ cup dry red wine or beef broth
- ½ cup mango chutney
- 3 tablespoons quick-cooking tapioca
- ¼ cup water
- 3 tablespoons brown sugar
- 3 tablespoons cider vinegar
- 1 tablespoon Worcestershire sauce
- ½ teaspoon salt
- ½ teaspoon ground mustard
- ½ teaspoon chili powder
- ½ teaspoon pepper
- 4 pounds bone-in beef short ribs
- 2 medium onions, sliced
  Hot cooked egg noodles

1. In a 5-qt. slow cooker, combine the first 11 ingredients. Add ribs and turn to coat. Top with onions.
2. Cover and cook on low for 8-10 hours or until meat is tender. Remove ribs from slow cooker. Skim fat from cooking juices; serve with ribs and noodles.

Texas-Style BBQ Brisket

A friend had tried this recipe and liked it, so I thought I would try it, too. When my husband told me how much he liked it, I knew I'd be making it often!

—VIVIAN WARNER ELKHART, KANSAS

PREP: 25 MIN. + MARINATING
COOK: 6½ HOURS
MAKES: 12 SERVINGS

- 3 tablespoons Worcestershire sauce
- 1 tablespoon chili powder
- 2 bay leaves
- 2 garlic cloves, minced
- 1 teaspoon celery salt
- 1 teaspoon pepper
- 1 teaspoon liquid smoke, optional
- 1 fresh beef brisket (6 pounds)
- ½ cup beef broth

BARBECUE SAUCE
- 1 medium onion, chopped
- 2 tablespoons canola oil
- 2 garlic cloves, minced
- 1 cup ketchup
- ½ cup molasses
- ¼ cup cider vinegar
- 2 teaspoons chili powder
- ½ teaspoon ground mustard

1. In a large resealable plastic bag, combine the Worcestershire sauce, chili powder, bay leaves, garlic, celery salt, pepper and liquid smoke if desired. Cut brisket in half and add to bag. Seal the bag and turn to coat. Refrigerate overnight.
2. Transfer beef to a 5- or 6-qt. slow cooker; add beef broth. Cover and cook on low for 6-8 hours or until tender.
3. For sauce, in a small saucepan, saute onion in oil until tender. Add garlic; cook 1 minute longer. Stir in the remaining ingredients; heat through.
4. Remove brisket from the slow cooker; discard bay leaves. Place 1 cup of the cooking juices in a measuring cup; skim fat. Add to the barbecue sauce. Discard remaining juices.
5. Return brisket to the slow cooker; top with sauce mixture. Cover and cook on high for 30 minutes to allow flavors to blend. Thinly slice beef across the grain; serve with sauce.
Editor's Note: *This is a fresh beef brisket, not corned beef.*

Smothered Round Steak

Try affordable round steak and gravy served over egg noodles for a hearty meal. Satisfying and chock-full of veggies, my easy creation takes the worry out of what's-for-dinner.

—KATHY GARRETT
CAMDEN, WEST VIRGINIA

PREP: 20 MIN. **COOK:** 7 HOURS
MAKES: 4 SERVINGS

- ⅓ cup all-purpose flour
- 1 teaspoon salt
- ¼ teaspoon pepper
- 1½ pounds beef top round steak, cut into 1½-inch strips
- 1 large onion, sliced
- 1 large green pepper, sliced
- 1 can (14½ ounces) diced tomatoes, undrained
- 1 jar (4 ounces) sliced mushrooms, drained
- 3 tablespoons soy sauce
- 2 tablespoons molasses
  Hot cooked egg noodles, optional

1. In a large resealable plastic bag, combine the flour, salt and pepper. Add beef and shake to coat. Transfer to a 3-qt. slow cooker. Add the onion, green pepper, tomatoes, mushrooms, soy sauce and molasses.
2. Cover and cook on low for 7-8 hours or until meat is tender. Serve with noodles if desired.

Mushroom 'n' Steak Stroganoff

I rely on this recipe whenever we have family visiting. I just put it in the slow cooker in the morning and when we get home from sightseeing all day, dinner's ready!

—MARILYN SHEHANE
COLORADO SPRINGS, COLORADO

PREP: 15 MIN. **COOK:** 6¼ HOURS
MAKES: 6 SERVINGS

- 2 tablespoons all-purpose flour
- ½ teaspoon garlic powder
- ½ teaspoon pepper
- ¼ teaspoon paprika
- 1¾ pounds beef top round steak, cut into 1½-inch strips
- 1 can (10¾ ounces) condensed cream of mushroom soup, undiluted
- ½ cup water
- ¼ cup Lipton onion mushroom soup mix
- 2 jars (4½ ounces each) sliced mushrooms, drained
- ½ cup sour cream
- 1 tablespoon minced fresh parsley
  Hot cooked egg noodles, optional

1. In a large resealable plastic bag, combine the flour, garlic powder, pepper and paprika. Add beef strips and shake to coat.
2. Transfer to a 3-qt. slow cooker. Combine the soup, water and soup mix; pour over beef. Cover and cook on low for 6-7 hours or until meat is tender.
3. Stir in the mushrooms, sour cream, and parsley. Cover and cook 15 minutes longer or until sauce is thickened. Serve with noodles if desired.

Mexican Taco Filling

My son's friends always requested this recipe when they planned to come over, and they're still talking about it over a decade later! It is perfect as a filling for tacos, burritos or enchiladas and also freezes well.

—**CONNIE DICAVOLI**
SHAWNEE, KANSAS

PREP: 25 MIN. **COOK:** 8 HOURS
MAKES: 9 SERVINGS

- 1½ teaspoons chili powder
- 1 teaspoon ground cumin
- ½ teaspoon smoked paprika
- ½ teaspoon crushed red pepper flakes
- ¼ teaspoon salt
- 1 boneless beef chuck roast (3 pounds)
- 1 can (4 ounces) chopped green chilies
- ½ cup chopped sweet onion
- 2 garlic cloves, minced
- ¾ cup beef broth
  Taco shells or flour tortillas (8 inches)
  Chopped tomatoes, shredded lettuce and shredded Mexican cheese blend

1. In a small bowl, combine the first five ingredients. Cut roast in half; rub spice mixture over meat. Transfer to a 3-qt. slow cooker. Top with chilies, onion and garlic. Pour broth over meat.
2. Cover and cook on low for 8-10 hours or until meat is tender.
3. Remove meat from slow cooker; shred with two forks. Skim fat from cooking juices. Return meat to slow cooker and heat through.
4. Using a slotted spoon, place ½ cup meat mixture on each taco shell. Top with tomatoes, lettuce and cheese.

FAST FIX ▶ Cider Mushroom Brisket

Apple juice and gingersnaps give an autumn feel to this brisket. It's quick to prep, and the pleasing aroma will linger for hours.

—**COLLEEN WESTON**
DENVER, COLORADO

PREP: 10 MIN. **COOK:** 6 HOURS
MAKES: 12 SERVINGS

- 1 fresh beef brisket (6 pounds)
- 2 jars (12 ounces each) mushroom gravy
- 1 cup apple cider or juice
- 1 envelope onion mushroom soup mix
- ⅓ cup crushed gingersnap cookies

1. Cut brisket into thirds; place in a 5- or 6-qt. slow cooker. In a large bowl, combine the gravy, cider, soup mix and cookie crumbs; pour over beef. Cover and cook on low for 6-8 hours or until tender.
2. Thinly slice meat across the grain. Skim fat from cooking juices; thicken if desired.
Editor's Note: *This is a fresh beef brisket, not corned beef.*

Melt-in-Your-Mouth Pot Roast

Slow-simmered and seasoned with rosemary, mustard and thyme, here's a tender and tasty pot roast that's a breeze to make.

—**JEANNIE KLUGH**
LANCASTER, PENNSYLVANIA

PREP: 10 MIN. **COOK:** 6 HOURS
MAKES: 6-8 SERVINGS

- 1 pound medium red potatoes, quartered
- 1 cup fresh baby carrots
- 1 boneless beef chuck roast (3 to 4 pounds)
- ¼ cup Dijon mustard
- 2 teaspoons dried rosemary, crushed
- 1 teaspoon garlic salt
- ½ teaspoon dried thyme
- ½ teaspoon pepper
- ⅓ cup chopped onion
- 1½ cups beef broth

1. Place potatoes and carrots in a 5-qt. slow cooker. Cut roast in half. In a small bowl, combine the mustard, rosemary, garlic salt, thyme and pepper; rub over roast.
2. Place beef in slow cooker; top with onion and broth. Cover and cook on low for 6-8 hours or until meat and vegetables are tender.

Round Steak Italiano

My mom used to make this wonderful dish, and it's always been one that I've enjoyed. I especially like how the thick gravy drapes both the meat and the potatoes.

—DEANNE STEPHENS
MCMINNVILLE, OREGON

PREP: 15 MIN. **COOK:** 7¼ HOURS
MAKES: 8 SERVINGS

- 2 **pounds beef top round steak**
- 1 **can (8 ounces) tomato sauce**
- 2 **tablespoons onion soup mix**
- 2 **tablespoons canola oil**
- 2 **tablespoons red wine vinegar**
- 1 **teaspoon ground oregano**
- ½ **teaspoon garlic powder**
- ¼ **teaspoon pepper**
- 8 **medium potatoes (7 to 8 ounces each)**
- 1 **tablespoon cornstarch**
- 1 **tablespoon cold water**

1. Cut steak into serving-size pieces; place in a 5-qt. slow cooker. In a large bowl, combine the tomato sauce, soup mix, oil, vinegar, oregano, garlic powder and pepper; pour over meat. Scrub and pierce potatoes; place over meat. Cover and cook on low for 7 to 8 hours or until meat and potatoes are tender.

2. Remove meat and potatoes; keep warm. For gravy, pour cooking juices into a small saucepan; skim fat. Combine cornstarch and water until smooth; gradually stir into juices. Bring to a boil; cook and stir for 2 minutes or until thickened. Serve with meat and potatoes.

Sloppy Joe Supper

What an easy way to serve up the flavor of sloppy joes in a one-dish dinner! It's great coming home to this simmering in the slow cooker.

—KARLA WIEDERHOLT
CUBA CITY, WISCONSIN

PREP: 15 MIN. **COOK:** 4 HOURS
MAKES: 8 SERVINGS

- 1 **package (32 ounces) frozen shredded hash brown potatoes, thawed**
- 1 **can (10¾ ounces) condensed cheddar cheese soup, undiluted**
- 1 **egg, lightly beaten**
- 1 **teaspoon salt**
- ½ **teaspoon pepper**
- 2 **pounds ground beef**
- 2 **tablespoons finely chopped onion**
- 1 **can (15½ ounces) sloppy joe sauce**

1. In a large bowl, combine the potatoes, soup, egg, salt and pepper. Spread into a lightly greased 5-qt. slow cooker. In a large skillet, cook beef and onion over medium heat until meat is no longer pink; drain. Stir in the sloppy joe sauce. Spoon over potato mixture.

2. Cover and cook on low for 4 to 4½ hours or until a thermometer reads 160°.

Enchilada Casserole

Tortilla chips and a side salad turn this casserole into a fun and festive meal with very little effort. It's perfect for a busy weeknight.

—DENISE WALLER
OMAHA, NEBRASKA

PREP: 20 MIN. **COOK:** 6 HOURS
MAKES: 4 SERVINGS

- 1 **pound ground beef**
- 2 **cans (10 ounces each) enchilada sauce**
- 1 **can (10¾ ounces) condensed cream of onion soup, undiluted**
- ¼ **teaspoon salt**
- 1 **package (8½ ounces) flour tortillas, torn**
- 3 **cups (12 ounces) shredded cheddar cheese**

1. In a large skillet, cook the beef over medium heat until no longer pink; drain. Stir in the enchilada sauce, soup and salt.
2. In a 3-qt. slow cooker coated with cooking spray, layer a third of the beef mixture, tortillas and cheese. Repeat the layers twice.
3. Cover and cook on low for 6-8 hours or until the casserole is heated through.

Dilled Pot Roast

It's hard to believe that this mouthwatering pot roast comes together so easily. A simple sour cream-and-dill sauce makes it delicious over rice or egg noodles.

—AMY LINGREN
JACKSONVILLE, FLORIDA

PREP: 15 MIN. **COOK:** 7½ HOURS
MAKES: 6-8 SERVINGS

- 2 **teaspoons dill weed, divided**
- 1 **teaspoon salt**
- ¼ **teaspoon pepper**
- 1 **boneless beef chuck roast (2½ pounds)**
- ¼ **cup water**
- 1 **tablespoon cider vinegar**
- 3 **tablespoons all-purpose flour**
- ¼ **cup cold water**
- 1 **cup (8 ounces) sour cream**
- ½ **teaspoon browning sauce, optional**
  Hot cooked rice

1. In a small bowl, combine 1 teaspoon dill, salt and pepper. Sprinkle over both sides of roast. Transfer to a 3-qt. slow cooker. Add water and vinegar. Cover and cook on low for 7-8 hours or until meat is tender.
2. Remove meat and keep warm. In a small bowl, combine flour and remaining dill; stir in cold water until smooth. Gradually stir into slow cooker.
3. Cover and cook on high for 30 minutes or until thickened. Stir in the sour cream and browning sauce if desired; heat through. Serve beef and sour cream sauce with rice.

ENCHILADA SAUCE

Enchilada sauce is a blend of tomatoes, oil and spices thickened with a little flour or cornstarch. Green enchilada sauce, which is made from tomatillos instead of tomatoes, is also available.

Double-Onion Beef Brisket

It's the slow cooking of this brisket that makes it so tender. The wonderfully sweet-tangy flavor comes from a combo of chili sauce, cider vinegar and brown sugar.

—ELAINE SWEET DALLAS, TEXAS

PREP: 35 MIN. **COOK:** 6 HOURS **MAKES:** 10 SERVINGS

- 1 fresh beef brisket (4 pounds)
- 1½ teaspoons kosher salt
- 1½ teaspoons coarsely ground pepper
- 2 tablespoons olive oil
- 3 medium onions, halved and sliced
- 3 celery ribs, chopped
- 1 cup chili sauce
- ¼ cup packed brown sugar
- ¼ cup cider vinegar
- 1 envelope onion soup mix

1. Cut brisket in half; sprinkle all sides with salt and pepper. In a large skillet, brown brisket in oil; remove and set aside. In the same skillet, cook and stir onions over low heat for 15-20 minutes or until caramelized.

2. Place half of the onions in a 5-qt. slow cooker; top with celery and brisket. Combine the chili sauce, brown sugar, vinegar and soup mix. Pour over brisket; top with remaining onions.

3. Cover and cook on low for 6-7 hours or until meat is tender. Let stand for 5 minutes before slicing. Skim fat from cooking juices; serve juices with meat.

Editor's Note: *This is a fresh beef brisket, not corned beef.*

Slow-Cooked Round Steak

Easy slow cooker recipes like this are a real plus, especially around the holidays. Serve these saucy steaks over mashed potatoes, rice or hot buttered noodles.

—DONA MCPHERSON SPRING, TEXAS

PREP: 15 MIN. **COOK:** 7 HOURS
MAKES: 6-8 SERVINGS

- ¼ cup all-purpose flour
- ½ teaspoon salt
- ⅛ teaspoon pepper
- 2 pounds boneless beef round steak, cut into serving-size pieces
- 6 teaspoons canola oil, divided
- 1 medium onion, thinly sliced
- 1 can (10¾ ounces) condensed cream of mushroom soup, undiluted
- ½ teaspoon dried oregano
- ¼ teaspoon dried thyme

1. In a large resealable plastic bag, combine the flour, salt and pepper. Add beef, a few pieces at a time, and shake to coat. In a large skillet, brown meat on both sides in 4 teaspoons oil. Place in a 5-qt. slow cooker.
2. In the same skillet, saute onion in remaining oil until lightly browned; place over beef. Combine the soup, oregano and thyme; pour over onion.
3. Cover and cook on low for 7-8 hours or until meat is tender.

VEGGIE ADDITIONS

You can easily customize round steak by sneaking in some of your favorite vegetables. Try doubling the onions, adding a julienned red pepper, or tossing in ½ pound of sliced baby portobello mushrooms.

Saucy Short Ribs

Smothered in a finger-licking-good barbecue sauce, these meaty ribs are a winner everywhere I take them. The recipe is great for a busy cook because once everything is combined, the slow cooker does all the work.

—PAM HALFHILL WAPAKONETA, OHIO

PREP: 25 MIN. **COOK:** 9 HOURS
MAKES: 12 SERVINGS

- ⅔ cup all-purpose flour
- 2 teaspoons salt
- ½ teaspoon pepper
- 4 to 4½ pounds boneless beef short ribs
- ¼ to ⅓ cup butter
- 1 large onion, chopped
- 1½ cups beef broth
- ¾ cup red wine vinegar
- ¾ cup packed brown sugar
- ½ cup chili sauce
- ⅓ cup ketchup
- ⅓ cup Worcestershire sauce
- 5 garlic cloves, minced
- 1½ teaspoons chili powder

1. In a large resealable plastic bag, combine the flour, salt and pepper. Add ribs in batches and shake to coat. In a large skillet, brown ribs in butter.
2. Transfer to a 6-qt. slow cooker. In the same skillet, combine the remaining ingredients. Cook and stir until mixture comes to a boil; pour over ribs.
3. Cover and cook on low for 9-10 hours or until meat is tender.

Slow-Cooked Sloppy Joes

Transform ground beef into a classic sandwich filling with just a few pantry staples—and slow cook your way to a crowd-pleasing entree! .

—JOEANNE STERAS
GARRETT, PENNSYLVANIA

PREP: 15 MIN. **COOK:** 4 HOURS
MAKES: 12 SERVINGS

- 2 **pounds ground beef**
- 1 **cup chopped green pepper**
- ⅔ **cup chopped onion**
- 2 **cups ketchup**
- 2 **envelopes sloppy joe mix**
- 2 **tablespoons brown sugar**
- 1 **teaspoon prepared mustard**
- 12 **hamburger buns, split**

1. In a large skillet, cook the beef, pepper and onion over medium heat until meat is no longer pink; drain. Stir in the ketchup, sloppy joe mix, brown sugar and mustard. Transfer mixture to a 3-qt. slow cooker
2. Cover and cook on low for 4-5 hours or until flavors are blended. Spoon ½ cup onto each bun.

Beef & Tortellini Marinara

Pasta stew made with fresh green beans is a meal in itself. It's great served with Italian bread to dip into the savory sauce and a nice big green salad.

—JOYCE FREY MACKSVILLE, KANSAS

PREP: 30 MIN. **COOK:** 6½ HOURS
MAKES: 11 SERVINGS

- 1 **pound beef stew meat**
- 2 **tablespoons olive oil**
- 2 **garlic cloves, minced**
- 1 **jar (26 ounces) marinara or spaghetti sauce**
- 2 **cups dry red wine or beef broth**
- 1 **pound fresh green beans, trimmed**
- 1 **can (14½ ounces) Italian diced tomatoes, undrained**
- ½ **pound small fresh mushrooms**
- 2 **envelopes thick and zesty spaghetti sauce mix**
- 2 **tablespoons minced fresh parsley**
- 1 **tablespoon dried minced onion**
- 2 **teaspoons minced fresh rosemary**
- 1 **teaspoon coarsely ground pepper**
- ¼ **teaspoon salt**
- 1 **package (9 ounces) refrigerated cheese tortellini**

1. In a large skillet, brown beef in oil until no longer pink. Add garlic; cook 1 minute longer. Place in a 5- or 6-qt. slow cooker.
2. Stir in the marinara sauce, wine, green beans, tomatoes, mushrooms, sauce mix, parsley, onion, rosemary, pepper and salt. Cover and cook on low for 6-8 hours or until meat is tender.
3. Stir in the tortellini. Cover and cook on high for 30 minutes or until the tortellini are heated through.

Old-World Corned Beef and Vegetables

This traditional corned beef dinner is a winner with my husband, family and friends. It's a nice meal in one.

—RUTH BURRUS ZIONSVILLE, INDIANA

PREP: 25 MIN. **COOK:** 8 HOURS
MAKES: 8 SERVINGS

- 2½ **pounds red potatoes, quartered**
- 2 **cups fresh baby carrots**
- 1 **package (10 ounces) frozen pearl onions**
- 1 **corned beef brisket with spice packet (3 to 3½ pounds)**
- ½ **cup water**
- 1 **tablespoon marinade for chicken**
- ⅛ **teaspoon pepper**
- 3 **tablespoons cornstarch**
- ¼ **cup cold water**

1. In a 5-qt. slow cooker, combine the potatoes, carrots and onions. Add beef; discard spice packet from corned beef or save for another use. Combine the water, marinade for chicken and pepper; pour over meat. Cover and cook on low for 8-10 hours or until meat and vegetables are tender.

2. Remove meat and vegetables to a serving platter; keep warm. Skim fat from cooking juices; transfer to a small saucepan. Bring liquid to a boil. Combine cornstarch and cold water until smooth. Gradually stir into the pan. Bring to a boil; cook and stir for 1-2 minutes or until thickened. Serve with meat and vegetables.

Editor's Note: *This recipe was tested with Lea & Perrins Marinade for Chicken.*

Short Ribs & Gravy

The whole family will love these ribs! The meat is so tender and delicious, and the gravy is perfect with either mashed potatoes or rice.

—HELENA IVY ST. LOUIS, MISSOURI

PREP: 15 MIN. **COOK:** 6 HOURS
MAKES: 6 SERVINGS

- 1 **large onion, sliced**
- 4 **pounds bone-in beef short ribs**
- ½ **pound sliced fresh mushrooms**
- 1 **can (10¾ ounces) condensed cream of mushroom soup, undiluted**
- ½ **cup water**
- 1 **envelope brown gravy mix**
- 1 **teaspoon minced garlic**
- ½ **teaspoon dried thyme**
- 1 **tablespoon cornstarch**
- 2 **tablespoons cold water**
  Hot mashed potatoes

1. Place onion in a 5-qt. slow cooker; top with ribs. Combine the mushrooms, soup, ½ cup water, gravy mix, garlic and thyme; pour over ribs. Cover and cook on low for 6 to 6½ hours or until meat is tender.

2. Remove meat to a serving platter; keep warm. Skim fat from cooking juices; transfer to a small saucepan. Bring to a boil.

3. Combine cornstarch and cold water until smooth. Gradually stir into pan. Bring to a boil. Cook and stir for 2 minutes or until thickened. Serve with meat and mashed potatoes.

Pot Roast with Mushroom Gravy

Is there anything better than the comforting goodness of pot roast—especially one that's simmered all day? Hearty vegetables like potatoes, carrots, mushrooms, celery and onion make this a great meal to come home to!

—TYLER SHERMAN
MADISON, WISCONSIN

PREP: 20 MIN. **COOK:** 8 HOURS
MAKES: 8 SERVINGS

- 1 **pound small red potatoes, halved**
- 2 **cups fresh baby carrots**
- ½ **pound sliced fresh mushrooms**
- 1 **medium onion, cut into six wedges**
- 2 **celery ribs, cut into 1-inch pieces**
- 1 **boneless beef chuck roast (3 pounds)**
- 1 **can (14½ ounces) reduced-sodium beef broth**
- 1 **can (10½ ounces) mushroom gravy**
- 1 **package (1½ ounces) beef stew seasoning mix**

1. Place the potatoes, carrots, mushrooms, onion and celery in a 5-qt. slow cooker. Cut roast in half; place over vegetables. In a small bowl, combine the broth, gravy and seasoning mix; pour over roast.

2. Cover and cook on low for 8-9 hours or until meat is tender.

Slow-Cooked Enchilada Dinner

This layered Southwestern meal just can't be beat. It amps up its spicy flavor with green chilies, seasoned beans, chili powder and cumin.

—JUDY RAGSDALE QUEEN CITY, TEXAS

PREP: 25 MIN. **COOK:** 2 HOURS
MAKES: 6 SERVINGS

- 1 **pound lean ground beef (90% lean)**
- 1 **small onion, chopped**
- 1 **can (15 ounces) Ranch Style beans (pinto beans in seasoned tomato sauce)**
- 1 **can (10 ounces) diced tomatoes with mild green chilies, undrained**
- ¼ **cup chopped green pepper**
- 1 **teaspoon chili powder**
- ½ **teaspoon salt**
- ½ **teaspoon ground cumin**
- ¼ **teaspoon pepper**
- 1 **cup (4 ounces) shredded Monterey Jack cheese**
- 1 **cup (4 ounces) shredded cheddar cheese**
- 6 **flour tortillas (6 inches)**

1. In a large skillet, cook beef and onion over medium heat until meat is no longer pink; drain. Stir in the beans, tomatoes, green pepper, chili powder, salt, cumin and pepper. In a small bowl, combine the cheeses; set aside.

2. Cut three 25-in. x 3-in. strips of heavy-duty foil; crisscross so they resemble spokes of a wheel. Place strips on the bottom and up the sides of a 5-qt. slow cooker. Coat strips with cooking spray. Place two tortillas in slow cooker, overlapping if necessary. Layer with a third of the beef mixture and cheese. Repeat layers twice.

3. Cover and cook on low for 2 to 2½ hours or until heated through. Using foil strips as handles, remove enchilada dinner to a platter.

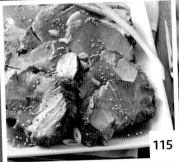

115

112

119

Pork

1. In a small bowl, combine the first four ingredients. Pour half into a greased 3-qt. slow cooker; top with pork chops and remaining mixture.

2. Cover and cook on low for 4-5 hours or until meat is tender.

Zesty Sausage & Beans

Looking for something hearty and delicious dish to feed your hungry family? Packed with sausage, beans and bacon, this is guaranteed to satisfy the heftiest appetites.

—MELISSA JUST MINNEAPOLIS, MINNESOTA

PREP: 30 MIN.   **COOK:** 5 HOURS   **MAKES:** 10 SERVINGS

- 2 pounds smoked kielbasa or Polish sausage, halved and sliced
- 2 cans (15 ounces each) black beans, rinsed and drained
- 1 can (15 ounces) great northern beans, rinsed and drained
- 1 can (15 ounces) thick and zesty tomato sauce
- 1 medium green pepper, chopped
- 1 medium onion, chopped
- 5 bacon strips, cooked and crumbled
- 3 tablespoons brown sugar
- 2 tablespoons cider vinegar
- 3 garlic cloves, minced
- ¼ teaspoon dried thyme
- ¼ teaspoon dried marjoram
- ¼ teaspoon cayenne pepper
  Hot cooked rice

In a large skillet, brown the sausage. Transfer to a 4-qt. slow cooker; add the beans, tomato sauce, green pepper, onion, bacon, brown sugar, vinegar, garlic, thyme, marjoram and cayenne. Cover and cook on low for 5-6 hours or until vegetables are tender. Serve with rice.

FAST FIX ▶ Secret's in the Sauce BBQ Ribs

A sweet, rich sauce makes these ribs so tender that the meat literally falls off the bones. And the aroma is just wonderful. Yum!

—TANYA REID WINSTON-SALEM, NORTH CAROLINA

PREP: 10 MIN.   **COOK:** 6 HOURS   **MAKES:** 5 SERVINGS

- 4½ pounds pork baby back ribs
- 1½ teaspoons pepper
- 2½ cups barbecue sauce
- ¾ cup cherry preserves
- 1 tablespoon Dijon mustard
- 1 garlic clove, minced

Cut ribs into serving-size pieces; sprinkle with pepper. Place in a 5- or 6-qt. slow cooker. Combine the remaining ingredients; pour over ribs. Cover and cook on low for 6-8 hours or until meat is tender. Serve with sauce.

FAST FIX ▶ Sweet 'n' Sour Pork Chops

These tangy, tender pork chops are moist and simply delicious. And with only five ingredients, they couldn't be much easier to make!

—LAURIE STAFFORD WATERVILLE, NEW YORK

PREP: 5 MIN.   **COOK:** 4 HOURS   **MAKES:** 4 SERVINGS

- 1 can (8 ounces) crushed pineapple, undrained
- 1 cup honey barbecue sauce
- ⅓ cup finely chopped onion
- 2 tablespoons chili sauce
- 4 bone-in pork loin chops (8 ounces each)

Herbed Pork Roast

The butter and herb rub adds flavor to juicy pork roast. I like to serve the pork with parsley-tossed new potatoes and a green salad.

—SHELIA LETCHWORTH VERSAILLES, MISSOURI

PREP: 25 MIN. **COOK:** 8 HOURS + STANDING
MAKES: 12 SERVINGS

- 1 **boneless pork loin roast (4 pounds)**
- 1 **cup water**
- ¼ **cup butter, softened**
- 2 **tablespoons rubbed sage**
- 2 **tablespoons dried parsley flakes**
- 2 **teaspoons pepper**
- 1 **teaspoon minced garlic**
- 1 **teaspoon dried oregano**
- ½ **teaspoon salt**
- 1 **small onion, thinly sliced**
- 1 **teaspoon browning sauce, optional**

Cut roast in half. Place pork and water in a 4-qt. slow cooker. Spread butter over meat. Combine the sage, parsley, pepper, garlic, oregano and salt; sprinkle over meat. Top with onion. Cover and cook on low for 8-10 hours or until meat is tender. If desired, thicken cooking juices. Stir in browning sauce if desired. Let meat stand 10 minutes before slicing.

Slow-Cooked Pork Barbecue

I need only five ingredients to fix this sweet and tender pork for sandwiches. I think it's perfect as is, but you can adjust seasonings to suit your own family's tastes.

—CONNIE JOHNSON
SPRINGFIELD, MISSOURI

PREP: 15 MIN. **COOK:** 5 HOURS
MAKES: 10 SERVINGS

- 1 boneless pork loin roast (3 to 4 pounds)
- 1½ teaspoons seasoned salt
- 1 teaspoon garlic powder
- 1 cup cola, divided
- 1 cup barbecue sauce
- 10 sandwich buns, split

1. Cut roast in half; place in a 5-qt. slow cooker. Sprinkle with seasoned salt and garlic powder. Pour ¼ cup cola over roast. Cover and cook on low for 4-5 hours or until meat is tender.

2. Remove roast; cool slightly. Shred meat with two forks and return to slow cooker. Combine barbecue sauce and remaining cola; pour over meat. Cover and cook on high for 1-2 hours or until sauce is thickened. Serve on rolls.

Robust Italian Sausage & Pasta

Sit back and let the slow cooker do all the hard work with my savory main dish. Since you don't even have to cook the pasta separately, there is one less pot to wash when dinner is over.

—LADONNA REED
PONCA CITY, OKLAHOMA

PREP: 15 MIN. **COOK:** 6½ HOURS
MAKES: 4 SERVINGS

- 4 Italian sausage links (4 ounces each), halved
- 1 jar (25.6 ounces) Italian sausage spaghetti sauce
- 1 can (10 ounces) diced tomatoes and green chilies, undrained
- 1 large green pepper, julienned
- 1 medium onion, diced
- 2 garlic cloves, minced
- 1 teaspoon Italian seasoning
- 2 cups uncooked spiral pasta

1. In a large nonstick skillet, brown sausage links. Transfer to a 3-qt. slow cooker. Add the spaghetti sauce, tomatoes, green pepper, onion, garlic and Italian seasoning.

2. Cover and cook on low for 6 hours. Stir in pasta. Cover and cook on high for 30-40 minutes or until pasta is tender.

Cabbage Kielbasa Supper

PREP: 15 MIN.   **COOK:** 8 HOURS
MAKES: 6-8 SERVINGS

   8   **cups coarsely shredded cabbage**
   3   **medium potatoes, cubed**
   1   **medium onion, chopped**
1¾   **teaspoons salt**
   ¼   **teaspoon pepper**
   1   **can (14½ ounces) chicken broth**
   2   **pounds smoked kielbasa or Polish sausage, cut into serving-size pieces**

1. In a 5-qt. slow cooker, combine the cabbage, potatoes, onion, salt and pepper. Pour broth over vegetables. Top with kielbasa (slow cooker will be full, but cabbage will cook down).
2. Cover and cook on low for 8-9 hours or until the cabbage and potatoes are tender.

❝This traditional German supper is so good. All you need is a bowl of fresh seasonal fruit and dinner's ready!❞
—MARGERY BRYAN
MOSES LAKE, WASHINGTON

Pork Chop Supper

My pork chop dinner is a perfect fall meal for two, and it features some of the season's best flavors.
—PAMELA SHANK
PARKERSBURG, WEST VIRGINIA

PREP: 20 MIN.   **COOK:** 3 HOURS
MAKES: 2 SERVINGS

   2   **boneless pork loin chops (5 ounces each)**
   2   **teaspoons canola oil**
   1   **medium sweet potato, peeled and thinly sliced**
   1   **small onion, sliced**
   1   **small tart apple, peeled and sliced**
   1   **tablespoon brown sugar**
   ½   **teaspoon ground cinnamon**
   ¼   **teaspoon salt**
   ¼   **teaspoon ground nutmeg**
   ¼   **teaspoon pepper**
   1   **can (8 ounces) sauerkraut, undrained**

1. In a small nonstick skillet, brown chops in oil. Meanwhile, place the sweet potato, onion and apple slices in a 1½-qt. slow cooker.
2. Combine the brown sugar, cinnamon, salt, nutmeg and pepper; sprinkle over the top. Layer with the pork chops and sauerkraut.
3. Cover and cook on low for 3-4 hours or until meat is tender.

Hoisin Pork Wraps

Flavorful pork with a tasty slaw is fun to serve at buffets because guests can make their own wraps. Even my grandchildren love this meal.

—LINDA WOO DERBY, KANSAS

PREP: 25 MIN. **COOK:** 7 HOURS
MAKES: 15 SERVINGS

- 1 **boneless pork loin roast (3 pounds)**
- 1 **cup hoisin sauce, divided**
- 1 **tablespoon minced fresh gingerroot**
- 6 **cups shredded red cabbage**
- 1½ **cups shredded carrots**
- ¼ **cup thinly sliced green onions**
- 3 **tablespoons rice vinegar**
- 4½ **teaspoons sugar**
- 15 **flour tortillas (8 inches), warmed**

1. Cut roast in half. Combine ⅓ cup hoisin sauce and ginger; rub over pork. Transfer to a 3-qt. slow cooker. Cover and cook on low for 7-8 hours or until tender.
2. Meanwhile, in a large bowl, combine the cabbage, carrots, onions, vinegar and sugar. Chill until serving.
3. Shred meat with two forks and return to the slow cooker; heat through. Place 2 teaspoons remaining hoisin sauce down the center of each tortilla; top with ⅓ cup shredded pork and ⅓ cup coleslaw. Roll up.

Cranberry-Dijon Pork Roast

Five everyday ingredients are all you need for my sweet and tangy pork roast.

—MARY-ELLEN STEELE
BRISTOL, CONNECTICUT

PREP: 15 MIN.
COOK: 4 HOURS + STANDING
MAKES: 6 SERVINGS

- 1 **boneless pork loin roast (2 to 3 pounds)**
- 2 **tablespoons butter**
- 1 **envelope golden onion soup mix**
- 1 **can (14 ounces) whole-berry cranberry sauce**
- 2 **teaspoons Dijon mustard**

1. In a large skillet, brown roast in butter on all sides. Transfer to a 5-qt. slow cooker; sprinkle with soup mix. Add cranberry sauce to skillet, stirring to loosen browned bits from pan. Pour over roast.
2. Cover and cook on low for 4-5 hours or until meat is tender. Remove roast to a serving platter; let stand for 10 minutes before slicing. Stir mustard into cooking juices. Serve with roast.

Sweet Sausage 'n' Beans

My simple, satisfying main dish is sweet, saucy and chock-full of beans, sausage and veggies.

—DORIS HEATH
FRANKLIN, NORTH CAROLINA

PREP: 10 MIN. **COOK:** 4 HOURS
MAKES: 4-6 SERVINGS

- ½ cup thinly sliced carrots
- ½ cup chopped onion
- 2 cups frozen lima beans, thawed
- 2 cups frozen cut green beans, thawed
- 1 pound smoked sausage, thinly sliced
- 1 can (16 ounces) baked beans
- ½ cup ketchup
- ⅓ cup packed brown sugar
- 1 tablespoon cider vinegar
- 1 teaspoon prepared mustard

1. In a 3-qt. slow cooker, layer the carrots, onion, lima beans, green beans, sausage and baked beans. Combine the ketchup, brown sugar, vinegar and mustard; pour over beans.
2. Cover and cook on high for 4 hours or until vegetables are tender. Stir before serving.

FAST FIX ▶ Sweet and Spicy Jerk Ribs

Here's a no-fuss ribs recipe that the whole family will love. The spicy rub and sweet sauce make it an instant favorite.

—GERI LESCH NEW PORT RICHEY, FLORIDA

PREP: 10 MIN. **COOK:** 6 HOURS
MAKES: 5 SERVINGS

- 4½ pounds pork baby back ribs
- 3 tablespoons olive oil
- ⅓ cup Caribbean jerk seasoning
- 3 cups honey barbecue sauce
- 3 tablespoons apricot preserves
- 2 tablespoons honey

1. Cut ribs into serving-size pieces; brush with oil and rub with jerk seasoning. Place in a 5- or 6-qt. slow cooker. Combine the remaining ingredients; pour over ribs.
2. Cover and cook on low for 6-8 hours or until meat is tender. Skim fat from sauce before serving.

FAST FIX ▶ Creamy Potatoes 'n' Kielbasa

In just 5 minutes, you can have this hearty meal started in your slow cooker. What's not to love about sausage, hash browns and cheese? Even picky eaters will dig in!

—BETH SINE FAULKNER, MARYLAND

PREP: 5 MIN. **COOK:** 6 HOURS
MAKES: 4-6 SERVINGS

- 1 package (28 ounces) frozen O'Brien potatoes
- 1 pound fully cooked kielbasa or Polish sausage, sliced
- 1 can (10¾ ounces) condensed cream of mushroom soup, undiluted
- 1 cup (4 ounces) shredded cheddar cheese
- ½ cup water

In a 3-qt. slow cooker, combine all ingredients. Cover and cook on low for 6-8 hours or until the potatoes are tender.

Thai-Style Pork

A creamy Thai peanut sauce coats tender pork in this delectable dish. The recipe is from a friend in my cooking club, and it's always a favorite with my family.

—**AMY VAN ORMAN** ROCKFORD, MICHIGAN

PREP: 15 MIN. **COOK:** 6¼ HOURS **MAKES:** 6 SERVINGS

- 2 **pounds boneless pork loin chops**
- ¼ **cup teriyaki sauce**
- 2 **tablespoons rice vinegar**
- 1 **teaspoon crushed red pepper flakes**
- 1 **teaspoon minced garlic**
- 1 **tablespoon cornstarch**
- ¼ **cup cold water**
- ¼ **cup creamy peanut butter**
  Hot cooked rice
- ½ **cup chopped green onions**
- ½ **cup dry roasted peanuts**
  Lime juice, optional

1. Place pork chops in a 3-qt. slow cooker. In a small bowl, combine the teriyaki sauce, vinegar, pepper flakes and garlic; pour over meat. Cover and cook on low for 6-8 hours or until meat is tender.

2. Remove pork and cut into bite-size pieces; keep warm. Place cooking juices in a small saucepan; bring to a boil. Combine cornstarch and water until smooth. Gradually stir into the pan. Bring to a boil; cook and stir for 2 minutes or until thickened. Stir in peanut butter; add meat.

3. Serve with rice. Sprinkle with onions and peanuts. Drizzle with lime juice if desired.

Orange Pork Roast

Overcooking can cause pork roasts to become dry and tough. But this recipe's succulent orange sauce guarantees that the meat turns out moist and tender.

—**NANCY MEDEIROS** SPARKS, NEVADA

PREP: 10 MIN. **COOK:** 8 HOURS
MAKES: 8 SERVINGS

- 1 **boneless pork shoulder butt roast (3 to 4 pounds)**
- ½ **teaspoon salt**
- ⅛ **teaspoon pepper**
- 1 **can (6 ounces) frozen orange juice concentrate, thawed**
- ¼ **cup honey**
- ⅛ **teaspoon ground cloves**
- ⅛ **teaspoon ground nutmeg**
- 3 **tablespoons all-purpose flour**
- ¼ **cup cold water**

1. Cut roast in half; sprinkle with salt and pepper. Place in a 5-qt. slow cooker. In a small bowl, combine the orange juice concentrate, honey, cloves and nutmeg; pour over pork. Cover and cook on high for 2 hours. Reduce heat to low and cook 6 hours longer or until meat is tender.

2. Remove meat to a serving platter; cover and keep warm. Skim fat from cooking liquid; pour liquid into a small saucepan. Combine flour and cold water until smooth; stir into cooking liquid. Bring to a boil; cook and stir for 2 minutes or until thickened. Serve with roast.

SAVE TIME
||||||||||||||||||||||||||||||||||||||||||||||||

When making sauce, heat the liquid to boiling before you stir in the cornstarch mixture. Since you only have to stir the liquid after cornstarch has been added, this gives you hands-free cooking time.

Conga Lime Pork

Nobody steps out of line when yummy pork slow-cooked in chipotle and molasses moves to the table.

—**JANICE ELDER**
CHARLOTTE, NORTH CAROLINA

PREP: 20 MIN. **COOK:** 4 HOURS
MAKES: 6 SERVINGS

- 1 **teaspoon salt, divided**
- ½ **teaspoon pepper, divided**
- 1 **boneless pork shoulder butt roast (2 to 3 pounds)**
- 1 **tablespoon canola oil**
- 1 **large onion, chopped**
- 3 **garlic cloves, peeled and thinly sliced**
- ½ **cup water**
- 2 **chipotle peppers in adobo sauce, seeded and chopped**
- 2 **tablespoons molasses**
- 2 **cups broccoli coleslaw mix**
- 1 **medium mango, peeled and chopped**
- 2 **tablespoons lime juice**
- 1½ **teaspoons grated lime peel**
- 6 **prepared corn muffins, halved**

1. Sprinkle ¾ teaspoon salt and ¼ teaspoon pepper over roast. In a large skillet, brown pork in oil on all sides. Transfer meat to a 3- or 4-qt. slow cooker.

2. In the same skillet, saute onion until tender. Add garlic; cook 1 minute longer. Add water, chipotle peppers and molasses, stirring to loosen browned bits from pan. Pour over pork. Cover and cook on high for 4-5 hours or until meat is tender.

3. Remove roast; cool slightly. Skim fat from cooking juices. Shred pork with two forks and return to slow cooker; heat through. In a large bowl, combine the coleslaw mix, mango, lime juice, lime peel and remaining salt and pepper.

4. Place muffin halves cut side down on an ungreased baking sheet. Broil 4 in. from the heat for 2-3 minutes or until lightly toasted. Serve pork with muffins; top with slaw.

FAST FIX ▶ Mushroom Pork Tenderloin

Juicy pork tenderloin in a savory mushroom gravy is simply the best! Prepared with canned soups, this entree couldn't be easier to make.

—DONNA HUGHES
ROCHESTER, NEW HAMPSHIRE

PREP: 5 MIN. **COOK:** 4 HOURS
MAKES: 6 SERVINGS

- 2 **pork tenderloins (1 pound each)**
- 1 **can (10¾ ounces) condensed cream of mushroom soup, undiluted**
- 1 **can (10¾ ounces) condensed golden mushroom soup, undiluted**
- 1 **can (10½ ounces) condensed French onion soup, undiluted**
  Hot mashed potatoes, optional

Place pork in a 3-qt. slow cooker. In a small bowl, combine soups; stir until smooth. Pour over pork. Cover and cook on low for 4-5 hours or until the meat is tender. Serve with mashed potatoes if desired.

FAST FIX ▶ Pork Spareribs

Who knew that five ingredients could be so delicious? These ribs are so tender, they literally fall off the bone.

—SHARI SIEG SILVER SPRINGS, FLORIDA

PREP: 5 MIN. **COOK:** 6 HOURS
MAKES: 6 SERVINGS

- 3 **pounds pork spareribs**
- 2 **cans (28 ounces each) diced tomatoes, undrained**
- 2 **cups barbecue sauce**
- ¼ **cup packed brown sugar**
- ¼ **cup white wine vinegar**

Place ribs in a 4- or 5-qt. slow cooker. Combine the remaining ingredients; pour over ribs. Cover and cook on low for 6-8 hours or until meat is tender. Serve with a slotted spoon.

Bavarian Pork Loin

I got the recipe for this wonderful pork roast from an aunt who used to make it all the time. What a delicious flavor combination with sauerkraut, carrots, onions and apples!

—EDIE DESPAIN LOGAN, UTAH

PREP: 25 MIN.
COOK: 6 HOURS + STANDING
MAKES: 10 SERVINGS

- 1 **boneless pork loin roast (3 to 4 pounds)**
- 1 **can (14 ounces) Bavarian sauerkraut, rinsed and drained**
- 1¾ **cups chopped carrots**
- 1 **large onion, finely chopped**
- ½ **cup unsweetened apple juice**
- 2 **teaspoons dried parsley flakes**
- 3 **large tart apples, peeled and quartered**

1. Cut roast in half; place in a 5-qt. slow cooker. In a small bowl, combine the sauerkraut, carrots, onion, apple juice and parsley; spoon over roast. Cover and cook on low for 4 hours.
2. Add apples to slow cooker. Cover and cook 2-3 hours longer or until meat is tender. Remove roast; let stand for 10 minutes before slicing. Serve with the sauerkraut mixture.

Pulled Pork Subs

Honey and ground ginger are the flavor boosters behind my easy, no-stress sandwiches. A bottle of barbecue sauce ties everything together.

—DENISE DAVIS PORTER, MAINE

PREP: 15 MIN.　**COOK:** 5 HOURS　**MAKES:** 8 SERVINGS

- 1　**small onion, finely chopped**
- 1　**boneless pork shoulder butt roast (2½ pounds)**
- 1　**bottle (18 ounces) barbecue sauce**
- ½　**cup water**
- ¼　**cup honey**
- 6　**garlic cloves, minced**
- 1　**teaspoon seasoned salt**
- 1　**teaspoon ground ginger**
- 8　**submarine buns, split**

1. Place onion and roast in a 5-qt. slow cooker. In a small bowl, combine the barbecue sauce, water, honey, garlic, seasoned salt and ginger; pour over meat. Cover and cook on high for 5-6 hours or until meat is tender.

2. Remove meat; cool slightly. Shred meat with two forks and return to the slow cooker; heat through. Serve on buns.

San Francisco Chops

Simmered all day in a tangy sauce, these irresistible chops are so moist and delicious, you'll want to make them often. They have just a hint of Asian flavor and are so nice to come home to!

—TARA BONESTEEL
DAYTON, NEW JERSEY

PREP: 20 MIN. **COOK:** 7½ HOURS
MAKES: 4 SERVINGS

- 4 bone-in pork loin chops (8 ounces each)
- 1 to 2 tablespoons canola oil
- 1 garlic clove, minced
- ¼ cup soy sauce
- ¼ cup red wine or chicken broth
- 2 tablespoons brown sugar
- ¼ teaspoon crushed red pepper flakes
- 1 tablespoon cornstarch
- 1 tablespoon cold water
  Hot cooked rice

1. In a large skillet, brown pork chops on both sides in oil; transfer to a 3-qt. slow cooker. Add garlic to drippings; cook and stir for 1 minute. Add the soy sauce, wine, brown sugar and pepper flakes; cook and stir until sugar is dissolved. Pour mixture over the pork chops.

2. Cover and cook on low for 7-8 hours or until meat is tender. Remove chops. Combine cornstarch and cold water until smooth; gradually stir into the slow cooker. Return chops to the slow cooker.

3. Cover and cook on high for 30 minutes or until sauce is slightly thickened. Serve with rice.

FAST FIX Chinese Pork Ribs

Add some Asian flair to this all-American dish. These ribs boast a wonderful taste from the salty touch of soy sauce and the sweetness of orange marmalade. I like to serve them with steamed broccoli and cooked white rice.

—JUNE ROSS
BELMONT, NORTH CAROLINA

PREP: 10 MIN. **COOK:** 6 HOURS
MAKES: 6 SERVINGS

- ¼ cup reduced-sodium soy sauce
- ⅓ cup reduced-sugar orange marmalade
- 3 tablespoons ketchup
- 2 garlic cloves, minced
- 3 to 4 pounds bone-in country-style pork ribs

1. In a small bowl, combine the soy sauce, marmalade, ketchup and garlic. Pour half into a 5-qt. slow cooker. Top with ribs; drizzle with remaining sauce.

2. Cover and cook on low for 6 hours or until tender. Thicken cooking juices if desired.

Simple Saucy Pork Chops

I serve these tender chops a couple of times a month because we love them! The rich and zesty sauce is delicious over mashed potatoes, rice or even noodles.

—SHARON POLK LAPEER, MICHIGAN

PREP: 10 MIN. **COOK:** 4 HOURS
MAKES: 8 SERVINGS

- 8 boneless pork loin chops (4 ounces each)
- ¼ teaspoon salt
- ⅛ teaspoon pepper
- 2 tablespoons canola oil
- 2 cans (10¾ ounces each) condensed cream of chicken soup, undiluted
- 1 medium onion, chopped
- ½ cup ketchup
- 2 tablespoons Worcestershire sauce
  Hot cooked mashed potatoes or rice

1. Sprinkle pork chops with salt and pepper. In a large skillet, cook chops in oil for 2-3 minutes on each side or until lightly browned. Transfer to a 3-qt. slow cooker.
2. Combine soup, onion, ketchup and Worcestershire sauce; pour over chops. Cover and cook on high for 4-5 hours or until tender. Serve with potatoes or rice.

MAKE IT YOUR WAY

These easy pork chops use pantry staples you probably have on hand. To dress them up a little more, add minced garlic to the sauce before cooking. Or substitute 1 can cream of mushroom soup for 1 can of chicken soup. Also try sprinkling the finished dish with chopped fresh chives or green onion tops.

Tender Teriyaki Pork

My children really loved this dish growing up: In fact, it was the only meat they would gladly eat besides hot dogs! I got the recipe from my mother.

—DEBBIE DUNAWAY
KETTERING, OHIO

PREP: 10 MIN. **COOK:** 6 HOURS
MAKES: 6-8 SERVINGS

- 1 boneless pork shoulder butt roast (3 to 4 pounds)
- 1 cup packed brown sugar
- ⅓ cup unsweetened apple juice
- ⅓ cup reduced-sodium soy sauce
- ½ teaspoon salt
- ¼ teaspoon pepper
- 2 tablespoons cornstarch
- 3 tablespoons cold water

1. Cut roast in half; rub with brown sugar. Place in a 5-qt. slow cooker. Pour apple juice and soy sauce over roast. Sprinkle with salt and pepper. Cover and cook on low for 6 to 8 hours or until meat is tender.
2. Remove roast; cover and keep warm. Skim fat from cooking juices; return to slow cooker. Mix cornstarch and water until smooth; stir into juices. Cover and cook on high for 15 minutes or until thickened. Serve with pork.

Slow and Easy BBQ Ribs

Take advantage of your slow cooker's convenience with these tender pork ribs coated in tangy barbecue sauce.

—KIMI SHORT PRIOR LAKE, MINNESOTA

PREP: 15 MIN. **COOK:** 5½ HOURS
MAKES: 4 SERVINGS

- 2 **pounds boneless country-style pork ribs**
- 1 **can (6 ounces) unsweetened pineapple juice**
- 1 **medium onion, thinly sliced**
- 1 **garlic clove, minced**
- ⅔ **cup barbecue sauce**
- ⅓ **cup plum jam**

1. In a large skillet coated with cooking spray, brown ribs on all sides. Transfer to a 3-qt. slow cooker; top with pineapple juice, onion and garlic. Cover and cook on low for 5-6 hours or until meat is tender.
2. Remove ribs; drain and discard cooking juices and onion. Return ribs to the slow cooker. Combine barbecue sauce and jam; pour over ribs. Cover and cook on high for 30 minutes.

FAST FIX ▶ Glazed Kielbasa

You'll need just three ingredients to whip up this delicious sausage.

—JODY SANDS TAYLOR
RICHMOND, VIRGINIA

PREP: 5 MIN. **COOK:** 4 HOURS
MAKES: 12 SERVINGS

- 3 **pounds smoked kielbasa or Polish sausage, cut into 1-inch chunks**
- ½ **cup packed brown sugar**
- 1½ **cups ginger ale**

Place sausage in a 3-qt. slow cooker; sprinkle with brown sugar. Add ginger ale. Cover and cook on low for 4-5 hours or until heated through.

Slow Cooker Pulled Pork Sandwiches

I like to bring this dish to potlucks because it can be made ahead, which I especially appreciate during the busy holiday season. But best of all, the sweet and spicy sauce is always a hit.

—MARTHA ANNE CARPENTER
MESA, ARIZONA

PREP: 20 MIN. **COOK:** 8½ HOURS
MAKES: 10 SERVINGS

- 1 **boneless pork loin roast (4 pounds)**
- 1 **can (14½ ounces) beef broth**
- ⅓ **cup plus ½ cup Worcestershire sauce, divided**
- ⅓ **cup plus ¼ cup Louisiana-style hot sauce, divided**
- 1 **cup ketchup**
- 1 **cup molasses**
- ½ **cup prepared mustard**
- 10 **kaiser rolls, split**

1. Cut roast in half; place in a 5-qt. slow cooker. In a small bowl, combine the broth, ⅓ cup Worcestershire sauce and ⅓ cup hot sauce; pour over roast. Cover and cook on low for 8-10 hours or until tender.
2. Remove pork; shred with two forks. Drain and discard cooking liquid. Return shredded pork to the slow cooker. For sauce, combine the ketchup, molasses, mustard and the remaining Worcestershire sauce and hot sauce. Pour over pork. Cover and cook on high for 30 minutes or until heated through. Serve on rolls.

Glazed Pork Roast

My roast has a hint of orange and is popular with adults and children alike. It's an excellent take-along meal for potlucks.

—RADELLE KNAPPENBERGER
OVIEDO, FLORIDA

PREP: 30 MIN. **COOK:** 4 HOURS
MAKES: 16 SERVINGS

- 1 **boneless pork loin roast (4 pounds), trimmed**
- 1 **tablespoon olive oil**
- 1 **tablespoon butter, melted**
- ⅔ **cup thawed orange juice concentrate**
- ⅓ **cup water**
- 3 **garlic cloves, minced**
- 1½ **teaspoons salt**
- ½ **teaspoon pepper**

GLAZE

- ¼ **cup packed brown sugar**
- 2 **tablespoons balsamic vinegar**
- 1 **tablespoon thawed orange juice concentrate**
- 1 **garlic clove, minced**
- 1 **can (11 ounces) mandarin oranges, drained, optional**

1. Cut roast in half. In a large skillet, brown roast in oil and butter on all sides.
2. Transfer to a 5-qt. slow cooker. Add the orange juice concentrate, water, garlic, salt and pepper. Cover and cook on low 4-6 hours or until meat is tender.
3. For glaze, in a small saucepan, combine the brown sugar, vinegar, orange juice concentrate and garlic. Bring to a boil. Reduce heat; simmer, uncovered, 3-5 minutes or until reduced to about ¼ cup. Brush over roast. Garnish with oranges if desired.

Italian Sausages with Provolone

Here's a casual dinner that everyone will rave about. These hot Italian sausages with their pepper-and-onion topping go so quickly, you'll want to double the batch!

—SHELLY BEVINGTON-FISHER
HERMISTON, OREGON

PREP: 15 MIN. **COOK:** 4 HOURS
MAKES: 10 SERVINGS

- 10 **Italian sausage links (4 ounces each)**
- 1 **tablespoon canola oil**
- 1 **each small sweet red, yellow and orange peppers, cut into strips**
- 2 **medium onions, halved and sliced**
- 2 **cups Italian salad dressing**
- 10 **slices provolone cheese**
- 10 **brat buns**

1. In a large skillet, brown sausages in batches in oil. Drain. Transfer to a 5-qt. slow cooker. Add the peppers, onions and salad dressing. Cover and cook on low for 4-5 hours or until a thermometer reads 160° and vegetables are tender.
2. Place sausages and cheese in buns; using a slotted spoon, top with pepper mixture.

FAST FIX ▶ Easy and Elegant Ham

I love to serve my large family this moist, tender ham. It can be readied quickly in the morning, frees up my oven, tastes outstanding and feeds a crowd. Pineapple, cherries and a sweet orange glaze make it a real showstopper!

—DENISE DIPACE
MEDFORD, NEW JERSEY

PREP: 5 MIN. **COOK:** 6 HOURS
MAKES: 18-20 SERVINGS

- 2 **cans (20 ounces each) sliced pineapple**
- 1 **fully cooked boneless ham (about 6 pounds), halved**
- 1 **jar (6 ounces) maraschino cherries, well drained**
- 1 **jar (12 ounces) orange marmalade**

1. Drain pineapple, reserving juice; set juice aside. Place half of the pineapple in an ungreased 5-qt. slow cooker. Top with the ham. Add cherries, remaining pineapple and reserved pineapple juice. Spoon marmalade over ham. Cover and cook on low 6-7 hours or until heated through.

2. Remove to a warm serving platter. Serve pineapple and cherries with the sliced ham.

Home-Style Ribs

A dear friend gave me the recipe for these tender ribs simmered in homemade barbecue sauce. They're great for summer because you don't have to turn on the oven and heat up the kitchen.

—RONI GOODELL
SPANISH FORK, UTAH

PREP: 10 MIN. **COOK:** 8 HOURS
MAKES: 6-8 SERVINGS

- 4 **to 5 pounds boneless pork spareribs, cut into pieces**
- 1 **medium onion, thinly sliced**
- 1 **cup ketchup**
- ½ **to 1 cup water**
- ¼ **cup packed brown sugar**
- ¼ **cup cider vinegar**
- 2 **tablespoons Worcestershire sauce**
- 2 **teaspoons ground mustard**
- 1½ **teaspoons salt**
- 1 **teaspoon paprika**

Place half of the ribs in a 5-qt. slow cooker; top with half of the onion. Repeat layers. Combine the remaining ingredients; pour over all. Cover and cook on low for 8-9 hours or until meat is tender.

Pork Chop Potato Dinner

This meal of tender pork chops on a bed of creamy potatoes is a snap to assemble with easy ingredients—and my family loves it!

—DAWN HUIZINGA
OWATONNA, MINNESOTA

PREP: 10 MIN. **COOK:** 5¼ HOURS
MAKES: 6 SERVINGS

- 6 **bone-in pork loin chops (8 ounces each)**
- 1 **tablespoon canola oil**
- 1 **package (30 ounces) frozen shredded hash brown potatoes, thawed**
- 1½ **cups (6 ounces) shredded cheddar cheese, divided**
- 1 **can (10¾ ounces) condensed cream of celery soup, undiluted**
- ½ **cup milk**
- ½ **cup sour cream**
- ½ **teaspoon seasoned salt**
- ⅛ **teaspoon pepper**
- 1 **can (2.8 ounces) French-fried onions, divided**

1. In a large skillet, brown chops in oil on both sides; set aside. In a large bowl, combine the potatoes, 1 cup cheese, soup, milk, sour cream, seasoned salt and pepper. Stir in half of the onions.
2. Transfer to a greased 5-qt. slow cooker; top with pork chops. Cover and cook on low for 5-6 hours or until meat is tender. Sprinkle with remaining cheese and onions. Cover and cook 15 minutes longer or until cheese is melted.

Apricot Pork Roast

Serve this delightful roast with rice or mashed potatoes and veggies. We like the leftovers served on buns the next day.

—PATRICIA DEFOSSE
WILMINGTON, DELAWARE

PREP: 15 MIN. **COOK:** 6 HOURS
MAKES: 6 SERVINGS

- 1 **boneless pork loin roast (2 to 3 pounds)**
- 1 **jar (12 ounces) apricot preserves**
- 1 **cup vegetable broth**
- 2 **tablespoons cornstarch**
- ¼ **cup cold water**

1. Place roast in a 3-qt. slow cooker. In a small bowl, combine preserves and broth; pour over roast. Cover and cook on low for 6-8 hours or until tender. Remove meat to a serving platter; keep warm.
2. Skim fat from cooking juices; transfer to a small saucepan. Bring liquid to a boil. Combine cornstarch and water until smooth. Gradually stir into pan. Bring to a boil; cook and stir for 2 minutes or until thickened. Serve with pork.

Maple Pork Ribs

Tender ribs are draped in a luscious maple-mustard sauce for a special entree. This is one of our favorite recipes.

—PHYLLIS SCHMALZ
KANSAS CITY, KANSAS

PREP: 10 MIN. **COOK:** 5 HOURS
MAKES: 2 SERVINGS

- 1 **pound boneless country-style pork ribs, trimmed and cut into 3-inch pieces**
- 2 **teaspoons canola oil**
- 1 **medium onion, sliced and separated into rings**
- 3 **tablespoons maple syrup**
- 2 **tablespoons spicy brown or Dijon mustard**

In a large skillet, brown ribs in oil on all sides; drain. Place ribs and onion in a 1½-qt. slow cooker. Combine syrup and mustard; pour over the ribs. Cover and cook on low for 5-6 hours or until meat is tender.

Baja Pork Tacos

Here's my copy-cat version of the best Mexican food we ever tasted. The original recipe used beef, but we prefer these succulent tacos with tender shredded pork.

—ARIELLA WINN MESQUITE, TEXAS

PREP: 10 MIN. **COOK:** 8 HOURS **MAKES:** 12 SERVINGS

- 1 boneless pork sirloin roast (3 pounds)
- 5 cans (4 ounces each) chopped green chilies
- 2 tablespoons reduced-sodium taco seasoning
- 1 tablespoon ground cumin
- 24 corn tortillas (6 inches), warmed
- 3 cups shredded lettuce
- 1½ cups (6 ounces) shredded part-skim mozzarella cheese

1. Cut roast in half; place in a 3- or 4-qt. slow cooker. In a small bowl, combine the chilies, taco seasoning and cumin; pour over pork. Cover and cook on low for 8-10 hours or until meat is tender.

2. Remove pork; cool slightly. Skim fat from cooking juices. Shred meat with two forks; return to the slow cooker and heat through. Spoon ¼ cup onto each tortilla; top each taco with 2 tablespoons lettuce and 1 tablespoon cheese.

Pork 'n' Pepper Tortillas

I season pork roast with onions, garlic and spices, then cook it slowly until tender. It's great in warm tortilla wraps with colorful peppers.

—RITA HAHNBAUM
MUSCATINE, IOWA

PREP: 20 MIN. **COOK:** 8 HOURS
MAKES: 12 SERVINGS

- 1 boneless pork shoulder butt roast (3 pounds), halved
- 1 cup boiling water
- 2 teaspoons beef bouillon granules
- 3 garlic cloves, minced
- 1 tablespoon dried basil
- 1 tablespoon dried oregano
- 1 teaspoon ground cumin
- 1 teaspoon pepper
- 1 teaspoon dried tarragon
- 1 teaspoon white pepper
- 2 medium onions, sliced
- 1 each large green, sweet red and yellow peppers, sliced
- 1 tablespoon butter
- 12 flour tortillas (8 inches), warmed
  Shredded lettuce, chopped ripe olives, sliced jalapeno peppers and sour cream, optional

1. Place roast in a 5-qt. slow cooker. Combine the water, bouillon, garlic and seasonings; pour over roast. Top with onions. Cover and cook on high for 1 hour. Reduce heat to low; cook 7-8 hours or until pork is very tender.
2. Remove meat; shred with two forks. Return to slow cooker; heat through. Meanwhile, in a skillet, saute peppers in butter until tender.
3. Using a slotted spoon, place about 1/2 cup pork and onion mixture down the center of each tortilla; top with peppers. Add toppings if desired. Fold sides of tortilla over filling; serve immediately.

Cantonese Sweet and Sour Pork

If you like sweet-and-sour pork, you'll love this easy slow-cooked creation. Tender vegetables, juicy pork and flavorful sauce are delicious over rice.

—NANCY TEWS ANTIGO, WISCONSIN

PREP: 20 MIN. **COOK:** 7 1/2 HOURS
MAKES: 6 SERVINGS

- 1 can (15 ounces) tomato sauce
- 1 medium onion, halved and sliced
- 1 medium green pepper, cut into strips
- 1 can (4 1/2 ounces) sliced mushrooms, drained
- 3 tablespoons brown sugar
- 4 1/2 teaspoons white vinegar
- 2 teaspoons steak sauce
- 1 teaspoon salt
- 1 1/2 pounds pork tenderloin, cut into 1-inch cubes
- 1 tablespoon olive oil
- 1 can (8 ounces) unsweetened pineapple chunks, drained
  Hot cooked rice

1. In a large bowl, combine the first eight ingredients; set aside.
2. In a large skillet, brown pork in oil in batches. Transfer to a 3- or 4-qt. slow cooker. Pour tomato sauce mixture over pork. Cover and cook on low for 7-8 hours or until meat is tender.
3. Add pineapple; cover and cook 30 minutes longer or until heated through. Serve with rice.

FAST FIX ▶ Lemon Pork Chops

These chops can simmer all day on low and be perfect by dinnertime. I serve them with a crisp salad and macaroni and cheese on the side.

—BARBARA DE FRANG
HAZEN, NORTH DAKOTA

PREP: 5 MIN. **COOK:** 6 HOURS
MAKES: 4 SERVINGS

- 4 bone-in pork chops (7 ounces each)
- ½ teaspoon salt
- ¼ teaspoon pepper
- 1 medium onion, thinly sliced
- 1 medium lemon, thinly sliced
- ¼ cup packed brown sugar
- ¼ cup ketchup

1. Place the pork chops in a 3-qt. slow cooker. Sprinkle with salt and pepper. Top with onion and lemon. Sprinkle with brown sugar; drizzle with ketchup.
2. Cover and cook on low for 6-8 hours or until meat is tender.

Saucy Pork Chops

I don't always have a lot of time to cook, so I've come to rely on my slow cooker a lot. I fix these tangy chops at least once a week. The meat's so tender, you can cut it with a fork.

—JENNIFER RUBERG
TWO HARBORS, MINNESOTA

PREP: 15 MIN. **COOK:** 4 HOURS
MAKES: 4 SERVINGS

- 4 bone-in pork loin chops (8 ounces each)
- 1 teaspoon garlic powder
- ½ teaspoon salt
- ¼ teaspoon pepper
- 2 tablespoons canola oil
- 2 cups ketchup
- ½ cup packed brown sugar
- 1 teaspoon liquid smoke, optional

1. Sprinkle pork chops with garlic powder, salt and pepper. In a large skillet, brown chops in oil on both sides; drain.
2. In a small bowl, combine the ketchup, brown sugar and liquid smoke if desired. Pour half of the sauce into a 3-qt. slow cooker. Top with pork chops and remaining sauce. Cover and cook on low for 4-5 hours or until meat is tender.

FAST FIX ▶ Christmas Carol Ham

This slow-cooked entree is simply delicious, and my family loves it! Simmered in pineapple juice, the ham slices are so flavorful.

—JULIE WILLIQUETTE
HARTSELLE, ALABAMA

PREP: 10 MIN. **COOK:** 2 HOURS
MAKES: 8 SERVINGS

- 2 pounds fully cooked boneless ham, cut into eight slices
- ½ cup packed brown sugar
- ¼ cup unsweetened pineapple juice
- 1½ teaspoons white vinegar
- ¼ teaspoon ground mustard

Place ham slices in a 3-qt. slow cooker. In a small bowl, combine the brown sugar, pineapple juice, vinegar and mustard; pour over ham. Cover and cook on low for 2-3 hours or until heated through.

Smoky Bean Stew

I start this satisfying sausage and bean stew in the slow cooker, then spend the afternoon curled up with a good book. It's an effortless meal that tastes great.

—**GLENDA HOLMES** RILEY, KANSAS

PREP: 10 MIN. **COOK:** 4 HOURS **MAKES:** 6-8 SERVINGS

- 1 **package (16 ounces) miniature smoked sausage links**
- 1 **can (16 ounces) baked beans**
- 2 **cups frozen cut green beans**
- 2 **cups frozen lima beans**
- ½ **cup packed brown sugar**
- ½ **cup thinly sliced fresh carrots**
- ½ **cup chopped onion**
- ½ **cup ketchup**
- 1 **tablespoon cider vinegar**
- 1 **teaspoon prepared mustard**

In a 3-qt. slow cooker, combine all ingredients. Cover and cook on high for 4-5 hours or until the vegetables are tender.

Italian Pork Chops

Not only is it easy to use my slow cooker, but the results are fabulous. Meat cooked this way is always so tender and juicy. These pork chops in a thick tomato sauce always turn out perfectly.

—BONNIE MARLOW
OTTOVILLE, OHIO

PREP: 15 MIN.   **COOK:** 5½ HOURS
MAKES: 6 SERVINGS

- 6 **boneless pork loin chops (6 ounces each)**
- 1 **tablespoon canola oil**
- 1 **medium green pepper, diced**
- 1 **can (6 ounces) tomato paste**
- 1 **jar (4½ ounces) sliced mushrooms, drained**
- ½ **cup water**
- 1 **envelope spaghetti sauce mix**
- ½ **to 1 teaspoon hot pepper sauce**

1. In a large skillet, brown pork chops in oil over medium heat for 3-4 minutes on each side; drain. In a 5-qt. slow cooker, combine the remaining ingredients. Top with pork chops.
2. Cover and cook on low for 5½ hours or until meat is tender.

Tasty Pork Ribs

The tantalizing aroma and zippy Cajun barbecue sauce on these tender ribs are sure to make them a favorite at your house. I like to serve them over rice.

—MICHELLE ROMINGER ALBIA, IOWA

PREP: 10 MIN.   **COOK:** 6 HOURS
MAKES: 8 SERVINGS

- 4 **pounds bone-in country-style pork ribs**
- 1 **cup ketchup**
- 1 **cup barbecue sauce**
- ¼ **cup packed brown sugar**
- ¼ **cup Worcestershire sauce**
- 1 **tablespoon balsamic vinegar**
- 1 **tablespoon molasses**
- 1 **garlic clove, minced**
- 2 **tablespoons dried minced onion**
- 1 **teaspoon Cajun seasoning**
- 1 **teaspoon ground mustard**
- ½ **teaspoon salt**
- ¼ **teaspoon pepper**

1. Place ribs in a 5-qt. slow cooker. Combine the remaining ingredients; pour over ribs.
2. Cover and cook on low for 6-7 hours or until meat is tender.

FAST FIX ▶ Polish Kraut and Apples

My family loves this hearty dinner on cold winter nights. The tender apples, kraut and smoked sausage give it a heartwarming Old World flavor. I like making it because the prep time is very short.

—**CAREN MARKEE** CARY, ILLINOIS

PREP: 10 MIN. **COOK:** 4 HOURS
MAKES: 4 SERVINGS

- 1 can (14 ounces) sauerkraut, rinsed and well drained
- 1 pound smoked Polish sausage or kielbasa, cut up
- 3 medium tart apples, peeled and cut into eighths
- ½ cup packed brown sugar
- ½ teaspoon caraway seeds, optional
- ⅛ teaspoon pepper
- ¾ cup apple juice

1. Place half of the sauerkraut in an ungreased 3-qt. slow cooker. Top with the sausage, apples, brown sugar, caraway seeds if desired and pepper. Top with the remaining sauerkraut. Pour apple juice over all.
2. Cover and cook on low for 4-5 hours or until apples are tender.

FAST FIX ▶ Honey-Glazed Ham

Here's an easy solution for feeding a large group. The simple ham is perfect for family dinners where time in the kitchen is as valuable as space in the oven.

—**JACQUIE STOLZ**
LITTLE SIOUX, IOWA

PREP: 10 MIN. **COOK:** 4½ HOURS
MAKES: 14 SERVINGS

- 1 boneless fully cooked ham (4 pounds)
- 1½ cups ginger ale
- ¼ cup honey
- ½ teaspoon ground mustard
- ½ teaspoon ground cloves
- ¼ teaspoon ground cinnamon

1. Cut ham in half; place in a 5-qt. slow cooker. Pour ginger ale over ham. Cover and cook on low for 4-5 hours or until heated through.
2. Combine the honey, mustard, cloves and cinnamon; stir until smooth. Spread mixture over ham; cook 30 minutes longer.

Busy-Day Barbecued Ribs

I don't have a lot of time on the weekends to prepare meals. That's when this recipe comes in handy. I put all the ingredients in the slow cooker, and before I know it, dinner is ready!

—**SHERRY SMALLEY** SOUTH MILWAUKEE, WISCONSIN

PREP: 10 MIN. **COOK:** 5 HOURS
MAKES: 6-8 SERVINGS

- 3½ to 4 pounds bone-in country-style pork ribs
- 1 can (10¾ ounces) condensed tomato soup, undiluted
- ½ cup packed brown sugar
- ⅓ cup cider vinegar
- 1 tablespoon soy sauce
- 1 teaspoon celery seed
- 1 teaspoon chili powder

1. Place ribs in a 5-qt. slow cooker. Combine the remaining ingredients; pour over ribs.
2. Cover and cook on high for 1 hour. Reduce heat to low; cook 4-5 hours longer or until meat is tender. Thicken the cooking liquid if desired.

Hot Ham Sandwiches

I came up with this crowd-pleasing recipe while trying to re-create a favorite sandwich from a restaurant near my hometown. The sandwiches are easy to serve in a buffet line because they don't really need condiments. They're so flavorful just as they are!

—SUSAN REHM
GRAHAMSVILLE, NEW YORK

PREP: 10 MIN. **COOK:** 4 HOURS
MAKES: 12 SERVINGS

- 3 **pounds thinly sliced deli ham (about 40 slices)**
- 2 **cups apple juice**
- ⅔ **cup packed brown sugar**
- ½ **cup sweet pickle relish**
- 2 **teaspoons prepared mustard**
- 1 **teaspoon paprika**
- 12 **kaiser rolls, split**
  Additional sweet pickle relish, optional

1. Separate ham slices and place in a 3-qt. slow cooker.
2. In a small bowl, combine the apple juice, brown sugar, relish, mustard and paprika. Pour over the ham.
3. Cover and cook on low for 4-5 hours or until heated through. Place 3-4 slices of ham on each roll. Serve sandwiches with additional relish if desired.

EASY POTLUCK

IIIIIIIIIIIIIIIIIIIIIIIIIIIIIIIIIIIIIIIIIII

When organizing a potluck, mark the tables with sticky notes labeled for main dishes, side dishes, salads, drinks, desserts, gifts, etc. Attendees will know where to place their items without having to ask. This will also help you plan a smooth flow of guests and reduce traffic jams.

Slow-Cooked Shredded Pork

The tasty pork filling for these sandwiches requires very little work because it's prepared in the slow cooker. The mild, sweet sauce appeals to all ages.

—SHIRLEYMAE HAEFNER
O'FALLON, MISSOURI

PREP: 15 MIN. **COOK:** 6 HOURS
MAKES: 8 SERVINGS

- 1 **boneless pork loin roast (2 to 3 pounds)**
- 1 **large onion, thinly sliced**
- 1 **cup beer or nonalcoholic beer**
- 1 **cup chili sauce**
- 2 **tablespoons brown sugar**
- 1 **tablespoon prepared horseradish**
- 8 **sandwich rolls, split**

1. Cut roast in half; place in a 3-qt. slow cooker. Top with onion. Combine the beer, chili sauce, brown sugar and horseradish; pour over pork and onion. Cover and cook on low for 6 to 6½ hours or until meat is tender.
2. Remove pork; shred with two forks. Return meat to cooking juices; heat through. Use a slotted spoon to serve on rolls.

Cranberry-Apricot Pork Roast with Potatoes

Here's a delightful meal-in-one dish that makes weeknight dining a snap. Apricots blend well with the whole-berry cranberry sauce for a delightful taste. Cayenne adds just the right touch of zing.

—**PAT BARNES** PANAMA CITY, FLORIDA

PREP: 15 MIN.
COOK: 5 HOURS + STANDING
MAKES: 8 SERVINGS

- 1 **boneless pork loin roast (3 pounds)**
- 4 **medium potatoes, peeled and quartered**
- 1 **can (14 ounces) whole-berry cranberry sauce**
- 1 **can (15 ounces) apricot halves, drained**
- 1 **medium onion, quartered**
- ½ **cup chopped dried apricots**
- 1 **tablespoon sugar**
- ½ **teaspoon ground mustard**
- ¼ **teaspoon cayenne pepper**

1. Cut roast in half. Place potatoes in a 5-qt. slow cooker. Add pork.
2. In a blender, combine the cranberry sauce, canned apricots, onion, dried apricots, sugar, mustard, and cayenne. Cover and process for 30 seconds or until mixture is almost smooth. Pour over pork.
3. Cover and cook on low for 5-6 hours or until meat is tender. Let meat stand for 10 minutes before slicing. Serve with potatoes and cooking juices.

Pulled Pork Sandwiches

Preparing pork roast in the slow cooker makes it moist and tender... so it's perfect for these sandwiches. The meat shreds easily, and the cumin and garlic add just the right flavor. Sourdough bread, chipotle mayonnaise, cheese and tomato make it complete.

—**TIFFANY MARTINEZ**
ALISO VIEJO, CALIFORNIA

PREP: 20 MIN. **COOK:** 6 HOURS
MAKES: 8 SERVINGS

- 1 **boneless pork loin roast (2 pounds)**
- 1 **cup barbecue sauce**
- ¼ **cup chopped onion**
- 2 **garlic cloves, minced**
- ½ **teaspoon ground cumin**
- ¼ **teaspoon salt**
- ⅛ **teaspoon pepper**
- 16 **slices sourdough bread**
- 1 **chipotle pepper in adobo sauce, chopped**
- ¾ **cup mayonnaise**
- 8 **slices cheddar cheese**
- 2 **plum tomatoes, thinly sliced**

1. Place pork in a 3-qt. slow cooker. Combine the barbecue sauce, onion, garlic, cumin, salt and pepper; pour over pork. Cover and cook on low for 6-7 hours or until meat is tender.
2. Remove meat. Shred with two forks and return to the slow cooker; heat through.
3. Place bread on ungreased baking sheets. Broil 4-6 in. from the heat for 2-3 minutes on each side or until golden brown.
4. Combine chipotle pepper and mayonnaise; spread over toast. Spoon ½ cup meat mixture onto each of eight slices of toast. Top with cheese, tomatoes and remaining toast.

Peachy Pork Steaks

My mom has been preparing this pork dish for years. She always found it a surefire way to get picky children to eat meat. No one can refuse these succulent steaks!

—SANDY MCKENZIE
BRAHAM, MINNESOTA

PREP: 10 MIN. **COOK:** 5 HOURS
MAKES: 4 SERVINGS

- 4 **pork blade steaks (½ inch thick and 7 ounces each), trimmed**
- 2 **tablespoons canola oil**
- ¾ **teaspoon dried basil**
- ¼ **teaspoon salt**
   Dash pepper
- 1 **can (15¼ ounces) sliced peaches in syrup, undrained**
- 2 **tablespoons white vinegar**
- 1 **tablespoon beef bouillon granules**
- 2 **tablespoons cornstarch**
- ¼ **cup cold water**
   Hot cooked rice

1. In a large skillet, brown pork in oil; sprinkle with the basil, salt and pepper. Drain peaches, reserving syrup. Place peaches in a 5-qt. slow cooker; top with pork. In a small bowl, combine the syrup, vinegar and bouillon; pour over pork.
2. Cover and cook on high for 1 hour. Reduce heat to low and cook 4 hours longer or until meat is tender. Remove pork and peaches to a serving platter and keep warm.
3. Skim fat from cooking liquid; place liquid in a small saucepan. Combine cornstarch and cold water until smooth; stir into cooking liquid. Bring to a boil; cook and stir for 2 minutes or until thickened. Serve the pork, peaches and sauce with rice.

Fruity Pork Roast

I like using the slow cooker because it gives me time for other dinner preparations and frees up the oven. Plus, it usually doesn't matter if you serve the food a little later than planned. This pork roast, which I created by adapting other recipes, gets a special flavor from the fruit.

—MARY JEPPESEN-DAVIS
ST. CLOUD, MINNESOTA

PREP: 25 MIN.
COOK: 8 HOURS + STANDING
MAKES: 8 SERVINGS

- ½ **medium lemon, sliced**
- ½ **cup dried cranberries**
- ⅓ **cup golden raisins**
- ⅓ **cup unsweetened apple juice**
- 3 **tablespoons sherry or additional unsweetened apple juice**
- 1 **teaspoon minced garlic**
- ½ **teaspoon ground mustard**
- 1 **boneless pork loin roast (3 pounds)**
- ½ **teaspoon salt**
- ¼ **teaspoon pepper**
- ⅛ to ¼ **teaspoon ground ginger**
- 1 **medium apple, peeled and sliced**
- ½ **cup packed fresh parsley sprigs**

1. In a small bowl, combine the first seven ingredients; set aside.
2. Cut roast in half; sprinkle with salt, pepper and ginger. Transfer to a 3-qt. slow cooker.
3. Pour fruit mixture over roast. Place apple and parsley around roast. Cover and cook on low for 8-10 hours or until meat is tender.
4. Transfer meat to a serving platter. Let stand for 10-15 minutes before slicing.

Country Rib Sandwiches

Perfect for a weekday dinner or a cozy weekend meal, these sandwiches are packed with delicious flavor—and so easy!

—MARGARET LUCHSINGER
JUPITER, FLORIDA

PREP: 30 MIN. **COOK:** 6¼ HOURS
MAKES: 8 SERVINGS

- 1 **large onion, chopped**
- 2 **pounds boneless country-style pork ribs**
- ½ **cup ketchup**
- ¼ **cup plum sauce**
- ¼ **cup chili sauce**
- 2 **tablespoons brown sugar**
- 1 **teaspoon celery seed**
- 1 **teaspoon garlic powder**
- 1 **teaspoon liquid smoke, optional**
- ½ **teaspoon ground allspice**
- 8 **kaiser rolls, split**

1. Place onion in a 3-qt. slow cooker; top with ribs. Combine the ketchup, plum sauce, chili sauce, brown sugar, celery seed, garlic powder, liquid smoke if desired and allspice; pour over ribs.
2. Cover and cook on low for 6-7 hours or until meat is tender. Shred meat with two forks and return to the slow cooker. Cover and cook 15 minutes longer or until heated through. Serve on rolls.

Tender Pork Chops

My family has enjoyed these simple pork chops for years. They are so tender and juicy, the meat falls right off the bone!

—PATRICIA DICK
ANDERSON, INDIANA

PREP: 20 MIN. **COOK:** 6 HOURS
MAKES: 6 SERVINGS

- ½ **cup all-purpose flour**
- 1½ **teaspoons ground mustard**
- 1 **teaspoon seasoned salt**
- ½ **teaspoon garlic powder**
- 6 **bone-in pork loin chops (8 ounces each)**
- 2 **tablespoons canola oil**
- 1 **can (10½ ounces) condensed chicken with rice soup, undiluted**

1. In a large resealable plastic bag, combine the flour, mustard, seasoned salt and garlic powder. Add pork chops, one at a time, and shake to coat.
2. In a large skillet, brown chops in oil on both sides. Place in a 3-qt. slow cooker. Pour soup over pork. Cover and cook on low for 6-7 hours or until meat is tender.

Pork Roast with Twist of Orange

Just a hint of citrus sets this pork shoulder roast apart.
It's my family's favorite!

—JANIE CANALS WEST JORDAN, UTAH

PREP: 25 MIN.   **COOK:** 4½ HOURS   **MAKES:** 8 SERVINGS

- 4 **bacon strips, diced**
- 1 **boneless pork shoulder butt roast (3 to 4 pounds)**
- 1 **large onion, thinly sliced**
- 1½ **teaspoons minced garlic**
- 1 **jalapeno pepper, seeded and finely chopped**
- 4½ **teaspoons chili powder**
- 1 **teaspoon salt**
- 1 **teaspoon pepper**
- 1 **cup chicken broth, divided**
- ⅔ **cup orange juice**
- ¼ **cup all-purpose flour**
     Hot mashed potatoes, optional

1. In a large skillet, cook bacon over medium heat until crisp. Remove to paper towels to drain; set aside.

2. Cut the roast in half. Brown meat in the bacon drippings on all sides.

3. Transfer to a 5-qt. slow cooker, reserving 1 tablespoon drippings. Brown onion in the drippings. Add garlic; cook 1 minute longer. Add the jalapeno, chili powder, salt and pepper. Stir in ½ cup chicken broth, the orange juice and bacon; pour over roast.

4. Cover and cook on low for 4½ to 5 hours or until meat is tender.

5. Remove pork and onion to a serving platter; keep warm. Skim fat from cooking juices; transfer to a small saucepan. Bring to a boil.

6. Combine flour and remaining broth until smooth. Gradually stir into the pan. Bring to a boil; cook and stir for 2 minutes or until thickened. Serve with pork and mashed potatoes if desired.

Editor's Note: *Wear disposable gloves when cutting hot peppers; the oils can burn skin. Avoid touching your face.*

Spaghetti Pork Chops

Tender pork chops are simmered to perfection in a tangy sauce and then served over pasta. This was one of Mother's most-cherished recipes.

—ELLEN GALLAVAN
MIDLAND, MICHIGAN

PREP: 20 MIN. **COOK:** 6 HOURS
MAKES: 6 SERVINGS

- 3 cans (8 ounces each) tomato sauce
- 1 can (10¾ ounces) condensed tomato soup, undiluted
- 1 small onion, finely chopped
- 1 bay leaf
- 1 teaspoon celery seed
- ½ teaspoon Italian seasoning
- 6 bone-in pork loin chops (8 ounces each)
- 2 tablespoons olive oil
  Hot cooked spaghetti

1. In a 5-qt. slow cooker, combine the tomato sauce, soup, onion, bay leaf, celery seed and Italian seasoning.
2. In a large skillet, brown pork chops in oil. Add to the slow cooker. Cover and cook on low for 6-8 hours or until meat is tender. Discard bay leaf. Serve chops and sauce over spaghetti.

Cheesy Ham & Potatoes

If you love scalloped potatoes but have a small household, this downsized version with tender chunks of ham is just for you.

—WENDY ROWLEY
GREEN RIVER, WYOMING

PREP: 20 MIN. **COOK:** 5 HOURS
MAKES: 2 SERVINGS

- 2 large red potatoes, cubed
- ⅓ cup cubed process cheese (Velveeta)
- ¾ cup cubed fully cooked ham
- 1 tablespoon dried minced onion
- ⅔ cup condensed cream of celery soup, undiluted
- ⅔ cup 2% milk
- 1 tablespoon all-purpose flour
- ¼ teaspoon pepper

1. In a greased 1½-qt. slow cooker, layer the potatoes, cheese, ham and onion.
2. In a small bowl, combine soup and milk; whisk in flour and pepper. Pour over potatoes. Cover and cook on low for 5-6 hours or until potatoes are tender. Stir before serving.

COOKING PASTA

To prevent pasta from sticking together when cooking, use a large pot and 3 quarts of water for each 8 ounces of pasta you plan to cook. Add 1 tablespoon cooking oil to the water. (This also prevents boiling over.) Bring the water to a full rolling boil before stirring in the pasta. Stir several times to separate the pasta until the water returns to a boil.

Cranberry Pork Tenderloin

Canned cranberry sauce creates a sweet, lightly spiced accompaniment for pork. I dress up the cranberries with orange juice, mustard, brown sugar and cloves.

—BETTY HELTON
MELBOURNE, FLORIDA

PREP: 10 MIN. **COOK:** 5¼ HOURS
MAKES: 4 SERVINGS

- 1 pork tenderloin (1 pound)
- 1 can (14 ounces) whole-berry cranberry sauce
- ½ cup orange juice
- ¼ cup sugar
- 1 tablespoon brown sugar
- 1 teaspoon ground mustard
- ¼ to ½ teaspoon ground cloves
- 2 tablespoons cornstarch
- 3 tablespoons cold water

1. Place pork tenderloin in a 3-qt. slow cooker. In a small bowl, combine the cranberry sauce, orange juice, sugars, mustard and cloves; pour over pork. Cover and cook on low for 5-6 hours or until meat is tender.

2. Remove pork and keep warm. Combine cornstarch and cold water until smooth; gradually stir into cranberry mixture. Cover and cook on high for 15 minutes or until thickened. Serve with pork.

Pork Baby Back Ribs

These ribs get a touch of sweetness from brown sugar and apricot preserves. It's one slow-cooked recipe that you will surely enjoy time and again.

—LAVERNE PARKIN
MANITOWOC, WISCONSIN

PREP: 10 MIN. **COOK:** 6 HOURS
MAKES: 5 SERVINGS

- 2½ pounds pork baby back ribs
- 2 tablespoons canola oil
- 1 medium onion, thinly sliced
- ½ cup apricot preserves
- ⅓ cup beef broth
- 3 tablespoons white vinegar
- 2 tablespoons Worcestershire sauce
- 1 tablespoon brown sugar

1. Cut ribs into serving-size pieces. In a large skillet, brown ribs in oil in batches. Place onion in a 5-qt. slow cooker; top with ribs. In a small bowl, combine the remaining ingredients. Pour over ribs.

2. Cover and cook on low for 6-7 hours or until meat is tender.

Hawaiian Pork Roast

This is one of my favorite slow cooker recipes. It's wonderful with rice or potatoes and any vegetable. It also reheats well for lunch the next day.

—RUTH CHIARENZA LA VALE, MARYLAND

PREP: 30 MIN. **COOK:** 4 HOURS **MAKES:** 8 SERVINGS

- 1 boneless pork loin roast (3 pounds)
- ½ teaspoon salt
- ¼ teaspoon pepper
- 3 tablespoons canola oil
- 2 cups unsweetened pineapple juice
- 1 can (8 ounces) unsweetened crushed pineapple, undrained
- ½ cup packed brown sugar
- ½ cup sliced celery
- ½ cup cider vinegar
- ½ cup reduced-sodium soy sauce
- ¼ cup cornstarch
- ⅓ cup cold water

1. Cut pork roast in half. Sprinkle with salt and pepper. In a large skillet, brown roast in oil on all sides; drain. Place in a 5-qt. slow cooker.
2. In a large bowl, combine the pineapple juice, pineapple, brown sugar, celery, vinegar and soy sauce. Pour over the roast. Cover and cook on low for 4-6 hours or until meat is tender.
3. Remove roast and keep warm. Strain cooking juices; transfer to a large saucepan. Combine cornstarch and water until smooth; stir into cooking juices. Bring to a boil; cook and stir for 2 minutes or until thickened. Serve with pork.

Pork and Sauerkraut With Potatoes

Down-home flavors of pork chops and sauerkraut are nicely complemented by potatoes and apples. The irresistible aroma makes this a wintertime favorite.

—VALERIE HAY
LONGMONT, COLORADO

PREP: 20 MIN. **COOK:** 5 HOURS
MAKES: 6 SERVINGS

- 2 cans (14 ounces each) sauerkraut, undrained
- 1 cup thinly sliced onion
- 2 medium tart apples, peeled and sliced
- ½ cup dark corn syrup
- 2 bay leaves
- 1 teaspoon caraway seeds
- ½ teaspoon pepper
- 3 large potatoes, peeled and cut into 2-inch chunks
- 6 bone-in pork loin chops (7 ounces each)

1. Combine the first seven ingredients. Spoon half of sauerkraut mixture into a 5-qt. slow cooker; top with potatoes.
2. Broil pork chops 6 in. from the heat for 3-4 minutes on each side or until browned; place over potatoes. Spoon remaining sauerkraut mixture over pork.
3. Cover and cook on high for 1 hour. Reduce heat to low; cook 4-5 hours longer or until meat is tender. Discard bay leaves.

COOK TIME

If you won't be home to lower the cook temperature after 1 hour, simply cook the pork chops on low for 6-7 hours instead. An hour of cooking on high is roughly equal to 2 hours on low.

Creole Black Beans 'n' Sausage

It's easy to add a taste of Louisiana to your table with my recipe. I brown the meat, cut up veggies and measure spices the night before, then assemble the dish and start cooking the next morning. When I get home, I just make the rice and dinner is served!

—CHERYL LANDERS
LATOUR, MISSOURI

PREP: 25 MIN. **COOK:** 6 HOURS
MAKES: 10 SERVINGS

- 2 pounds smoked sausage, cut into 1-inch slices
- 3 cans (15 ounces each) black beans, rinsed and drained
- 1½ cups each chopped onions, celery and green peppers
- 1 cup water
- 1 can (8 ounces) tomato sauce
- 4 garlic cloves, minced
- 2 teaspoons dried thyme
- 1 teaspoon chicken bouillon granules
- 1 teaspoon white pepper
- ¼ teaspoon cayenne pepper
- 2 bay leaves
  Hot cooked rice

1. In a large skillet, brown sausage over medium heat; drain. Transfer to a 5-qt. slow cooker. Stir in the beans, onion, celery, green pepper, water, tomato sauce, garlic, thyme, bouillon, white pepper, cayenne and bay leaves.
2. Cover and cook on low for 6-8 hours or until vegetables are tender. Discard bay leaves. Serve with rice.

Mom's Scalloped Potatoes and Ham

Whenever I have leftover ham to use up, this is my go-to recipe!

—KELLY GRAHAM
ST. THOMAS, ONTARIO

PREP: 20 MIN. **COOK:** 8 HOURS
MAKES: 9 SERVINGS

- 10 **medium potatoes, peeled and thinly sliced**
- 3 **cups cubed fully cooked ham**
- 2 **large onions, thinly sliced**
- 2 **cups (8 ounces) shredded cheddar cheese**
- 1 **can (10¾ ounces) condensed cream of mushroom soup, undiluted**
- ½ **teaspoon paprika**
- ¼ **teaspoon pepper**

1. In a greased 6-qt. slow cooker, layer half of the potatoes, ham, onions and cheese. Repeat layers. Pour soup over top. Sprinkle with paprika and pepper.
2. Cover and cook on low for 8-10 hours or until potatoes are tender.

FAST FIX ▶ Chipotle Pomegranate Pulled Pork

One day I was making pulled pork and wanted to kick it up a bit. Pomegranate jelly and smoky chipotles were the perfect addition!

—TATIANA KUSHNIR
MONTARA, CALIFORNIA

PREP: 10 MIN. **COOK:** 8½ HOURS
MAKES: 10 SERVINGS

- 1 **boneless pork shoulder butt roast (3 pounds)**
- 2 **tablespoons steak seasoning**
- ½ **cup water**
- 1 **cup pomegranate or red currant jelly**
- 3 **tablespoons minced chipotle peppers in adobo sauce**
- 10 **kaiser rolls, split**

1. Cut roast in half. Place in a 5-qt. slow cooker; sprinkle with steak seasoning. Add water. Cover and cook on low for 8-10 hours or until meat is tender.
2. In a small saucepan, combine jelly and peppers. Cook over medium heat for 5 minutes or until heated through.
3. Remove meat from slow cooker; discard cooking liquid. Shred pork with two forks. Return to the slow cooker; top with jelly mixture. Cover and cook on low for 30 minutes or until heated through. Spoon about ⅔ cup meat onto each roll.

Editor's Note: *This recipe was tested with McCormick's Montreal Steak Seasoning. Look for it in the spice aisle.*

Switch-and-Go Ribs

A slightly sweet teriyaki sauce makes these boneless ribs simply delicious.

—LIL NEULS CABALLO, NEW MEXICO

PREP: 10 MIN. **COOK:** 6 HOURS
MAKES: 3 SERVINGS

- 1½ **pounds boneless country-style pork ribs**
- 1 **tablespoon canola oil**
- ⅓ **cup orange marmalade**
- ⅓ **cup teriyaki sauce**
- 1 **teaspoon minced garlic**

1. In a large skillet, brown ribs in oil on both sides. Combine marmalade, teriyaki sauce and garlic; pour half of mixture into a 3-qt. slow cooker. Top with ribs and remaining sauce.
2. Cover and cook on low for 6-8 hours or until meat is tender.

Fruited Pork Chops

Here's one of my favorite recipes for the slow cooker. I often prepare these tender pork chops for guests and then serve with brown rice.

—CINDY RAGAN
NORTH HUNTINGDON, PENNSYLVANIA

PREP: 10 MIN.   **COOK:** 6¼ HOURS
MAKES: 6 SERVINGS

- 3 tablespoons all-purpose flour
- 1½ teaspoons dried oregano
- ¾ teaspoon salt
- ¼ teaspoon garlic powder
- ¼ teaspoon pepper
- 6 boneless pork loin chops (5 ounces each)
- 1 tablespoon olive oil
- 1 can (20 ounces) unsweetened pineapple chunks
- ¾ cup unsweetened pineapple juice
- ¼ cup water
- 2 tablespoons brown sugar
- 2 tablespoons dried minced onion
- 2 tablespoons tomato paste
- ¼ cup raisins

1. In a large resealable plastic bag, combine the flour, oregano, salt, garlic powder and pepper; add the pork chops, one at a time, and shake to coat. In a nonstick skillet, brown chops in oil on both sides. Transfer to a 5-qt. slow cooker.

2. Drain pineapple, reserving juice; set pineapple aside. In a bowl, combine the ¾ cup pineapple juice with reserved pineapple juice. Stir in the water, brown sugar, onion and tomato paste; pour over chops. Sprinkle with raisins.

3. Cover and cook on low for 6-8 hours or until meat is tender. Stir in reserved pineapple. Cover and cook 15 minutes longer or until heated through.

All-Day Red Beans & Rice

My family loves New Orleans-style cooking, so I make this authentic dish often. Being a busy woman, I appreciate how simple it is. And its smoky ham flavor is scrumptious!

—CELINDA DAHLGREN
NAPA, CALIFORNIA

PREP: 20 MIN. + SOAKING
COOK: 8½ HOURS
MAKES: 6 SERVINGS

- 1 cup dried red beans
- 7 cups water, divided
- 2 smoked ham hocks
- 1 medium onion, chopped
- 1½ teaspoons minced garlic
- 1 teaspoon ground cumin
- 1 medium tomato, chopped
- 1 medium green pepper, chopped
- 1 teaspoon salt
- 4 cups hot cooked rice

1. Sort beans and rinse in cold water. Place beans in a 3-qt. slow cooker. Add 4 cups water; cover and let stand overnight.

2. Drain and rinse beans, discarding liquid. Return beans to slow cooker; add the ham hocks, onion, garlic, cumin and remaining water. Cover and cook on low for 8-10 hours or until beans are tender.

3. Remove ham hocks; cool slightly. Remove meat from bones. Finely chop meat and return to slow cooker; discard bones. Stir in the tomato, green pepper and salt; cover and cook on high for 30 minutes or until pepper is tender. Serve with rice.

No-Fuss Pork and Sauerkraut

PREP: 10 MIN. **COOK:** 4 HOURS
MAKES: 12-16 SERVINGS

- 1 boneless pork loin roast (4 to 5 pounds), cut into quarters
- ⅓ cup Dijon mustard
- 1 teaspoon garlic powder
- 1 teaspoon rubbed sage
- 1 can (27 ounces) sauerkraut, rinsed and well drained
- 2 medium tart apples, sliced
- 1 cup apple juice

1. Rub roast on all sides with mustard; sprinkle with garlic powder and sage.
2. Place sauerkraut and half of the apples in a 6-qt. slow cooker. Top with pork. Pour apple juice around pork; top with remaining apples.
3. Cover and cook on high for 4-5 hours or until meat is tender.

❝I once tasted a similar dish at a restaurant and decided to try making it at home. This is the fabulous result!❞

—**JOAN PEREIRA**
AVON, MASSACHUSETTS

Pork Chili Verde

Pork slowly stews with jalapenos, onion, green enchilada sauce and spices in this flavor-packed Mexican dish. It's great on its own or stuffed into a warm tortilla with sour cream, grated cheese and olives on the side.

—**KIMBERLY BURKE**
CHICO, CALIFORNIA

PREP: 25 MIN. **COOK:** 6½ HOURS
MAKES: 8 SERVINGS

- 1 boneless pork sirloin roast (3 pounds), cut into 1-inch cubes
- 4 medium carrots, sliced
- 1 medium onion, thinly sliced
- 4 garlic cloves, minced
- 3 tablespoons canola oil
- 1 can (28 ounces) green enchilada sauce
- 2 jalapeno peppers, seeded and chopped
- 1 cup minced fresh cilantro
- 1 tablespoon cornstarch
- ¼ cup cold water
    Hot cooked rice
    Flour tortillas, warmed

1. In a large skillet, saute the pork, carrots, onion and garlic in oil in batches until pork is browned. Transfer to a 5-qt. slow cooker. Add the enchilada sauce, jalapenos and cilantro. Cover and cook on low for 6 hours or until meat is tender.
2. In a small bowl, combine cornstarch and water until smooth; stir into pork mixture. Cover and cook on high for 30 minutes or until thickened. Serve with rice and tortillas.

Editor's Note: *Wear disposable gloves when cutting hot peppers; the oils can burn skin. Avoid touching your face.*

Sesame Pork Roast

Marinating a boneless cut of pork in a tangy sauce overnight, then cooking it slowly the next day will result in this tasty roast that's fall-apart tender.

—**SUE BROWN** SAN MIGUEL, CALIFORNIA

PREP: 10 MIN. + MARINATING **COOK:** 9 HOURS
MAKES: 8 SERVINGS

- 1 **boneless pork shoulder butt roast (4 pounds)**
- 2 **cups water**
- ½ **cup soy sauce**
- ¼ **cup sesame seeds, toasted**
- ¼ **cup molasses**
- ¼ **cup cider or white wine vinegar**
- 4 **green onions, sliced**
- 2 **teaspoons garlic powder**
- ¼ **teaspoon cayenne pepper**
- 3 **tablespoons cornstarch**
- ¼ **cup cold water**

1. Cut roast in half; place in a large resealable plastic bag. In a small bowl, combine the water, soy sauce, sesame seeds, molasses, vinegar, onions, garlic powder and cayenne. Pour half over the roast. Seal bag and turn to coat; refrigerate overnight. Cover and refrigerate remaining marinade.

2. Drain and discard marinade. Place roast in a 5-qt. slow cooker; add the reserved marinade. Cover and cook on high for 1 hour. Reduce temperature to low; cook 8-9 hours longer or until meat is tender.

3. Remove meat to a serving platter; keep warm. Skim fat from cooking juices; transfer to a small saucepan. Bring liquid to a boil. Combine cornstarch and cold water until smooth. Gradually stir into the pan. Bring to a boil; cook and stir for 2 minutes or until thickened. Serve with meat.

Brats with Sauerkraut

I've made many variations of brats and kraut over the years. The bratwurst can be plain or smoked, served whole or cut into slices, with a bun or without—but it's always popular at parties and potlucks.

—DARLENE DIXON
HANOVER, MINNESOTA

PREP: 10 MIN. **COOK:** 6 HOURS
MAKES: 8 SERVINGS

- 8 uncooked bratwurst links
- 1 can (14 ounces) sauerkraut, rinsed and well drained
- 2 medium apples, peeled and finely chopped
- 3 bacon strips, cooked and crumbled
- ¼ cup packed brown sugar
- ¼ cup finely chopped onion
- 1 teaspoon ground mustard
- 8 brat buns, split

1. Place the bratwurst in a 5-qt. slow cooker. In a large bowl, combine the sauerkraut, apples, bacon, brown sugar, onion and mustard; spoon over bratwurst.
2. Cover and cook on low for 6-8 hours or until a thermometer inserted in the sausage reads 160°.
3. Place brats in buns; using a slotted spoon, top each with the sauerkraut mixture.

Sweet Onion & Cherry Pork Chops

When I want to jump-start supper, I opt for these tender pork chops. The sweet and savory cherry sauce makes this recipe a keeper. Try serving it with wild rice pilaf.

—STEPHANIE RAY NAPLES, FLORIDA

PREP: 15 MIN. **COOK:** 3 HOURS
MAKES: 2 SERVINGS

- ½ cup fresh or frozen pitted tart cherries, thawed
- 2 tablespoons chopped sweet onion
- 1 tablespoon honey
- ½ teaspoon seasoned salt
- ¼ teaspoon pepper
- 2 boneless pork loin chops (5 ounces each)
- 1 teaspoon cornstarch
- 1 teaspoon cold water

1. In a 1½-qt. slow cooker, combine the first five ingredients; top with pork chops. Cover and cook on low for 3-4 hours or until meat is tender.
2. Remove meat to a serving platter; keep warm. Skim fat from cooking juices; transfer to a small saucepan. Bring liquid to a boil. Combine cornstarch and water until smooth. Gradually stir into the pan. Bring to a boil; cook and stir for 2 minutes or until thickened. Serve with meat.

Slow-Cooked Pork Roast

Here's a meal that's wonderful for summer, as the oven never needs heating. It's so flavorful, it's sure to become a favorite with your gang!

—MARION LOWERY
MEDFORD, OREGON

PREP: 20 MIN.
COOK: 6 HOURS + STANDING
MAKES: 12 SERVINGS

- 2 cans (8 ounces each) unsweetened crushed pineapple, undrained
- 1 cup barbecue sauce
- 2 tablespoons unsweetened apple juice
- 1 tablespoon minced fresh rosemary or 1 teaspoon dried rosemary, crushed
- 1 teaspoon minced garlic
- 2 teaspoons grated lemon peel
- 1 teaspoon liquid smoke, optional
- ½ teaspoon salt
- ¼ teaspoon pepper
- 1 boneless pork loin roast (3 to 4 pounds)

1. In a large saucepan, combine the first nine ingredients. Bring to a boil. Reduce heat; simmer, uncovered, for 3 minutes.

2. Meanwhile, cut roast in half. In a nonstick skillet coated with cooking spray, brown pork roast on all sides.

3. Place roast in a 5-qt. slow cooker. Pour sauce over roast and turn to coat. Cover and cook on low for 6-7 hours or until meat is tender. Let stand for 10 minutes before slicing.

Pork Sandwiches with Root Beer Barbecue Sauce

My tasty recipe is sure to please a crowd! People say they love the subtle heat and hint of sweetness in these saucy sandwiches. I like to serve them up with coleslaw and pickles.

—KAREN CURRIE
KIRKWOOD, MISSOURI

PREP: 30 MIN. **COOK:** 9½ HOURS
MAKES: 8 SERVINGS

- 2 pounds boneless pork sirloin roast
- 1 medium onion, sliced
- 2 tablespoons dried minced garlic
- 3 cups root beer, divided
- 1 bottle (12 ounces) chili sauce
- ⅛ teaspoon hot pepper sauce
- 8 kaiser rolls, split

1. Place roast in a 3-qt. slow cooker. Add the onion, garlic and 1 cup root beer. Cover and cook on low for 9-10 hours or until the meat is tender.

2. In a small saucepan, combine the chili sauce, hot pepper sauce and remaining root beer. Bring to a boil. Reduce heat; simmer, uncovered, for 20-25 minutes or until thickened.

3. Remove meat from slow cooker; cool slightly. Discard cooking juices. Shred pork with two forks and return to slow cooker. Stir in barbecue sauce. Cover and cook on low for 30 minutes or until heated through. Serve on rolls.

Southwestern Pulled Pork

The best way to describe this shredded pork recipe is "yummy!" Barbecue sauce, sweet onion and green chilies deliver a lot of flavor with little prep work for the cook. We like to wrap the pulled pork in warm flour tortillas.

—JILL HARTUNG
COLORADO SPRINGS, COLORADO

PREP: 10 MIN. **COOK:** 8 HOURS
MAKES: 6-8 SERVINGS

> 2 **cans (4 ounces each) chopped green chilies**
> 1 **can (8 ounces) tomato sauce**
> 1 **cup barbecue sauce**
> 1 **large sweet onion, thinly sliced**
> ¼ **cup chili powder**
> 1 **teaspoon ground cumin**
> 1 **teaspoon dried oregano**
> 1 **boneless pork loin roast (2 to 2½ pounds)**
> **Flour tortillas**
> TOPPINGS
> **Sour cream, shredded lettuce and chopped tomatoes, optional**

1. In a 3-qt. slow cooker, combine the chilies, tomato sauce, barbecue sauce, onion, chili powder, cumin and oregano. Cut pork in half; place on top of tomato sauce mixture.
2. Cover and cook on low for 8-9 hours or until meat is tender.
3. Remove pork. When cool enough to handle, shred meat with two forks. Return to slow cooker; heat through. Serve on tortillas with toppings if desired.

Slow Cooker Pork Chops

Everyone will go for these fork-tender pork chops with a light and creamy gravy. I also like to prepare the recipe with boneless chicken breasts instead of pork, substituting poultry seasoning for the ground mustard.

—SUE BINGHAM
MADISONVILLE, TENNESSEE

PREP: 15 MIN. **COOK:** 3 HOURS
MAKES: 4 SERVINGS

> ¾ **cup all-purpose flour, divided**
> ½ **teaspoon ground mustard**
> ½ **teaspoon garlic pepper blend**
> ¼ **teaspoon seasoned salt**
> 4 **boneless pork loin chops (4 ounces each)**
> 2 **tablespoons canola oil**
> 1 **can (14½ ounces) chicken broth**

1. In a large resealable plastic bag, combine ½ cup flour, mustard, garlic pepper and seasoned salt. Add pork chops, one at a time, and shake to coat. In a large skillet, brown chops in oil on both sides.
2. Transfer to a 5-qt. slow cooker. Place remaining flour in a small bowl; whisk in broth until smooth. Pour over chops. Cover and cook on low for 3-4 hours or until meat is tender.
3. Remove chops to a serving plate and keep warm. Whisk cooking liquid until smooth; serve with chops.

Bandito Chili Dogs

These deluxe chili dogs are a surefire hit at family functions! Adults and children alike love the cheesy chili sauce, and it's fun to customize your dog with the different toppings.

—MARION LOWERY
MEDFORD, OREGON

PREP: 15 MIN. **COOK:** 4 HOURS
MAKES: 10 SERVINGS

- 1 package (1 pound) hot dogs
- 2 cans (15 ounces each) chili without beans
- 1 can (10¾ ounces) condensed cheddar cheese soup, undiluted
- 1 can (4 ounces) chopped green chilies
- 10 hot dog buns, split
- 1 medium onion, chopped
- 1 to 2 cups corn chips, coarsely crushed
- 1 cup (4 ounces) shredded cheddar cheese

1. Place hot dogs in a 3-qt. slow cooker. In a large bowl, combine the chili, soup and green chilies; pour over hot dogs. Cover and cook on low for 4-5 hours.
2. Serve hot dogs in buns; top with chili mixture, onion, corn chips and cheese.

Oktoberfest Pork Roast

So many of my favorite fall flavors, such as apples, pork roast, sauerkraut and potatoes, are combined in this one sensational dish. I took my mom's recipe and changed it for the slow cooker.

—TONYA SWAIN SEVILLE, OHIO

PREP: 35 MIN. **COOK:** 8 HOURS
MAKES: 8 SERVINGS

- 16 small red potatoes
- 1 can (14 ounces) sauerkraut, rinsed and well drained
- 2 large tart apples, peeled and cut into wedges
- 1 pound smoked kielbasa or Polish sausage, cut into 16 slices
- 2 tablespoons brown sugar
- 1 teaspoon caraway seeds
- 1 teaspoon salt, divided
- 1 teaspoon pepper, divided
- 1 boneless pork loin roast (3 pounds)
- 3 tablespoons canola oil

1. Place potatoes in a greased 6-qt. slow cooker. Top with sauerkraut, apples and kielbasa. Sprinkle with brown sugar, caraway seeds, ½ teaspoon salt and ½ teaspoon pepper.
2. Cut roast in half; sprinkle with remaining salt and pepper. In a large skillet, brown meat in oil on all sides. Transfer to slow cooker.
3. Cover and cook on low for 8-10 hours or until meat and vegetables are tender. Skim fat and thicken the cooking liquid if desired.

125

144

151

Poultry

||||||||||||||||||||||||||||||||||||||||||||||||||||||||||||||||||||||||||||||||||||||||||||||||||||||||||||||||||||||||||||||||||||

Stuffed Chicken Rolls

The wonderful aroma of this delightful chicken always sparks our appetites. The ham and cheese rolled inside is a tasty surprise.

—**JEAN SHERWOOD** KENNETH CITY, FLORIDA

PREP: 25 MIN. **COOK:** 4 HOURS **MAKES:** 6 SERVINGS

- 6 boneless skinless chicken breast halves (8 ounces each)
- 6 slices fully cooked ham
- 6 slices Swiss cheese
- ¼ cup all-purpose flour
- ¼ cup grated Parmesan cheese
- ½ teaspoon rubbed sage
- ¼ teaspoon paprika
- ¼ teaspoon pepper
- ¼ cup canola oil
- 1 can (10¾ ounces) condensed cream of chicken soup, undiluted
- ½ cup chicken broth
  Chopped fresh parsley, optional

1. Flatten chicken breasts to ⅛-in. thickness; top with ham and cheese. Roll up and tuck in ends; secure with toothpicks.
2. In a shallow bowl, combine the flour, cheese, sage, paprika and pepper; coat chicken on all sides.
3. In a large skillet, brown chicken in oil over medium-high heat. Transfer to a 5-qt. slow cooker. Combine soup and broth; pour over chicken. Cover and cook on low for 4-5 hours or until chicken is tender. Remove toothpicks. Garnish with parsley if desired.

Zesty Chicken Marinara

A friend served this delicious Italian-style chicken before a church social, and I fell in love with it. My husband says it tastes like something you'd get at a restaurant.

—**LINDA BAUMANN** RICHFIELD, WISCONSIN

PREP: 15 MIN. **COOK:** 4 HOURS **MAKES:** 4 SERVINGS

- 4 bone-in chicken breast halves (12 to 14 ounces each), skin removed
- 2 cups marinara sauce
- 1 medium tomato, chopped
- ½ cup Italian salad dressing
- 1½ teaspoons Italian seasoning
- 1 garlic clove, minced
- ½ pound uncooked angel hair pasta
- ½ cup shredded part-skim mozzarella cheese

1. Place chicken in a 4-qt. slow cooker. In a small bowl, combine the marinara sauce, tomato, salad dressing, Italian seasoning and garlic; pour over chicken. Cover and cook on low for 4-5 hours or until chicken is tender.
2. Cook pasta according to package directions; drain. Serve chicken and sauce with pasta; sprinkle with cheese.

Creamy Tarragon Chicken

Start the week off on an easy note with this delicious slow-cooked recipe. A cup of chicken broth may be substituted for the water and chicken bouillon granules.

—TASTE OF HOME TEST KITCHEN

PREP: 10 MIN. **COOK:** 6¼ HOURS **MAKES:** 6 SERVINGS

- 6 boneless skinless chicken breast halves (6 ounces each)
- 1 cup chopped onion
- 1 cup water
- 2 ounces prosciutto or deli ham, chopped
- 3 tablespoons quick-cooking tapioca
- 2 teaspoons chicken bouillon granules
- 2 teaspoons dried tarragon
- 1 teaspoon minced garlic
- ¼ teaspoon salt
- ¼ teaspoon pepper
- 3 cups frozen broccoli-cauliflower blend, thawed
- ½ cup half-and-half cream
- 1½ cups uncooked orzo pasta

1. In a 5-qt. slow cooker, combine the first 10 ingredients. Cover and cook on low for 6-7 hours or until chicken juices run clear.

2. Stir vegetables and cream into the slow cooker. Cover and cook 15 minutes longer or until vegetables are heated through. Meanwhile, cook orzo according to package directions. Serve with chicken and vegetables.

Teriyaki Chicken Thighs

Chicken, rice and a sweet-salty sauce create an entree that's packed with Asian flavor. Your family will love this simple meal.

—GIGI MILLER
STOUGHTON, WISCONSIN

PREP: 15 MIN. **COOK:** 4 HOURS
MAKES: 6 SERVINGS

- 12 boneless skinless chicken thighs (about 3 pounds)
- ¾ cup sugar
- ¾ cup soy sauce
- 6 tablespoons cider vinegar
- ¾ teaspoon ground ginger
- ¾ teaspoon minced garlic
- ¼ teaspoon pepper
- 4½ teaspoons cornstarch
- 4½ teaspoons cold water
  Hot cooked rice, optional

1. Place chicken in a 4-qt. slow cooker. Combine the sugar, soy sauce, vinegar, ginger, garlic and pepper; pour over chicken. Cover and cook on low for 4-5 hours or until chicken is tender.

2. Remove chicken to a serving platter; keep warm. Skim fat from cooking juices; transfer to a small saucepan. Bring liquid to a boil. Combine cornstarch and water until smooth. Gradually stir into the pan. Bring to a boil; cook and stir for 2 minutes or until thickened. Serve with chicken and rice if desired.

Chicken Cacciatore

Here's an all-time-favorite Italian dish made easy in the slow cooker! The herbs and garlic give it such a wonderful aroma as it slowly simmers away.

—DENISE HOLLEBEKE
PENHOLD, ALBERTA

PREP: 20 MIN. **COOK:** 4 HOURS
MAKES: 6 SERVINGS

- ⅓ cup all-purpose flour
- 1 broiler/fryer chicken (3 to 4 pounds), cut up
- 2 tablespoons canola oil
- 2 medium onions, cut into wedges
- 1 medium green pepper, cut into strips
- 1 jar (6 ounces) sliced mushrooms, drained
- 1 can (14½ ounces) diced tomatoes, undrained
- 2 garlic cloves, minced
- ½ teaspoon salt
- ½ teaspoon dried oregano
- ¼ teaspoon dried basil
- ½ cup shredded Parmesan cheese

1. Place flour in a large resealable plastic bag. Add chicken, a few pieces at a time, and shake to coat. In a large skillet, brown chicken in oil on all sides.

2. Transfer to a 5-qt. slow cooker. Top with onions, green pepper and mushrooms. In a small bowl, combine the tomatoes, garlic, salt, oregano and basil; pour over vegetables. Cover and cook on low for 4-5 hours or until chicken juices run clear and vegetables are tender. Serve with cheese.

Honey Pineapple Chicken

I adapted a dinnertime favorite for my slow cooker because it's so much easier to do the preparation in advance, then let the chicken cook on its own while I do other things. Your family will love the combination of sweet and savory flavors.

—CAROL GILLESPIE
CHAMBERSBURG, PENNSYLVANIA

PREP: 15 MIN. **COOK:** 3 HOURS
MAKES: 12 SERVINGS

- 3 **pounds boneless skinless chicken breast halves**
- 2 **tablespoons canola oil**
- 1 **can (8 ounces) unsweetened crushed pineapple, undrained**
- 1 **cup packed brown sugar**
- ½ **cup honey**
- ⅓ **cup lemon juice**
- ¼ **cup butter, melted**
- 2 **tablespoons prepared mustard**
- 2 **teaspoons reduced-sodium soy sauce**

1. In a large skillet, brown chicken in oil in batches on both sides; transfer to a 5-qt. slow cooker. In a small bowl, combine the remaining ingredients; pour over chicken.
2. Cover and cook on low for 3-4 hours or until meat is tender. Strain pan juices, reserving pineapple. Serve pineapple with the chicken.

FAST FIX ▶ Apricot-Orange Salsa Chicken

This easy entree is just five ingredients away! Sweet oranges and apricots blend perfectly with zippy salsa. Keep the heat to your liking with mild, medium or hot salsa.

—LADONNA REED
PONCA CITY, OKLAHOMA

PREP: 10 MIN. **COOK:** 2½ HOURS
MAKES: 2 SERVINGS

- ¾ **cup salsa**
- ⅓ **cup apricot preserves**
- ¼ **cup orange juice**
- 2 **boneless skinless chicken breast halves (5 ounces each)**
- 1 **cup hot cooked rice**

1. In a small bowl, combine the salsa, preserves and orange juice. In a 1½-qt. slow cooker coated with cooking spray, layer ⅓ cup salsa mixture and a chicken breast. Repeat layers. Top with remaining salsa.
2. Cover and cook on low for 2½ to 3 hours or until chicken is tender. If desired, thicken cooking liquid. Serve with rice.

Best Italian Sausage Sandwiches

Need a different type of sandwich for your next party? Everyone will be complimenting these easy and great-tasting sausages smothered in rich tomato sauce.

—TASTE OF HOME TEST KITCHEN

PREP: 10 MIN. **COOK:** 4 HOURS
MAKES: 10 SERVINGS

- 2 **jars (24 ounces each) meatless spaghetti sauce**
- 2 **medium green peppers, cut into strips**
- 2 **medium onions, thinly sliced**
- ½ **teaspoon garlic powder**
- ½ **teaspoon fennel seed, crushed**
- 2 **packages (20 ounces each) Italian turkey sausage links**
- 10 **sandwich buns, split**

1. In a 3-qt. slow cooker, combine the spaghetti sauce, green peppers, onions, garlic powder and fennel seed. Cover and cook on low for 4 hours or until vegetables are tender.
2. Grill sausages according to package directions. Serve on buns with sauce.

Turkey with Mushroom Sauce

When we were first married, I didn't have an oven, so I made this tender turkey in the slow cooker. These days, I rely on this recipe because it frees up the oven to make other dishes for large get-togethers.

—**MYRA INNES** AUBURN, KANSAS

PREP: 20 MIN. **COOK:** 4 HOURS **MAKES:** 8 SERVINGS

- 1 boneless skinless turkey breast half (2½ pounds)
- 2 tablespoons butter, melted
- 2 tablespoons dried parsley flakes
- ½ teaspoon salt
- ½ teaspoon dried tarragon
- ⅛ teaspoon pepper
- 1 jar (4½ ounces) sliced mushrooms, drained or 1 cup sliced fresh mushrooms
- ½ cup white wine or chicken broth
- 2 tablespoons cornstarch
- ¼ cup cold water

1. Place turkey in a 5-qt. slow cooker. Brush with butter. Sprinkle with parsley, salt, tarragon and pepper. Top with mushrooms. Pour wine over all. Cover and cook on low for 4-6 hours or until a thermometer reads 170°.

2. Remove turkey to a serving platter; keep warm. Skim fat from cooking juices; transfer to a small saucepan. Bring liquid to a boil. Combine cornstarch and water until smooth. Gradually stir into the pan. Bring to a boil; cook and stir for 2 minutes or until thickened. Serve with turkey.

Slow Cooker Cranberry-Orange Chicken

My family loves this delicious recipe that I created. Also try shredding the tasty chicken and serving it on buns.

—FRANCES ROBERTS
SILVER SPRING, MARYLAND

PREP: 15 MIN. **COOK:** 5 HOURS
MAKES: 6 SERVINGS

- 1 teaspoon garlic powder
- 1 teaspoon poultry seasoning
- ½ teaspoon salt
- ⅛ to ¼ teaspoon pepper
- 3½ pounds bone-in chicken breast halves, skin removed
- 1 can (14 ounces) jellied cranberry sauce
- ½ cup chili sauce
- ¼ cup Thai chili sauce
- ⅓ cup orange marmalade
- 4 teaspoons cornstarch
- 2 tablespoons cold water

1. Combine the garlic powder, poultry seasoning, salt and pepper; rub over chicken. Transfer to a 5- to 6-qt. slow cooker.

2. In a small bowl, combine the cranberry sauce, chili sauces and marmalade; pour over chicken. Cover and cook on low for 5-6 hours or until a thermometer reads 170°.

3. Remove chicken to a serving platter; keep warm.

4. Skim fat from cooking juices; transfer juices to a small saucepan. Bring to a boil. Combine cornstarch and water until smooth; gradually stir into cooking juices. Return to a boil; cook and stir for 2 minutes or until thickened. Serve with chicken.

Citrus Chicken

Bold-flavored ingredients are tempered by the flavor of oranges, creating a mouthwatering dish that's guaranteed to impress.

—BARBARA EASTON
NORTH VANCOUVER, BRITISH COLUMBIA

PREP: 15 MIN. **COOK:** 4 HOURS
MAKES: 4 SERVINGS

- 2 medium oranges, cut into wedges
- 1 medium green pepper, chopped
- 1 broiler/fryer chicken (3 to 4 pounds), cut up and skin removed
- 1 cup orange juice
- ½ cup chili sauce
- 2 tablespoons soy sauce
- 1 tablespoon molasses
- 1 teaspoon ground mustard
- 1 teaspoon minced garlic
- ¼ teaspoon pepper
    Hot cooked rice

Place oranges and green pepper in a 5-qt. slow cooker coated with cooking spray. Top with chicken. Combine the next seven ingredients; pour over chicken. Cover and cook on low for 4-5 hours or until chicken juices run clear. Serve with rice.

Saucy Chicken Thighs

Everyone raves about the sweet sauce with these tender, slow-cooked chicken thighs. Add your favorite side dish for a nice meal.

—KIM PUCKETT REAGAN, TENNESSEE

PREP: 20 MIN. **COOK:** 4 HOURS
MAKES: 9 SERVINGS

- 9 bone-in chicken thighs (about 3¼ pounds)
- ½ teaspoon salt
- ¼ teaspoon pepper
- 1½ cups barbecue sauce
- ½ cup honey
- 2 teaspoons prepared mustard
- 2 teaspoons Worcestershire sauce
- ⅛ to ½ teaspoon hot pepper sauce

1. Sprinkle chicken with salt and pepper. Place on a broiler pan. Broil 4-5 in. from the heat for 3-4 minutes on each side or until lightly browned. Transfer to a 5-qt. slow cooker.
2. In a small bowl, combine the barbecue sauce, honey, mustard, Worcestershire sauce and pepper sauce. Pour over chicken; stir to coat. Cover and cook on low for 4-5 hours or until chicken is tender.

Zesty Mexican Chicken

A hint of lime juice helps tame the heat of spicy chicken breasts with crunchy vegetables. And because it's all prepared in the slow cooker, you and your kitchen will stay cool, too!

—MICHELLE SHELDON MIDDLETOWN, DELAWARE

PREP: 15 MIN. **COOK:** 3½ HOURS
MAKES: 6 SERVINGS

- 6 boneless skinless chicken breast halves (4 ounces each)
- 1 can (14½ ounces) diced tomatoes, undrained
- 1 large onion, chopped
- 1 medium green pepper, chopped
- 3 garlic cloves, minced
- 2 tablespoons lime juice
- 1 tablespoon hot pepper sauce
- ¼ teaspoon salt
- ¼ teaspoon pepper
- 3 cups hot cooked rice

1. Place chicken in a 4-qt. slow cooker coated with cooking spray. In a large bowl, combine the tomatoes, onion, green pepper, garlic, lime juice, pepper sauce, salt and pepper. Pour over the chicken.

2. Cover and cook on low for 3-4 hours or until chicken is tender. Serve with rice.

FAST FIX ▶ Moist & Tender Turkey Breast

Your family will love the taste of this easy dish, and you'll love how quickly it comes together.

—HEIDI VAWDREY RIVERTON, UTAH

PREP: 10 MIN. **COOK:** 4 HOURS
MAKES: 12 SERVINGS

- 1 bone-in turkey breast (6 to 7 pounds)
- ½ cup water
- 4 fresh rosemary sprigs
- 4 garlic cloves, peeled
- 1 tablespoon brown sugar
- ½ teaspoon coarsely ground pepper
- ¼ teaspoon salt

Place turkey and water in a 6-qt. slow cooker. Place rosemary and garlic around turkey. Combine the brown sugar, pepper and salt; sprinkle over turkey. Cover and cook on low for 4-6 hours or until turkey is tender.

Turkey Thigh Supper

This family-pleasing meal has it all—tender turkey thighs, tasty vegetables and a homemade sauce. You can substitute chicken breasts for the turkey or a honey-flavored barbecue sauce for the soup mixture.

—BETTY GINGRICH OXFORD, ARKANSAS

PREP: 10 MIN. **COOK:** 6 HOURS **MAKES:** 4 SERVINGS

- **3 medium red potatoes, cut into chunks**
- **½ pound fresh baby carrots**
- **2 medium onions, cut into chunks**

- **4 turkey thighs, skin removed**
- **1 can (10¾ ounces) condensed tomato soup, undiluted**
- **⅓ cup water**
- **1 teaspoon minced garlic**
- **1 teaspoon Italian seasoning**
- **½ to 1 teaspoon salt**

In a 5-qt. slow cooker, layer the potatoes, carrots and onions. Top with turkey. Combine the soup, water, garlic, Italian seasoning and salt; pour over turkey. Cover and cook on low for 6-8 hours or until a thermometer reads 180° and vegetables are tender.

Sweet 'n' Sour Curry Chicken

A little mango chutney goes a long way in adding a zesty twist to chicken. I also add some curry powder to give this dish real flair.

—CAROL CONRAD
EDMONTON, ALBERTA

PREP: 15 MIN. **COOK:** 4½ HOURS
MAKES: 4 SERVINGS

- 1 **pound boneless skinless chicken breasts, cut into 1-inch pieces**
- 1 **can (14½ ounces) stewed tomatoes, cut up**
- 1 **large green pepper, cut into 1-inch pieces**
- 1 **large onion, sliced**
- ½ **cup mango chutney**
- 1½ **teaspoons curry powder**
- 2 **tablespoons cornstarch**
- ¼ **cup cold water**

1. In a 3-qt. slow cooker, combine the chicken, tomatoes, green pepper, onion, chutney and curry powder. Cover and cook on low for 4-5 hours or until chicken is no longer pink.
2. Combine cornstarch and water until smooth; stir into slow cooker. Cover and cook on high for 30 minutes or until thickened.

FAST FIX Turkey with Cranberry Sauce

Here's a tasty and easy way to cook turkey breast in the slow cooker. Ideal for holiday potlucks, the sweet cranberry sauce complements the turkey nicely.

—MARIE RAMSDEN
FAIRGROVE, MICHIGAN

PREP: 15 MIN. **COOK:** 4½ HOURS
MAKES: 15 SERVINGS

- 2 **boneless skinless turkey breast halves (3 pounds each)**
- 1 **can (14 ounces) jellied cranberry sauce**
- ½ **cup plus 2 tablespoons water, divided**
- 1 **envelope onion soup mix**
- 2 **tablespoons cornstarch**

1. Place turkey breasts in a 5-qt. slow cooker. In a large bowl, combine the cranberry sauce, ½ cup water and soup mix. Pour over turkey. Cover and cook on low for 4-6 hours or meat is tender. Remove turkey and keep it warm.
2. Combine the cornstarch and remaining water until smooth; stir into cooking juices. Cover and cook on high for 30 minutes or until thickened. Slice turkey; serve with cranberry sauce. Leftovers may be frozen for up to 3 months.

Turkey in Cream Sauce

I've relied on this recipe for tender turkey since I first moved out on my own years ago. I serve it whenever I invite new guests to the house, and I'm always asked to share the recipe!

—**KATHY-JO WINTERBOTTOM**
POTTSTOWN, PENNSYLVANIA

PREP: 20 MIN. **COOK:** 7 HOURS
MAKES: 9 SERVINGS

- 1¼ cups white wine or chicken broth
- 1 medium onion, chopped
- 2 garlic cloves, minced
- 2 bay leaves
- 2 teaspoons dried rosemary, crushed
- ½ teaspoon pepper
- 3 turkey breast tenderloins (¾ pound each)
- 3 tablespoons cornstarch
- ½ cup half-and-half cream or whole milk
- ½ teaspoon salt

1. In a 3-qt. slow cooker, combine the wine, onion, garlic and bay leaves. Combine rosemary and pepper; rub over turkey. Place in slow cooker.
2. Cover and cook on low for 7-9 hours or until turkey is tender.
3. Remove turkey to a serving platter; keep warm.
4. Strain and skim fat from cooking juices; transfer to a small saucepan. Bring liquid to a boil. Combine the cornstarch, cream and salt until smooth. Gradually stir into the pan. Bring to a boil; cook and stir for 2 minutes or until thickened. Serve with turkey.

Chicken with Wild Rice

My family is always busy, so it's nice when we can come home to a meal that's already prepared and ready to eat. I just open up a bag of salad greens and dinner is ready!

—**BECKY GIFFORD**
CONWAY, ARKANSAS

PREP: 20 MIN. **COOK:** 4 HOURS
MAKES: 6 SERVINGS

- 1 package (6 ounces) long grain and wild rice mix
- 6 boneless skinless chicken breast halves (5 ounces each)
- 1 tablespoon canola oil
- 1 teaspoon butter
- ½ pound sliced fresh mushrooms
- 1 can (10¾ ounces) condensed cream of chicken soup, undiluted
- 1 cup water
- 3 bacon strips, cooked and crumbled
- 1 teaspoon dried parsley flakes
- ½ teaspoon dried thyme
- ¼ teaspoon dried tarragon

1. Place rice in a 5-qt. slow cooker; set aside seasoning packet. In large skillet, brown chicken in oil and butter. Add to slow cooker. In the same skillet, saute mushrooms until tender; place over chicken.
2. In a small bowl, combine soup, water, bacon, herbs and contents of seasoning packet. Pour over top. Cover and cook on low for 4-5 hours or until chicken is tender.

Creamy Herbed Chicken

I'm a nurse and work nights, so I count on my slow cooker for good meals that fit my schedule. This chicken is moist and tender, and the rich sauce, seasoned with garlic and thyme, is delicious.

—**MARY HUMENIUK-SMITH** PERRY HALL, MARYLAND

PREP: 5 MIN.   **COOK:** 4 HOURS   **MAKES:** 4 SERVINGS

- 4   **boneless skinless chicken breast halves (4 ounces each)**
- 1   **can (10¾ ounces) condensed cream of chicken soup, undiluted**
- 1   **cup milk**
- 1   **envelope garlic and herb pasta sauce mix**
- 1   **teaspoon dried thyme**
- 1   **teaspoon dried parsley flakes**
   Hot cooked fettuccine

Place chicken in a 3-qt. slow cooker. Combine the soup, milk, sauce mix, thyme and parsley; pour over chicken. Cover and cook on low for 4-5 hours or until chicken is tender. Serve with fettuccine.

Editor's Note: *This recipe was tested with Knorr Garlic Herb Pasta Sauce Mix.*

GO-TO PANTRY MEALS

Good cooks like to keep some go-to meals on hand that don't require a special trip to the store. Creamy Herbed Chicken uses pantry ingredients. Keep chicken breasts in the freezer and you'll always be ready.

Squash 'n' Chicken Stew

We've created a satisfying stew that's nutritious, full-flavored and family-friendly with this recipe. Chicken thighs are slowly simmered with stewed tomatoes, butternut squash, green peppers and onion for meal-in-one convenience.

—TASTE OF HOME TEST KITCHEN

PREP: 15 MIN. **COOK:** 6 HOURS
MAKES: 5 SERVINGS

- 2 **pounds boneless skinless chicken thighs, cut into ½-inch pieces**
- 1 **can (28 ounces) stewed tomatoes, cut up**
- 3 **cups cubed butternut squash**
- 2 **medium green peppers, cut into ½-inch pieces**
- 1 **small onion, sliced and separated into rings**
- 1 **cup water**
- 1 **teaspoon salt**
- 1 **teaspoon ground cumin**
- ½ **teaspoon ground coriander**
- ½ **teaspoon pepper**
- 2 **tablespoons minced fresh parsley**
  Hot cooked couscous, optional

1. In a 5-qt. slow cooker, combine the first 10 ingredients.
2. Cover and cook on low for 6-7 hours or until the chicken is no longer pink.
3. Sprinkle each serving with parsley. Serve stew with couscous if desired.

Red, White and Brew Slow-Cooked Chicken

Thrifty whole chicken is cut up and simmered in a spicy tomato sauce. I serve it with crusty bread so we can mop up and enjoy every last drop of sauce.

—GILDA LESTER
MILLSBORO, DELAWARE

PREP: 25 MIN. **COOK:** 6 HOURS
MAKES: 6 SERVINGS

- 1 **can (14½ ounces) fire-roasted diced tomatoes, undrained**
- 1 **medium onion, chopped**
- 1 **jalapeno pepper, seeded and chopped**
- 3 **tablespoons brown sugar**
- 3 **tablespoons balsamic vinegar**
- 1 **tablespoon ground mustard**
- 1 **teaspoon dried basil**
- ¼ **teaspoon crushed red pepper flakes**
- 1 **cup beer or nonalcoholic beer**
- 1 **broiler/fryer chicken (3 to 4 pounds), cut up and skin removed**
- 1 **envelope (1¼ ounces) chili seasoning**
  Hot cooked pasta

1. Place first eight ingredients in a food processor; cover and process until pureed. Stir in beer; set aside.
2. Rub chicken pieces with chili seasoning. Place in a 5-qt. slow cooker. Pour tomato mixture over chicken. Cover and cook on low for 6-7 hours or until chicken is tender.
3. Thicken cooking liquid if desired. Serve chicken with pasta.
Editor's Note: *Wear disposable gloves when cutting hot peppers; the oils can burn skin. Avoid touching your face.*

Herbed Chicken and Shrimp

Tender chicken and shrimp make a flavorful combination that's easy to prepare, yet elegant enough to serve at a dinner party. While I clean the house, it practically cooks itself! I like to serve it over hot cooked rice with a green salad.

—DIANA KNIGHT RENO, NEVADA

PREP: 15 MIN.
COOK: 4¼ HOURS
MAKES: 4 SERVINGS

- 1 **teaspoon salt**
- 1 **teaspoon pepper**
- 1 **broiler/fryer chicken (3 to 4 pounds), cut up and skin removed**
- ¼ **cup butter**
- 1 **large onion, chopped**
- 1 **can (8 ounces) tomato sauce**
- ½ **cup white wine or chicken broth**
- 1 **garlic clove, minced**
- 1 **teaspoon dried basil**
- 1 **pound uncooked medium shrimp, peeled and deveined**

1. Combine salt and pepper; rub over the chicken pieces. In a large skillet, brown chicken on all sides in butter. Transfer to an ungreased 5-qt. slow cooker.
2. In a large bowl, combine onion, tomato sauce, wine, garlic and basil; pour over chicken. Cover and cook on low for 4-5 hours or until chicken is tender.
3. Stir in the shrimp. Cover and cook on high for 15-30 minutes or until shrimp turn pink.

Flavorful Lemon Chicken

This easy and attractive meal is bound to become a staple in your home. Made with everyday ingredients, there's nothing complicated or fancy about this great find.

—ELIZABETH HOKANSON ARBORG, MANITOBA

PREP: 20 MIN. **COOK:** 4¼ HOURS
MAKES: 6 SERVINGS

- 1 **teaspoon dried oregano**
- ½ **teaspoon seasoned salt**
- ¼ **teaspoon pepper**
- 6 **boneless skinless chicken breast halves (6 ounces each)**
- 2 **teaspoons chicken bouillon granules**
- ¼ **cup boiling water**
- 3 **tablespoons lemon juice**
- 1½ **teaspoons minced garlic**
- 1½ **cups (12 ounces) sour cream**
- 2 **teaspoons minced fresh parsley**
  Hot cooked brown rice, optional

1. Combine the oregano, seasoned salt and pepper; rub mixture over chicken. Place in a 3-qt. slow cooker.
2. In small bowl, dissolve the bouillon in boiling water. Stir in lemon juice and garlic. Pour over chicken. Cover and cook on low for 4-5 hours or until the chicken is tender.
3. Remove chicken and keep warm. Stir in sour cream and parsley; cover and cook for 15 minutes or until heated through. Serve chicken with sauce and brown rice if desired.

Lime Chicken Tacos

Lime juice adds bright flavor to an easy taco filling that's surprisingly healthy. This fun recipe is great for a casual dinner with friends and family.
—**TRACY GUNTER** BOISE, IDAHO

PREP: 10 MIN. **COOK:** 5½ HOURS **MAKES:** 6 SERVINGS

- 1½ **pounds boneless skinless chicken breasts**
- 3 **tablespoons lime juice**
- 1 **tablespoon chili powder**
- 1 **cup frozen corn**
- 1 **cup chunky salsa**
- 12 **flour tortillas (6 inches), warmed**
  Sour cream, shredded cheddar cheese and shredded lettuce, optional

1. Place the chicken in a 3-qt. slow cooker. Combine lime juice and chili powder; pour over chicken. Cover and cook on low for 5-6 hours or until chicken is tender.
2. Remove chicken; cool slightly. Shred meat with two forks and return to the slow cooker; heat through. Stir in corn and salsa.
3. Cover and cook on low for 30 minutes or until heated through. Serve in tortillas with sour cream, cheese and lettuce if desired.

Italian Turkey Sandwiches

I hope you enjoy these tasty sandwiches as much as our family does. The recipe makes plenty, so it's great for potlucks. Leftovers are delicious the next day.
—**CAROL RILEY** OSSIAN, INDIANA

PREP: 10 MIN. **COOK:** 5 HOURS **MAKES:** 12 SERVINGS

- 1 **bone-in turkey breast (6 pounds), skin removed**
- 1 **medium onion, chopped**
- 1 **small green pepper, chopped**
- ¼ **cup chili sauce**
- 3 **tablespoons white vinegar**
- 2 **tablespoons dried oregano or Italian seasoning**
- 4 **teaspoons beef bouillon granules**
- 12 **kaiser or hard rolls, split**

1. Place turkey breast in a greased 5-qt. slow cooker. Add onion and green pepper.
2. Combine the chili sauce, vinegar, oregano and bouillon; pour over turkey and vegetables. Cover and cook on low for 5-6 hours or until turkey is tender.
3. Shred turkey with two forks and return to the slow cooker; heat through. Spoon ½ cup onto each roll.

Slow-Cooked Asian Chicken

Tender chicken is treated to a slightly sweet sauce and crunchy almonds in this easy recipe. It's so nice to find simple, tasty ways to serve chicken. I prepare this often for both family and guests.

—RUTH SEITZ
COLUMBUS JUNCTION, IOWA

PREP: 20 MIN. **COOK:** 5 HOURS
MAKES: 4-6 SERVINGS

- 1 broiler/fryer chicken (3 to 4 pounds), cut up
- 2 tablespoons canola oil
- ⅓ cup soy sauce
- 2 tablespoons brown sugar
- 2 tablespoons water
- 1 garlic clove, minced
- 1 teaspoon ground ginger
- ¼ cup slivered almonds

1. In a large skillet over medium heat, brown the chicken in oil on all sides.
2. Transfer to a 5-qt. slow cooker. Combine the soy sauce, brown sugar, water, garlic and ginger; pour over chicken.
3. Cover and cook on low for 5-6 hours or until chicken juices run clear. Remove chicken to a serving platter; sprinkle with almonds.

Moist Drumsticks

I found this in my mom's recipe box years ago. It's very quick to prepare and fills the house with a wonderful aroma while it's cooking.

—LIANNE FELTON
RIVERSIDE, CALIFORNIA

PREP: 10 MIN. **COOK:** 5 HOURS
MAKES: 6 SERVINGS

- 3 pounds chicken drumsticks, skin removed
- 1 can (8 ounces) tomato sauce
- ½ cup soy sauce
- ¼ cup packed brown sugar
- 1 teaspoon minced garlic
- 3 tablespoons cornstarch
- ¼ cup cold water

1. Place drumsticks in a 5-qt. slow cooker. In a small bowl, combine the tomato sauce, soy sauce, brown sugar and garlic; pour over chicken. Cover and cook on low for 5-6 hours or until a thermometer reads 180°.
2. Remove chicken to a serving platter; keep warm.
3. Skim fat from cooking juices; transfer to saucepan. Bring liquid to a boil. Combine cornstarch and water until smooth. Gradually stir into pan. Bring to a boil; cook and stir for 2 minutes or until thickened. Serve with chicken.

Barbecue Chicken Sandwiches

PREP: 20 MIN. **COOK:** 5 HOURS
MAKES: 10 SERVINGS

- 3 **pounds boneless skinless chicken thighs**
- 1 **cup ketchup**
- 1 **small onion, chopped**
- ¼ **cup water**
- ¼ **cup cider vinegar**
- 2 **tablespoons Worcestershire sauce**
- 1 **tablespoon brown sugar**
- 1 **garlic clove, minced**
- 1 **bay leaf**
- 2 **teaspoons paprika**
- 1 **teaspoon dried oregano**
- 1 **teaspoon chili powder**
- ½ **teaspoon salt**
- ½ **teaspoon pepper**
- 10 **kaiser rolls, split**

1. Place chicken in a 5-qt. slow cooker. Combine the ketchup, onion, water, vinegar, Worcestershire sauce, brown sugar, garlic, bay leaf and seasonings. Pour over chicken. Cover and cook on low for 5 hours or until tender.
2. Discard bay leaf. Remove chicken; shred with two forks and return to slow cooker. Heat through. Serve on rolls.

> ❝I love to use my slow cooker. In fact, I have three in various sizes! These saucy sandwiches are popular.❞
>
> —LYNN IRELAND
> LEBANON, WISCONSIN

Sweet and Saucy Chicken

I can't remember where this recipe came from, but I've been making it for several years. Everyone who tries it, enjoys it. When the chicken is done cooking, it's so tender it falls off the bone.

—PATRICIA WEIR
CHILLIWACK, BRITISH COLUMBIA

PREP: 30 MIN. **COOK:** 6 HOURS
MAKES: 6 SERVINGS

- 1 **broiler/fryer chicken (4 pounds), cut up and skin removed**
- ¾ **cup packed brown sugar**
- ¼ **cup all-purpose flour**
- ⅔ **cup water**
- ⅓ **cup white vinegar**
- ⅓ **cup reduced-sodium soy sauce**
- 2 **tablespoons ketchup**
- 1 **tablespoon dried minced onion**
- 1 **teaspoon prepared mustard**
- ¼ **teaspoon garlic powder**
- ¼ **teaspoon salt**
- ¼ **teaspoon pepper**
  Hot cooked rice or egg noodles, optional

1. Place chicken in a 3-qt. slow cooker. In a small saucepan, combine brown sugar and flour. Stir in the water, vinegar and soy sauce. Add the ketchup, onion, mustard, garlic powder, salt and pepper. Bring to a boil; cook and stir for 1-2 minutes or until thickened.
2. Pour over chicken. Cover and cook on low for 6-8 hours or until chicken juices run clear. Serve with rice or noodles if desired.

Spicy Beans with Turkey Sausage

Here's a jambalaya-type dish that comes together in the slow cooker. It's a wonderful way to warm up cold winter nights and works equally well for casual get-togethers or family dinners. For extra pizzazz, top each bowlful with sour cream or shredded cheese.

—DOROTHY JORDAN COLLEGE STATION, TEXAS

PREP: 25 MIN. **COOK:** 5 HOURS **MAKES:** 6 SERVINGS

- 1 **pound smoked turkey sausage, halved and sliced**
- 1 **can (16 ounces) kidney beans, rinsed and drained**
- 1 **can (15½ ounces) great northern beans, rinsed and drained**
- 1 **can (15 ounces) black beans, rinsed and drained**
- 1½ **cups frozen corn**
- 1½ **cups salsa**
- 1 **large green pepper, chopped**
- 1 **large onion, chopped**
- ½ **to 1 cup water**
- 3 **garlic cloves, minced**
- 1 **teaspoon ground cumin**

In a 5-qt. slow cooker, combine all ingredients. Cover and cook on low for 5-6 hours or until heated through. Stir before serving.

Prosciutto Chicken Cacciatore

I changed my mother's original recipe so it can be made in the slow cooker. This hearty result is perfect for busy weeknights.

—SANDRA PUTNAM
CORVALLIS, MONTANA

PREP: 30 MIN. **COOK:** 4 HOURS
MAKES: 6-8 SERVINGS

- 2 **pounds boneless skinless chicken thighs**
- 1½ **pounds boneless skinless chicken breast halves**
- ½ **cup all-purpose flour**
- 1 **teaspoon salt**
- ¼ **teaspoon pepper**
- 3 **tablespoons olive oil**
- 1 **can (14½ ounces) chicken broth**
- 1 **can (14½ ounces) diced tomatoes, undrained**
- 1 **cup sliced fresh mushrooms**
- 1 **medium onion, chopped**
- 1 **package (3 ounces) thinly sliced prosciutto or deli ham, coarsely chopped**
- 1 **tablespoon diced pimientos**
- 2 **garlic cloves, minced**
- ½ **teaspoon Italian seasoning**
  Hot cooked linguine
  Grated Parmesan cheese

1. Cut chicken into serving-size pieces. In a large resealable plastic bag, combine the flour, salt and pepper. Add chicken, a few pieces at a time, and shake to coat.
2. In a large skillet, brown chicken in oil in batches. Transfer to a 5-qt. slow cooker.
3. Stir in the broth, tomatoes, mushrooms, onion, prosciutto, pimientos, garlic and Italian seasoning. Cover and cook on low for 4 to 4½ hours or until chicken juices run clear. Serve with a slotted spoon over linguine; sprinkle with cheese.

Herbed Slow Cooker Chicken

I use my slow cooker to prepare these well-seasoned chicken breasts that cook up moist and tender. My daughter, who has two young sons to keep up with, shared the recipe with me, and I make it often.

—SUNDRA HAUCK
BOGALUSA, LOUISIANA

PREP: 5 MIN. **COOK:** 4 HOURS
MAKES: 4 SERVINGS

- 1 **tablespoon olive oil**
- 1 **teaspoon paprika**
- ½ **teaspoon garlic powder**
- ½ **teaspoon seasoned salt**
- ½ **teaspoon dried thyme**
- ½ **teaspoon dried basil**
- ½ **teaspoon pepper**
- ½ **teaspoon browning sauce, optional**
- 4 **bone-in chicken breast halves (8 ounces each)**
- ½ **cup chicken broth**

In a small bowl, combine the first eight ingredients; rub over chicken. Place in a 5-qt. slow cooker; add broth. Cover and cook on low for 4-5 hours or until chicken is tender.

Nacho Chicken & Rice

Simmer up a nutritious and tasty meal with just a few basic ingredients. Your family is sure to love this tender chicken and peppers in the nacho cheese sauce.

—LINDA FOREMAN
LOCUST GROVE, OKLAHOMA

PREP: 20 MIN. **COOK:** 5 HOURS
MAKES: 6 SERVINGS

- 2½ pounds boneless skinless chicken breast halves, cubed
- 1 each small green, sweet red and orange peppers, cut into thin strips
- 1 can (10¾ ounces) condensed nacho cheese soup, undiluted
- ½ cup chunky salsa
- ⅛ teaspoon chili powder
- 4½ cups hot cooked rice

In a 3-qt. slow cooker, combine the chicken, peppers, soup, salsa and chili powder. Cover and cook on low for 5-6 hours or until chicken is tender. Serve with rice.

Tender Chicken Dinner

This all-in-one poultry dinner provides lots of family appeal. Best of all, it can be put together fast before you leave for school or work.

—WANDA SANNER AMARILLO, TEXAS

PREP: 15 MIN. **COOK:** 5¼ HOURS
MAKES: 4 SERVINGS

- 4 boneless skinless chicken breast halves (4 ounces each)
- 1 can (14½ ounces) chicken broth
- 1 can (14½ ounces) chicken gravy
- 2 cups sliced peeled potatoes
- 1 package (16 ounces) frozen sliced carrots, thawed
- 1 package (16 ounces) frozen cut green beans, thawed
- 1 teaspoon pepper
- 2 tablespoons cornstarch
- ⅓ cup cold water
- 1 cup french-fried onions

1. Place chicken in a 5-qt. slow cooker. Add the broth, gravy, potatoes, carrots, beans and pepper. Cover and cook on low for 5 to 5½ hours or until the chicken is tender.

2. Mix cornstarch and water until smooth; stir into cooking juices. Sprinkle with onions. Cover and cook on high for 15 more minutes or until thickened.

FAST FIX ▶ Maple Mustard Chicken

This recipe is one of my husband's favorites. It only calls for four ingredients, and we try to have them on hand all the time for a delicious and cozy dinner anytime!

—JENNIFER SEIDEL
MIDLAND, MICHIGAN

PREP: 5 MIN. **COOK:** 3 HOURS
MAKES: 6 SERVINGS

- 6 boneless skinless chicken breast halves (6 ounces each)
- ½ cup maple syrup
- ⅓ cup stone-ground mustard
- 2 tablespoons quick-cooking tapioca
    Hot cooked brown rice

Place chicken in a 3-qt. slow cooker. In a small bowl, combine the syrup, mustard and tapioca; pour over chicken. Cover and cook on low for 3-4 hours or until tender. Serve with rice.

Stuffed Sweet Peppers

Italian sausage and feta cheese give zest to the rice filling in these tender peppers I've prepared often over the years. When I was married in 1970, slow cookers were the rage. In our home, it's one appliance that has never gone out of style.

—**JUDY EARL** SARASOTA, FLORIDA

PREP: 15 MIN. **COOK:** 4 HOURS **MAKES:** 5 SERVINGS

- 3 **medium sweet red peppers**
- 2 **medium sweet yellow peppers**
- 1 **jar (14 ounces) spaghetti sauce, divided**
- ¾ **pound Italian turkey sausage links, casings removed**
- ¾ **cup uncooked instant rice**
- ½ **cup crumbled feta cheese**
- ½ **cup chopped onion**
- ¼ **cup chopped tomato**
- ¼ **cup minced fresh parsley**
- 2 **tablespoons sliced ripe olives**
- ¼ **to ½ teaspoon garlic powder**
- ½ **teaspoon salt**
- ½ **teaspoon Italian seasoning**
- ½ **teaspoon crushed red pepper flakes**

1. Cut tops off peppers; chop tops and set aside. Discard stems and seeds; set pepper cups aside. Set aside ¾ cup spaghetti sauce; pour the remaining sauce into a 5-qt. slow cooker.

2. Combine the sausage, rice, cheese, onion, tomato, parsley, olives, garlic powder, salt, Italian seasoning, pepper flakes and reserved chopped peppers and spaghetti sauce. Spoon into peppers.

3. Transfer peppers to a 3-qt. slow cooker. Cover and cook on low for 4-5 hours or until the sausage is no longer pink and the peppers are tender.

Chicken with Noodles and Gravy

PREP: 15 MIN. **COOK:** 6 HOURS
MAKES: 4 SERVINGS

- 4 chicken leg quarters
- 2 cans (10¾ ounces each) condensed cream of chicken soup, undiluted
- 2 envelopes chicken gravy mix
- 2 teaspoons dried celery flakes
- 1¾ teaspoons Creole seasoning
- 1 teaspoon dried minced onion
- ¼ teaspoon pepper
- 3 cups uncooked egg noodles

1. With a sharp knife, cut leg quarters at the joints if desired. Place in a 4- or 5-qt. slow cooker. Combine the soup, gravy mix and seasonings; pour over chicken.

2. Cover and cook on low for 6-8 hours or until chicken is tender. Cook noodles according to package directions; serve with chicken and sauce.

Editor's Note: *The following spices may be substituted for 1 teaspoon Creole seasoning: ¼ teaspoon each salt, garlic powder and paprika; and a pinch each of dried thyme, ground cumin and cayenne pepper.*

❝ Here's a classic comfort food recipe. The rich golden gravy makes it perfect over hot noodles. ❞

—GLENDA PRINCE
GRAVETTE, ARKANSAS

Tex-Mex Chicken & Rice

I came up with this recipe for my sister, who just got her first slow cooker and cooks mostly by throwing canned goods into a pot. It's a delicious go-to recipe for busy days.

—ELIZABETH DUMONT
BOULDER, COLORADO

PREP: 15 MIN. **COOK:** 7 HOURS
MAKES: 6 SERVINGS

- 6 chicken leg quarters, skin removed
- 1 envelope taco seasoning, divided
- 1 can (14½ ounces) Mexican diced tomatoes, undrained
- 1 can (10¾ ounces) condensed cream of chicken soup, undiluted
- 1 large onion, chopped
- 1 can (4 ounces) chopped green chilies
- 1 cup uncooked instant rice
- 1 cup canned black beans, rinsed and drained
- 1 container (8 ounces) sour cream
- 1 cup (4 ounces) shredded cheddar cheese
- 1½ cups crushed tortilla chips
  Minced fresh cilantro

1. Sprinkle chicken with 1 tablespoon taco seasoning; transfer to a 5- or 6-qt. slow cooker. In a large bowl, combine tomatoes, soup, onion, chilies and remaining taco seasoning; pour over chicken. Cover and cook on low for 7-9 hours or until chicken is tender.

2. Prepare rice according to package directions; stir in beans and heat through.

3. Remove chicken from cooking juices; stir sour cream into cooking juices. Serve chicken with rice mixture and sauce. Sprinkle servings with cheese, tortilla chips and cilantro.

Savory Lemonade Chicken

I don't know where this recipe originally came from, but my mother used to prepare this chicken when I was little. Now I love to make it! The sweet and tangy sauce is delightful on chicken.

—JENNY COOK
EAU CLAIRE, WISCONSIN

PREP: 10 MIN. **COOK:** 3 HOURS
MAKES: 6 SERVINGS

- 6 **boneless skinless chicken breast halves (4 ounces each)**
- ¾ **cup thawed lemonade concentrate**
- 3 **tablespoons ketchup**
- 2 **tablespoons brown sugar**
- 1 **tablespoon cider vinegar**
- 2 **tablespoons cornstarch**
- 2 **tablespoons cold water**

1. Place chicken in a 5-qt. slow cooker. In a small bowl, combine the lemonade concentrate, ketchup, brown sugar and vinegar; pour over chicken. Cover and cook on low for 2½ hours or until chicken is tender.
2. Remove chicken and keep warm. Combine cornstarch and water until smooth; gradually stir into cooking juices. Cover and cook on high for 30 minutes or until thickened. Return chicken to the slow cooker; heat through.

Tangy Chicken Thighs

I love this dish because it turns affordable chicken thighs into a rich and delicious meal! The creamy and tangy sauce is what makes it so special. Serve with a crisp salad or fresh vegetables.

—DUTCHMOM4MI
TASTE OF HOME ONLINE COMMUNITY

PREP: 25 MIN. **COOK:** 4¾ HOURS
MAKES: 6 SERVINGS

- 1 **envelope Italian salad dressing mix**
- ½ **teaspoon pepper**
- 6 **boneless skinless chicken thighs (about 1½ pounds)**
- 2 **tablespoons butter, melted**
- 1 **large onion, chopped**
- 2 **garlic cloves, minced**
- 1 **can (10¾ ounces) condensed cream of chicken soup, undiluted**
- 1 **package (8 ounces) cream cheese, softened and cubed**
- ¼ **cup chicken broth**
  Hot cooked noodles or rice, optional

1. Combine salad dressing mix and pepper. In a 3-qt. slow cooker, layer half of the chicken, butter, salad dressing mixture, onion and garlic. Repeat layers. Cover and cook on low for 4-5 hours or until chicken is tender. Skim fat.
2. In a small bowl, combine the soup, cream cheese and broth until blended; add to slow cooker. Cover and cook for 45 minutes or until heated through.
3. Remove chicken to a serving platter; stir sauce until smooth. Serve chicken with sauce and noodles or rice if desired.

Slow-Cooked Orange Chicken

I created this recipe to prepare a flavorful chicken dish that's lower in calories and fat. Everyone likes the taste, including my grandchildren. It's a favorite of mine. It travels well, and I often take it to potluck suppers.
—**NANCY WIT** FREMONT, NEBRASKA

PREP: 15 MIN. **COOK:** 4½ HOURS **MAKES:** 6 SERVINGS

- 1 broiler/fryer chicken (3 pounds), cut up and skin removed
- 3 cups orange juice
- 1 cup chopped celery
- 1 cup chopped green pepper
- 1 can (4 ounces) mushroom stems and pieces, drained
- 4 teaspoons dried minced onion
- 1 tablespoon minced fresh parsley or 1 teaspoon dried parsley flakes
- ½ teaspoon salt, optional
- ¼ teaspoon pepper
- 3 tablespoons cornstarch
- 3 tablespoons cold water
  Hot cooked rice, optional
  Additional minced fresh parsley, optional

1. In a 3-qt. slow cooker, combine the first nine ingredients. Cover and cook on low for 4-5 hours or until chicken juices run clear.
2. Combine cornstarch and water until smooth; gradually stir into cooking liquid. Cover and cook on high for 30-45 minutes or until thickened. Serve with rice and sprinkle with parsley if desired.

ONIONS ON HAND

If you don't have dried minced onion, substitute ⅓ cup of minced fresh onion or a scant teaspoon of onion powder. Consider adding some chopped green onion tops as a tasty garnish.

Fiesta Chicken Burritos

Looking for some heat with supper but still want a cool kitchen? Try my burritos with a spicy touch the whole family will love! The recipe is easy to double if you're serving a crowd. If you prefer a more spicy dish, add a teaspoon of cayenne pepper.

—MARGARET LATTA PADUCAH, KENTUCKY

PREP: 30 MIN. **COOK:** 4¼ HOURS **MAKES:** 8 SERVINGS

1½ **pounds boneless skinless chicken breasts**
1 **can (15¼ ounces) whole kernel corn, drained**
1 **can (15 ounces) black beans, rinsed and drained**
1 **can (10 ounces) diced tomatoes and green chilies, undrained**
1 **jalapeno pepper, seeded and finely chopped**
3 **tablespoons ground cumin**
1 **teaspoon salt**
1 **teaspoon paprika**
½ **teaspoon pepper**
   Dash cayenne pepper
   Dash crushed red pepper flakes
1 **package (8 ounces) reduced-fat cream cheese, cubed**
8 **flour tortillas (8 inches), warmed**
   Optional toppings: sour cream, shredded cheddar cheese, shredded lettuce and chopped tomatoes

1. Place chicken breasts in a greased 4-qt. slow cooker. In a large bowl, combine the corn, beans, tomatoes, jalapeno and seasonings; pour over chicken. Cover and cook on low for 4-5 hours or until chicken is tender.

2. Remove chicken; cool slightly. Shred chicken with two forks and return to the slow cooker. Stir in the cream cheese. Cover and cook for 15 minutes or until heated through.

3. Spoon ¾ cup chicken mixture down the center of each tortilla; add toppings of your choice. Fold sides and ends over filling and roll up.

Editor's Note: *Wear disposable gloves when cutting hot peppers; the oils can burn skin. Avoid touching your face.*

Sweet Orange Chicken

Barbecue sauce and marmalade make this chicken an irresistible dish. Serve it with rice or rice noodles.

—LOUISE GILBERT
QUESNEL V2J6L4, BRITISH COLUMBIA

PREP: 15 MIN. **COOK:** 6 HOURS
MAKES: 6 SERVINGS

- 3 tablespoons all-purpose flour
- 1 broiler/fryer chicken (3 to 4 pounds), cut up and skin removed
- ⅔ cup orange marmalade
- ⅔ cup barbecue sauce
- ¼ cup soy sauce
- 2 tablespoons minced fresh gingerroot
  Hot cooked rice or rice noodles, optional

1. Place flour in a large resealable plastic bag. Add chicken, a few pieces at a time, and shake to coat. Place in a 3-qt. slow cooker.
2. In a small bowl, combine the orange marmalade, barbecue sauce, soy sauce and ginger; pour over chicken. Cover and cook on low for 6-8 hours or until chicken juices run clear. Serve with rice or noodles if desired.

Curried Chicken with Peaches

I'm always looking for dinners I can prepare ahead of time. The chicken in this recipe cooks for hours in delicious seasonings, and sweet peaches and raisins round out the amazing flavors.

—HEIDI MARTINEZ
COLORADO SPRINGS, COLORADO

PREP: 15 MIN. **COOK:** 3¼ HOURS
MAKES: 4 SERVINGS

- 1 broiler/fryer chicken (3 pounds), cut up
- ⅛ teaspoon salt
- ⅛ teaspoon pepper
- 1 can (29 ounces) sliced peaches
- ½ cup chicken broth
- 2 tablespoons butter, melted
- 1 tablespoon dried minced onion
- 2 teaspoons curry powder
- 2 garlic cloves, minced
- ¼ teaspoon ground ginger
- 3 tablespoons cornstarch
- 3 tablespoons cold water
- ¼ cup raisins
  Toasted flaked coconut, optional

1. Place chicken in a 5-qt. slow cooker; sprinkle with salt and pepper. Drain peaches, reserving ½ cup juice; set peaches aside. In a small bowl, combine the broth, butter, onion, curry, garlic, ginger and reserved juice; pour over chicken. Cover and cook on low for 3-4 hours or until chicken juices run clear.
2. Remove chicken to a serving platter; keep warm. Mix cornstarch and water until smooth; stir into cooking juices. Add raisins. Cover and cook on high for 10-15 minutes or until thickened. Stir in peaches and heat through. Serve with chicken. Garnish with coconut if desired.

Turkey Enchiladas

I've discovered a new and different way to serve economical turkey thighs. I simmer them in tomato sauce, green chilies and seasonings until they're tender and flavorful, then serve them in tortillas with our favorite fresh toppings!

—**STELLA SCHAMS** TEMPE, ARIZONA

PREP: 10 MIN. **COOK:** 6 HOURS
MAKES: 4 SERVINGS

- 2 **pounds turkey thighs or drumsticks**
- 1 **can (8 ounces) tomato sauce**
- 1 **can (4 ounces) chopped green chilies**
- ⅓ **cup chopped onion**
- 2 **tablespoons Worcestershire sauce**
- 1 **to 2 tablespoons chili powder**
- ¼ **teaspoon garlic powder**
- 8 **flour tortillas (6 inches), warmed**
  Optional toppings: chopped green onions, sliced ripe olives, chopped tomatoes, shredded cheddar cheese, sour cream and/or shredded lettuce

1. Remove skin from turkey; place turkey in a 5-qt. slow cooker. In a small bowl, combine the tomato sauce, chilies, onion, Worcestershire sauce, chili powder and garlic powder; pour over turkey. Cover and cook on low for 6-8 hours or until turkey is tender.
2. Remove turkey; shred meat with two forks and return to the slow cooker. Heat through.
3. Spoon about ½ cup of turkey mixture down the center of each tortilla. Fold bottom of tortilla over filling and roll up. Add toppings of your choice.

Chicken Merlot with Mushrooms

A dear friend who liked cooking as much as I do shared this recipe with me, and I think of her every time I make it. My friends and family love it and request it often.

—**SHELLI MCWILLIAM**
SALEM, OREGON

PREP: 10 MIN. **COOK:** 5 HOURS
MAKES: 5 SERVINGS

- ¾ **pound sliced fresh mushrooms**
- 1 **large onion, chopped**
- 2 **garlic cloves, minced**
- 3 **pounds boneless skinless chicken thighs**
- 1 **can (6 ounces) tomato paste**
- ¾ **cup chicken broth**
- ¼ **cup merlot or additional chicken broth**
- 2 **tablespoons quick-cooking tapioca**
- 2 **teaspoons sugar**
- 1½ **teaspoons dried basil**
- ½ **teaspoon salt**
- ¼ **teaspoon pepper**
- 2 **tablespoons grated Parmesan cheese**
  Hot cooked pasta, optional

1. Place the mushrooms, onion and garlic in a 5-qt. slow cooker. Top with chicken.
2. In a small bowl, combine the tomato paste, broth, wine, tapioca, sugar, basil, salt and pepper. Pour over chicken. Cover and cook on low for 5-6 hours or until chicken is tender.
3. Sprinkle with cheese. Serve with pasta if desired.

Best Italian Chicken

A friend gave me this easy recipe years ago, and I've adjusted the spices over time to better suit my family's tastes. Now, they ask me to make it at least twice a month!

—JUDI GUIZADO
RANCHO CUCAMONGA, CALIFORNIA

PREP: 20 MIN. **COOK:** 3 HOURS
MAKES: 6 SERVINGS

- 6 boneless skinless chicken breast halves
- 1 can (14½ ounces) Italian stewed tomatoes
- ¾ cup plus 3 tablespoons water, divided
- 2 tablespoons dried minced onion
- 2 teaspoons chicken bouillon granules
- 2 teaspoons chili powder
- ½ teaspoon dried tarragon
- ½ teaspoon Italian seasoning
- ¼ teaspoon garlic powder
- 3 tablespoons cornstarch
  Hot cooked rice

1. Place chicken in a 5-qt. slow cooker. Combine the tomatoes, ¾ cup water, onion, bouillon and seasonings; pour over chicken. Cover and cook on low for 3-4 hours or until chicken is tender.
2. Transfer chicken to a serving platter; keep warm. Place cooking juices in a saucepan; bring to a boil. Combine cornstarch and remaining water until smooth. Gradually stir into pan. Bring to a boil; cook and stir for 2 minutes or until thickened. Serve with chicken and rice.

ITALIAN TOMATOES

If you don't have Italian stewed tomatoes, use regular stewed tomatoes instead and bump up the Italian seasoning to ¾ to 1 teaspoon.

FAST FIX ▶ Sesame Orange Chicken

The enticing aroma of sweet orange and barbecue sauce awaits. Enjoy this dish in summer—and without heating up your kitchen. If you have a rice cooker, use it to prepare rice on the side. Easy!

—DARLENE BRENDEN
SALEM, OREGON

PREP: 20 MIN. **COOK:** 4 HOURS
MAKES: 8 SERVINGS

- ½ cup all-purpose flour
- 4 pounds boneless skinless chicken thighs
- ⅔ cup honey barbecue sauce
- ⅔ cup orange marmalade
- ½ cup orange juice
- ¼ cup reduced-sodium soy sauce
- 1 tablespoon minced fresh gingerroot
- ½ teaspoon crushed red pepper flakes
- 2 tablespoons sesame seeds, toasted
  Hot cooked rice

1. Place flour in a large resealable plastic bag. Add chicken, a few pieces at a time, and shake to coat. Transfer to a or 5-qt. slow cooker.
2. Combine the barbecue sauce, marmalade, orange juice, soy sauce, ginger and pepper flakes. Pour over chicken. Cover and cook on low for 4-6 hours or until chicken is tender. Sprinkle with sesame seeds. Serve with rice.

Italian Chicken Chardonnay

One day, I needed to have dinner ready when we walked in the door. So I altered a skillet dish that my family likes into a delicious slow cooker meal. It's perfect for a weeknight but nice enough for company, too.

—**JUDY ARMSTRONG** PRAIRIEVILLE, LOUISIANA

PREP: 20 MIN. **COOK:** 5 HOURS **MAKES:** 6 SERVINGS

- 2 teaspoons paprika
- 1 teaspoon salt
- 1 teaspoon pepper
- ¼ teaspoon cayenne pepper
- 3 pounds bone-in chicken breast halves, skin removed
- ½ pound baby portobello mushrooms, quartered
- 1 medium sweet red pepper, chopped
- 1 medium onion, chopped
- 1 can (14 ounces) water-packed artichoke hearts, rinsed and drained
- 1½ cups chardonnay
- 1 can (6 ounces) tomato paste
- 3 garlic cloves, minced
- 2 tablespoons minced fresh thyme or 2 teaspoons dried thyme
- ¼ cup minced fresh parsley
  Hot cooked pasta
  Shredded Romano cheese

1. Combine the paprika, salt, pepper and cayenne; sprinkle over chicken. Place the chicken, mushrooms, red pepper, onion and artichokes in a 5-qt. slow cooker. In a small bowl, combine the chardonnay, tomato paste, garlic and thyme; pour over vegetables.
2. Cover and cook on low for 5-6 hours or until chicken is tender. Stir in parsley. Serve with pasta; sprinkle with cheese.

Chicken Athena

With olives, sun-dried tomatoes, lemon juice and garlic, Greek flavors abound in my easy chicken dish that's prepared in the slow cooker. Serve it with orzo or couscous for a tasty accompaniment.

—RADELLE KNAPPENBERGER
OVIEDO, FLORIDA

PREP: 15 MIN. **COOK:** 4 HOURS
MAKES: 6 SERVINGS

- 6 **boneless skinless chicken breast halves (6 ounces each)**
- 2 **medium onions, chopped**
- ⅓ **cup sun-dried tomatoes (not packed in oil), chopped**
- ⅓ **cup pitted Greek olives, chopped**
- 2 **tablespoons lemon juice**
- 1 **tablespoon balsamic vinegar**
- 3 **garlic cloves, minced**
- ½ **teaspoon salt**

Place chicken in a 3-qt. slow cooker. Add the remaining ingredients. Cover and cook on low for 4 hours or until a thermometer reads 170°.

Turkey Leg Pot Roast

Well-seasoned turkey legs and tender veggies make this an ideal dinner for a crisp fall day. Tender and satisfying, the recipe couldn't be easier!

—RICK AND VEGAS PEARSON
CADILLAC, MICHIGAN

PREP: 20 MIN. **COOK:** 5 HOURS
MAKES: 3 SERVINGS

- 3 **medium potatoes, peeled and quartered**
- 2 **cups fresh baby carrots**
- 2 **celery ribs, cut into 2½-inch pieces**
- 1 **medium onion, peeled and quartered**
- 3 **garlic cloves, peeled and quartered**
- ½ **cup chicken broth**
- 3 **turkey drumsticks (12 ounces each), skin removed**
- 2 **teaspoons seasoned salt**
- 1 **teaspoon dried thyme**
- 1 **teaspoon dried parsley flakes**
- ¼ **teaspoon pepper**

In a greased 5-qt. slow cooker, combine the first six ingredients. Place drumsticks over vegetables. Sprinkle with the seasoned salt, thyme, parsley and pepper. Cover and cook on low for 5 to 5½ hours or until turkey is tender.

Rosemary Chicken with White Beans

With a full-time job and young child, I'm known as the Slow Cooker Queen in my family. I use my slow cookers at least twice a week and sometimes have two or three going at a time with different dishes. I've made this recipe for years. It's a treasured favorite.

—SHARON JOHANNES
ASHLEY, ILLINOIS

PREP: 15 MIN. **COOK:** 3 HOURS
MAKES: 6 SERVINGS

- 6 boneless skinless chicken breast halves (6 ounces each)
- 1 tablespoon canola oil
- 2 cans (15½ ounces each) great northern beans, rinsed and drained
- 1 cup sliced fresh carrots
- ½ cup sliced celery
- ⅔ cup Italian salad dressing
- 2 teaspoons dried rosemary, crushed
- ½ teaspoon salt
- 1 teaspoon pepper

1. In a large skillet, brown chicken in oil in batches on both sides. Place the beans, carrots and celery in a 5-qt. slow cooker; top with chicken.
2. Combine the salad dressing, rosemary, salt and pepper; pour over chicken. Cover and cook on low for 3-4 hours or until a thermometer reads 170°.

Satisfying Chicken and Veggies

This satisfying dish is all your family needs for dinner...so there's only one pot to clean. Love that!

—KAT SADI
SAN LUIS OBISPO, CALIFORNIA

PREP: 20 MIN. **COOK:** 4 HOURS
MAKES: 6 SERVINGS

- 2 medium potatoes, peeled and cut into 1-inch pieces (about 1½ cups)
- 1 cup thickly sliced onion
- ½ cup sliced celery
- 1 medium carrot, cut into 1-inch pieces
- 1 medium sweet yellow pepper, cut into 1-inch pieces
- 1 broiler/fryer chicken (3 to 4 pounds), cut up and skin removed
- 1 jar (24 ounces) meatless spaghetti sauce
- 1 cup water
- 1½ teaspoons minced garlic
- ¼ teaspoon salt
- ¼ teaspoon dried oregano
- ¼ teaspoon dried basil
- ¼ teaspoon pepper

1. Place the potatoes, onion, celery, carrot and yellow pepper in a 5-qt. slow cooker. Top with chicken. Combine the remaining ingredients; pour over chicken.
2. Cover and cook on low for 4-5 hours or until chicken and vegetables are tender.

FAST FIX ▶ Soy-Garlic Chicken

Because I'm a full-time mom and help my husband on our ranch, I'm always looking for simple yet hearty meals for the slow cooker. My family really likes this one.
—**COLLEEN FABER** BUFFALO, MONTANA

PREP: 10 MIN. **COOK:** 4 HOURS **MAKES:** 6 SERVINGS

- 6 chicken leg quarters, skin removed
- 1 can (8 ounces) tomato sauce
- ½ cup soy sauce
- ¼ cup packed brown sugar
- 2 teaspoons minced garlic

1. With a sharp knife, cut leg quarters at the joints if desired. Place in a 4-qt. slow cooker. In a small bowl, combine the tomato sauce, soy sauce, brown sugar and garlic; pour over chicken.
2. Cover and cook on low for 4-5 hours or until chicken is tender.

Chicken, Bean and Rice Nachos

When you're craving nachos but need more than a snack, my recipe makes a fun and zesty meal. You can't go wrong with it.
—**BARBARA SCHWEITZER** CHESAPEAKE, VIRGINIA

PREP: 15 MIN. **COOK:** 5 HOURS **MAKES:** 6 SERVINGS

- 1½ pounds boneless skinless chicken breasts
- 1 jar (16 ounces) salsa
- 1 can (15 ounces) black beans, rinsed and drained
- 1 can (7 ounces) Mexicorn, drained
- 1 package (8 ounces) cream cheese, cubed
- 3 cups cooked rice
- ¾ cup shredded Mexican cheese blend
   Tortilla chips

1. Place chicken in a 3-qt. slow cooker. Combine the salsa, beans and corn; pour over chicken. Cover and cook on low for 5-6 hours or until chicken is tender.
2. Shred chicken with two forks. Stir cream cheese into mixture until blended.
3. To serve, place rice in serving bowls; top with chicken mixture and cheese blend. Serve with chips.

Chicken and Red Potatoes

Try this moist and tender chicken-and-potato dish with scrumptious gravy tonight! Just fix it early in the day, and you can forget about it until mealtime.

—MICHELE TRANTHAM WAYNESVILLE, NORTH CAROLINA

PREP: 20 MIN. **COOK:** 3½ HOURS **MAKES:** 4 SERVINGS

- 3 tablespoons all-purpose flour
- 4 boneless skinless chicken breast halves
  (6 ounces each)
- 2 tablespoons olive oil
- 4 medium red potatoes, cut into wedges
- 2 cups fresh baby carrots, halved lengthwise
- 1 can (4 ounces) mushroom stems and pieces, drained
- 4 canned whole green chilies, cut into ½-inch slices
- 1 can (10¾ ounces) condensed cream of onion soup,
  undiluted
- ¼ cup 2% milk
- ½ teaspoon chicken seasoning
- ¼ teaspoon salt
- ¼ teaspoon dried rosemary, crushed
- ¼ teaspoon pepper

1. Place flour in a large resealable plastic bag. Add chicken, one piece at a time; shake to coat. In a large skillet, brown chicken in oil on both sides.
2. Meanwhile, place the potatoes, carrots, mushrooms and chilies in a greased 5-qt. slow cooker. In a small bowl, combine the remaining ingredients. Pour half of soup mixture over vegetables.
3. Transfer chicken to slow cooker; top with remaining soup mixture. Cover and cook on low for 3½ to 4 hours or until a thermometer reads 170°.
Editor's Note: *This recipe was tested with McCormick's Montreal Chicken Seasoning. Look for it in the spice aisle.*

Citrus Turkey Roast

I was skeptical at first about making turkey in the slow cooker. But once I tasted this dish, I was hooked!

—**KATHY KITTELL** LENEXA, KANSAS

PREP: 15 MIN. **COOK:** 5¼ HOURS
MAKES: 12 SERVINGS

- 1 frozen boneless turkey roast, thawed (3 pounds)
- 1 tablespoon garlic powder
- 1 tablespoon paprika
- 1 tablespoon olive oil
- 2 teaspoons Worcestershire sauce
- ½ teaspoon salt
- ½ teaspoon pepper
- 8 garlic cloves, peeled
- 1 cup chicken broth, divided
- ¼ cup water
- ¼ cup white wine or additional chicken broth
- ¼ cup orange juice
- 1 tablespoon lemon juice
- 2 tablespoons cornstarch

1. Cut roast in half. Combine the garlic powder, paprika, oil, Worcestershire sauce, salt and pepper; rub over turkey. Place in a 5-qt. slow cooker. Add the garlic, ½ cup broth, water, wine, orange juice and lemon juice. Cover and cook on low for 5-6 hours or until a thermometer reads 170°.
2. Remove turkey and keep warm. Discard garlic cloves. For gravy, combine cornstarch and remaining broth until smooth; stir into cooking juices. Cover and cook on high for 15 minutes or until thickened. Slice turkey; serve with gravy.

Louisiana Red Beans and Rice

Smoked turkey sausage and red pepper flakes add zip to this saucy, slow-cooked version of the New Orleans classic. For extra heat, add red pepper sauce at the table.

—**JULIA BUSHREE**
GEORGETOWN, TEXAS

PREP: 20 MIN. **COOK:** 8 HOURS
MAKES: 9 SERVINGS

- 4 cans (16 ounces each) kidney beans, rinsed and drained
- 1 can (14½ ounces) diced tomatoes, undrained
- 1 package (14 ounces) smoked turkey sausage, sliced
- 1 cup chicken broth
- 3 celery ribs, chopped
- 1 large onion, chopped
- 1 medium green pepper, chopped
- 1 small sweet red pepper, chopped
- 6 garlic cloves, minced
- 1 bay leaf
- ½ teaspoon crushed red pepper flakes
- 2 green onions, chopped
  Hot cooked rice

1. In a 4-qt. slow cooker, combine the first 11 ingredients. Cover and cook on low for 8-10 hours or until vegetables are tender. Stir before serving. Discard bay leaf.
2. Sprinkle each serving with onions. Serve with rice.

PREP: 10 MIN. **COOK:** 5 HOURS
MAKES: 14 SERVINGS

- 1 **bone-in turkey breast (6 to 7 pounds), skin removed**
- 1 **tablespoon olive oil**
- 1 **teaspoon dried minced garlic**
- 1 **teaspoon seasoned salt**
- 1 **teaspoon paprika**
- 1 **teaspoon Italian seasoning**
- 1 **teaspoon pepper**
- ½ **cup water**

Brush turkey with oil. Combine the garlic, seasoned salt, paprika, Italian seasoning and pepper; rub over turkey. Transfer to a 6-qt. slow cooker; add water. Cover and cook on low for 5-6 hours or until tender.

❝Here's an easy recipe to try when you're craving turkey. It uses pantry ingredients, which is handy.❞

—**MARIA JUCO**
MILWAUKEE, WISCONSIN

FAST FIX ▶ Southwest Chicken

Chicken is cooked until tender and combined with corn, beans, cheese, and salsa for a delicious dinner with Southwestern flair. The garnishes really complete the meal.

—**MADDYMOO**
TASTE OF HOME ONLINE COMMUNITY

PREP: 15 MIN. **COOK:** 4 HOURS
MAKES: 6 SERVINGS

- 1 **can (15¼ ounces) whole kernel corn, drained**
- 1 **can (15 ounces) black beans, rinsed and drained**
- 1 **jar (16 ounces) mild salsa**
- 1¼ **pounds boneless skinless chicken breast halves**
    Sweet red and yellow pepper strips, sour cream, shredded cheddar cheese and sliced green onions, optional

1. In a 3-qt. slow cooker, layer three-fourths each of the corn and beans and half of the salsa. Arrange chicken over salsa; top with remaining corn, beans and salsa. Cover and cook on low for 4-5 hours or until chicken is tender.
2. Shred chicken with two forks and return to the slow cooker; heat through. Top with the peppers, sour cream, cheese and onions if desired.

Cornish Game Hens with Couscous

When I invite people to dinner, they often ask if we're going to have these delightful hens. They think I've worked all day in the kitchen, and I don't tell them any different. I suppose my secret's out now!

—BARBARA LENTO
HOUSTON, PENNSYLVANIA

PREP: 40 MIN. **COOK:** 3 HOURS
MAKES: 4 SERVINGS

- 2 tablespoons all-purpose flour
- ½ teaspoon salt
- ½ teaspoon pepper
- ¼ teaspoon chili powder
- 2 Cornish game hens (20 to 24 ounces each), thawed
- 1 tablespoon olive oil
- 1 can (14½ ounces) reduced-sodium chicken broth
- 2 cups cubed peeled eggplant
- 2 large tomatoes, cut into wedges and seeded
- 2 cups sliced baby portobello mushrooms
- 1 medium onion, sliced
- 1 medium green pepper, chopped
- 1 garlic clove, minced
- 1 bay leaf
- 2 cups hot cooked couscous

1. In a large resealable plastic bag, combine flour, salt, pepper and chili powder. Add hens, one at a time, and shake to coat. In a large skillet, brown hens in oil on all sides.
2. Transfer to a 5- or 6-qt. slow cooker. Add broth to the skillet, stirring to loosen browned bits from pan. Bring to a boil. Reduce heat; simmer, uncovered, for 1-2 minutes. Add to slow cooker.
3. Stir in the eggplant, tomatoes, mushrooms, onion, green pepper, garlic and bay leaf. Cover and cook on low for 3-4 hours or until a thermometer reads 180° and vegetables are tender. Discard bay leaf. To serve, split hens in half. Serve with couscous and vegetables.

Slow-Cooked Turkey Sandwiches

These sandwiches have been such a hit at office potlucks that I keep copies of the recipe in my desk to hand out!

—DIANE TWAIT NELSEN
RINGSTED, IOWA

PREP: 15 MIN. **COOK:** 3 HOURS
MAKES: 18 SERVINGS

- 6 cups cubed cooked turkey
- 2 cups cubed process cheese (Velveeta)
- 1 can (10¾ ounces) condensed cream of chicken soup, undiluted
- 1 can (10¾ ounces) condensed cream of mushroom soup, undiluted
- ½ cup finely chopped onion
- ½ cup chopped celery
- 18 wheat sandwich buns, split

In a 4-qt. slow cooker, combine the first six ingredients. Cover and cook on low for 3-4 hours or until vegetables are tender and cheese is melted. Stir mixture; spoon ½ cup onto each bun.

Chipotle-Marmalade Chicken

Big on flavor and easy on the cook's time, my chicken recipe is so appealing! The sweet-hot sauce gets its heat from chipotle pepper. I like to serve the chicken with a side of rice to use up every delectable drop of sauce.

—CITTIE TASTE OF HOME ONLINE COMMUNITY

PREP: 15 MIN. **COOK:** 4 HOURS **MAKES:** 4 SERVINGS

- **4 boneless skinless chicken breast halves (6 ounces each)**
- **¼ teaspoon salt**
- **Dash pepper**
- **½ cup chicken broth**
- **⅓ cup orange marmalade**
- **1 tablespoon canola oil**
- **1 tablespoon balsamic vinegar**
- **1 tablespoon minced chipotle pepper in adobo sauce**
- **1 tablespoon honey**
- **1 teaspoon chili powder**
- **¼ teaspoon garlic powder**
- **4 teaspoons cornstarch**
- **2 tablespoons cold water**

1. Sprinkle chicken with salt and pepper. Transfer to a 4- or 5-qt. slow cooker. In a small bowl, combine the broth, marmalade, oil, vinegar, chipotle pepper, honey, chili powder and garlic powder; pour over chicken. Cover and cook on low for 4-5 hours or until a thermometer reads 170°.

2. Remove chicken to a serving platter and keep warm. Place cooking juices in a small saucepan; bring to a boil. Combine cornstarch and water until smooth. Gradually stir into the pan. Bring to a boil; cook and stir for 2 minutes or until thickened. Serve sauce with chicken.

FAST FIX ▶ Creamy Chicken and Carrots

PREP: 5 MIN. **COOK:** 4 HOURS
MAKES: 2 SERVINGS

- 2 boneless skinless chicken breast halves (6 ounces each)
- ½ pound fresh baby carrots, cut in half lengthwise
- 1 can (10¾ ounces) condensed cream of mushroom soup, undiluted
- 1 can (4 ounces) mushroom stems and pieces, drained
  Hot cooked rice, optional

Place chicken in a 1½-qt. slow cooker. Top with carrots, soup and mushrooms. Cover and cook on low for 4-5 hours or until chicken is tender. Serve over rice if desired.

66 Mushroom soup makes a creamy gravy for my tender chicken breasts. Use other vegetables or thickly sliced potatoes for a change. 99

—**VALMA O'NEILL** UTICA, MICHIGAN

Italian Chicken and Peppers

I put this chicken recipe together one day when I had leftover peppers and wanted something easy. To my delight, the taste reminded me of pizza—something I love but can no longer eat! It's great with a side of steamed broccoli.

—**BRENDA NOLEN**
SIMPSONVILLE, SOUTH CAROLINA

PREP: 20 MIN. **COOK:** 4 HOURS
MAKES: 6 SERVINGS

- 6 boneless skinless chicken breast halves (4 ounces each)
- 1 jar (24 ounces) garden-style spaghetti sauce
- 1 medium onion, sliced
- ½ each small green, sweet yellow and red peppers, julienned
- ¼ cup grated Parmesan cheese
- 2 garlic cloves, minced
- 1 teaspoon dried oregano
- 1 teaspoon dried basil
- ½ teaspoon salt
- ¼ teaspoon pepper
- 4½ cups uncooked spiral pasta
  Shaved Parmesan cheese, optional

1. Place chicken in a 3-qt. slow cooker. In a large bowl, combine the spaghetti sauce, onion, peppers, cheese, garlic, oregano, basil, salt and pepper. Pour over chicken. Cover and cook on low for 4-5 hours or until a thermometer reads 170°.
2. Cook pasta according to package directions; drain. Serve with chicken and sauce. Top each serving with shaved Parmesan cheese if desired.

BELL PEPPERS

Bell peppers add crunch, sweetness, color and vitamin C to recipes. Green bell peppers are actually unripened versions of the sweeter-tasting colored peppers. They're less expensive than sweet peppers because they're faster to market. To save time and money, go ahead and use whatever color pepper you like instead of mixing the different colors. Or check your store's salad bar for ready-chopped peppers.

Chicken with Mushroom Gravy

This deliciously moist chicken is a longtime favorite with family and friends. It's so easy, comforting and rich. A friend shared the recipe years ago, and I adapted it by adding a few new ingredients. I like to serve it over mashed potatoes or rice.

—**DAROLYN JONES** FISHERS, INDIANA

PREP: 10 MIN.   **COOK:** 4¼ HOURS
MAKES: 4 SERVINGS

- 4 **boneless skinless chicken breast halves (6 ounces each)**
- 1 **can (12 ounces) mushroom gravy**
- 1 **cup 2% milk**
- 1 **can (8 ounces) mushroom stems and pieces, drained**
- 1 **can (4 ounces) chopped green chilies**
- 1 **envelope Italian salad dressing mix**
- 1 **package (8 ounces) cream cheese, cubed**

1. In a 3-qt. slow cooker, combine the chicken, gravy, milk, mushrooms, chilies and dressing mix. Cover and cook on low for 4-5 hours or until chicken is tender.
2. Stir in cream cheese; cover and cook 15 minutes longer or until cheese is melted.

Italian Sausage and Vegetables

This easy and complete meal in a pot is both healthy and delicious. It's wonderful served with a slice of hot garlic bread. I found the recipe in a magazine and made just a few adjustments to suit myself. Enjoy!

—**GINNY STUBY**
ALTOONA, PENNSYLVANIA

PREP: 20 MIN.   **COOK:** 5½ HOURS
MAKES: 6 SERVINGS

- 1¼ **pounds sweet or hot Italian turkey sausage links**
- 1 **can (28 ounces) diced tomatoes, undrained**
- 2 **medium potatoes, cut into 1-inch pieces**
- 4 **small zucchini, cut into 1-inch slices**
- 1 **medium onion, cut into wedges**
- ½ **teaspoon garlic powder**
- ¼ **teaspoon crushed red pepper flakes**
- ¼ **teaspoon dried oregano**
- ¼ **teaspoon dried basil**
- 1 **tablespoon dry bread crumbs**
- ¾ **cup shredded pepper jack cheese**

1. In a nonstick skillet, brown sausages over medium heat. Place in a 5-qt. slow cooker. Add vegetables and seasonings. Cover and cook on low for 5½ to 6½ hours or until a thermometer reads 165°.
2. Remove sausages and cut into 1-in. pieces; return to slow cooker. Stir in bread crumbs. Serve in bowls; sprinkle with cheese.

Southern Shredded BBQ Chicken

My family loves traditional pork barbecue served on mashed potatoes. But I like using chicken instead of pork, and serving it over moist and delicious corn bread. The result? It's better than ever!

—ANGELA SPENGLER CLOVIS, NEW MEXICO

PREP: 30 MIN. **COOK:** 6 HOURS **MAKES:** 6 SERVINGS

- 4 **pounds bone-in chicken breast halves, skin removed**
- 1 **can (10¾ ounces) condensed tomato soup, undiluted**
- ½ **cup packed brown sugar**
- ½ **cup cider vinegar**
- 1½ **teaspoons chili powder**
- 1 **teaspoon salt**
- 1 **teaspoon celery seed**
- 1 **teaspoon soy sauce**
- ¼ **teaspoon cayenne pepper**

CORN BREAD
- 1 **cup all-purpose flour**
- 1 **cup yellow cornmeal**
- 2 **tablespoons sugar**
- 2 **teaspoons baking powder**
- ¼ **teaspoon salt**
- 2 **eggs**
- 1 **cup 2% milk**
- 6 **tablespoons butter, melted, divided**

1. Place chicken in a 4-qt. slow cooker. In a small bowl, combine the tomato soup, brown sugar, vinegar, chili powder, salt, celery seed, soy sauce and cayenne. Pour over chicken. Cover and cook on low for 6-8 hours or until tender.

2. In a large bowl, combine the flour, cornmeal, sugar, baking powder and salt. Combine the eggs, milk and 4 tablespoons butter; stir into dry ingredients just until combined.

3. Pour into a greased 8-in. square baking pan. Bake at 350° for 18-20 minutes or until a toothpick inserted near the center comes out clean. Drizzle remaining butter over warm bread.

4. Remove chicken from slow cooker. When cool enough to handle, remove meat from bones; discard bones. Shred meat with two forks; return to slow cooker. Using a slotted spoon, serve the chicken over the corn bread.

162

165

171

Other Entrees

In a 5-qt. slow cooker, combine the first 16 ingredients. Cover and cook on low for 6-7 hours or until chicken is no longer pink. Stir in shrimp. Cover and cook 15 minutes longer or until heated through. Discard bay leaves. Serve with rice.

Red Clam Sauce

This luscious sauce tastes like you've worked on it all day. Instead, it cooks hands-free while you do other things. What a great way to jazz up pasta!

—**JOANN BROWN** LATROBE, PENNSYLVANIA

PREP: 25 MIN. **COOK:** 3 HOURS **MAKES:** 4 SERVINGS

- 1 medium onion, chopped
- 1 tablespoon canola oil
- 2 garlic cloves, minced
- 2 cans (6½ ounces each) chopped clams, undrained
- 1 can (14½ ounces) diced tomatoes, undrained
- 1 can (6 ounces) tomato paste
- ¼ cup minced fresh parsley
- 1 bay leaf
- 1 teaspoon sugar
- 1 teaspoon dried basil
- ½ teaspoon dried thyme
- 6 ounces linguine, cooked and drained

1. In a small skillet, saute onion in oil until tender. Add garlic; cook 1 minute longer.
2. Transfer to a 1½- or 2-qt. slow cooker. Stir in the clams, tomatoes, tomato paste, parsley, bay leaf, sugar, basil and thyme.
3. Cover and cook on low for 3-4 hours or until heated through. Discard bay leaf. Serve with linguine.

Hearty Jambalaya

I love anything with Cajun spices, so I came up with a slow-cooker jambalaya that's just as good as that served in restaurants. If you can't find andouille sausage, try hot links, smoked sausage or chorizo instead.

—**JENNIFER FULK** MORENO VALLEY, CALIFORNIA

PREP: 20 MIN. **COOK:** 6¼ HOURS **MAKES:** 8 SERVINGS

- 1 can (28 ounces) diced tomatoes, undrained
- 1 pound fully cooked andouille sausage links, cubed
- ½ pound boneless skinless chicken breasts, cut into 1-inch cubes
- 1 can (8 ounces) tomato sauce
- 1 cup diced onion
- 1 small sweet red pepper, diced
- 1 small green pepper, diced
- 1 cup chicken broth
- 1 celery rib with leaves, chopped
- 2 tablespoons tomato paste
- 2 teaspoons dried oregano
- 2 teaspoons Cajun seasoning
- 1½ teaspoons minced garlic
- 2 bay leaves
- 1 teaspoon Louisiana-style hot sauce
- ½ teaspoon dried thyme
- 1 pound cooked medium shrimp, peeled and deveined
  Hot cooked rice

Egg and Broccoli Casserole

For years, I've prepared this hearty casserole for brunches and potlucks. It's an unusual recipe for the slow cooker, but it's always welcomed wherever I serve it. Folks always go back for seconds.

—JANET SLITER
KENNEWICK, WASHINGTON

PREP: 10 MIN. **COOK:** 3½ HOURS
MAKES: 6 SERVINGS

- 3 **cups (24 ounces) 4% cottage cheese**
- 3 **cups frozen chopped broccoli, thawed and drained**
- 2 **cups (8 ounces) shredded cheddar cheese**
- 6 **eggs, lightly beaten**
- ⅓ **cup all-purpose flour**
- ¼ **cup butter, melted**
- 3 **tablespoons finely chopped onion**
- ½ **teaspoon salt**
  Additional shredded cheddar cheese, optional

1. In a large bowl, combine the first eight ingredients. Pour into a greased 3-qt. slow cooker. Cover and cook on high for 1 hour. Stir.
2. Reduce heat to low; cover and cook 2½ to 3 hours longer or until a thermometer reads 160°. Sprinkle with cheese if desired.

Forgotten Jambalaya

During the winter, I make jambalaya at least once a month. It's so easy—just chop the vegetables, dump everything in the slow cooker and forget it! Even my sons, who are picky about spicy things, like this.

—CINDI COSS COPPELL, TEXAS

PREP: 35 MIN. **COOK:** 4¼ HOURS
MAKES: 11 SERVINGS

- 1 **can (14½ ounces) diced tomatoes, undrained**
- 1 **can (14½ ounces) beef or chicken broth**
- 1 **can (6 ounces) tomato paste**
- 3 **celery ribs, chopped**
- 2 **medium green peppers, chopped**
- 1 **medium onion, chopped**
- 5 **garlic cloves, minced**
- 3 **teaspoons dried parsley flakes**
- 2 **teaspoons dried basil**
- 1½ **teaspoons dried oregano**
- 1¼ **teaspoons salt**
- ½ **teaspoon cayenne pepper**
- ½ **teaspoon hot pepper sauce**
- 1 **pound boneless skinless chicken breasts, cut into 1-inch cubes**
- 1 **pound smoked sausage, halved and cut into ¼-inch slices**
- ½ **pound uncooked medium shrimp, peeled and deveined**
  Hot cooked rice

1. In a 5-qt. slow cooker, combine the tomatoes, broth and tomato paste. Add the celery, green peppers, onion, garlic and seasonings. Stir in the chicken and sausage.
2. Cover and cook on low for 4-6 hours or until chicken is no longer pink. Stir in shrimp. Cover and cook 15-30 minutes longer or until shrimp turn pink. Serve with rice.

Corn Bread-Topped Frijoles

My family often requests this economical slow-cooker favorite. It's loaded with fresh Southwestern flavors. One batch makes eight hearty servings, but it still never lasts long at our house!

—**SUZANNE CALDWELL** ARTESIA, NEW MEXICO

PREP: 20 MIN. **COOK:** 3 HOURS **MAKES:** 8 SERVINGS

- 1 **medium onion, chopped**
- 1 **medium green pepper, chopped**
- 1 **tablespoon canola oil**
- 2 **garlic cloves, minced**
- 1 **can (16 ounces) kidney beans, rinsed and drained**
- 1 **can (15 ounces) pinto beans, rinsed and drained**
- 1 **can (14½ ounces) diced tomatoes, undrained**
- 1 **can (8 ounces) tomato sauce**
- 1 **teaspoon chili powder**
- ½ **teaspoon pepper**
- ⅛ **teaspoon hot pepper sauce**

CORN BREAD TOPPING

- 1 **cup all-purpose flour**
- 1 **cup yellow cornmeal**
- 1 **tablespoon sugar**
- 1½ **teaspoons baking powder**
- ½ **teaspoon salt**
- 2 **eggs, lightly beaten**
- 1¼ **cups fat-free milk**
- 1 **can (8¼ ounces) cream-style corn**
- 3 **tablespoons canola oil**

1. In a large skillet, saute onion and green pepper in oil until tender. Add garlic; cook 1 minute longer. Transfer to a greased 5-qt. slow cooker.

2. Stir in the beans, tomatoes, tomato sauce, chili powder, pepper and pepper sauce. Cover and cook on high for 1 hour.

3. In a large bowl, combine the flour, cornmeal, sugar, baking powder and salt. Combine the eggs, milk, corn and oil; add to dry ingredients and mix well. Spoon evenly over bean mixture.

4. Cover and cook on high for 2 hours or until a toothpick inserted near the center of corn bread comes out clean.

Hearty Cheese Tortellini

Simple enough for an everyday meal but good enough for company, my recipe feeds plenty of people. I serve it with steamed broccoli and hot fresh bread.

—CHRISTINE EILERTS
TULSA, OKLAHOMA

PREP: 30 MIN. **COOK:** 6¼ HOURS
MAKES: 6 SERVINGS

- ½ **pound bulk Italian sausage**
- ½ **pound lean ground beef (90% lean)**
- 1 **jar (24 ounces) marinara sauce**
- 1 **can (14½ ounces) Italian diced tomatoes**
- 1 **cup sliced fresh mushrooms**
- 1 **package (9 ounces) refrigerated cheese tortellini**
- 1 **cup (4 ounces) shredded part-skim mozzarella cheese**

1. In a small skillet, cook sausage and beef over medium heat until no longer pink; drain. Transfer to a 3-qt. slow cooker. Stir in marinara sauce, tomatoes and mushrooms. Cover and cook on low for 6-7 hours or until heated through.

2. Prepare tortellini according to package directions; stir into meat mixture. Sprinkle with cheese. Cover and cook for 15 minutes or until cheese is melted.

Overnight Flax Oatmeal

Fans of the healthy benefits of flaxseed will enjoy this hearty oatmeal. It's full of yummy raisins and dried cranberries, too!

—SUSAN SMITH
OCEAN VIEW, NEW JERSEY

PREP: 10 MIN. **COOK:** 7 HOURS
MAKES: 4 SERVINGS

- 3 **cups water**
- 1 **cup old-fashioned oats**
- 1 **cup raisins**
- ½ **cup dried cranberries**
- ½ **cup ground flaxseed**
- ½ **cup 2% milk**
- 1 **teaspoon vanilla extract**
- 1 **teaspoon molasses**

In a 3-qt. slow cooker, combine all ingredients. Cover and cook on low for 7-8 hours or until liquid is absorbed and oatmeal is tender.

Vegetarian Tortilla Lasagna

You won't miss the meat in this savory delight. The layered main course is as tasty as it is impressive. Serve warm wedges alongside chips and salsa or a green salad.

—CONNIE MCDOWELL
GREENWOOD, DELAWARE

PREP: 20 MIN. **COOK:** 3 HOURS
MAKES: 8 SERVINGS

- 1 **can (14½ ounces) diced tomatoes with basil, oregano and garlic**
- 1 **cup chunky salsa**
- 1 **can (6 ounces) tomato paste**
- ½ **teaspoon ground cumin**
- 2 **cans (15½ ounces each) hominy, rinsed and drained**
- 1 **can (15 ounces) black beans, rinsed and drained**
- 3 **flour tortillas (10 inches)**
- 2 **cups (8 ounces) shredded Monterey Jack cheese**
- ¼ **cup sliced ripe olives**

1. Cut three 25-in. x 3-in. strips of heavy-duty foil; crisscross so they resemble spokes of a wheel. Place strips on the bottom and up the sides of a round 5-qt. slow cooker. Coat strips with cooking spray.
2. In a large bowl, combine the tomatoes, salsa, tomato paste and cumin. Stir in hominy and beans.
3. Place one tortilla in slow cooker. Top with a third of the hominy mixture and ⅔ cup cheese. Repeat layers twice. Sprinkle with olives. Cover and cook on low for 3 to 3½ hours or until heated through.
4. Using foil strips as handles, remove the lasagna to a platter. Let stand for 5 minutes before cutting into wedges.

Thai Shrimp and Rice

Raisins and coconut milk add a lovely hint of sweetness to shrimp, while fresh lime and ginger give this dish a wonderful aroma. It adds a fun flair to weeknight menus.

—PAULA MARCHESI
LENHARTSVILLE, PENNSYLVANIA

PREP: 30 MIN. **COOK:** 3¼ HOURS
MAKES: 8 SERVINGS

- 2 cans (14½ ounces each) chicken broth
- 2 cups uncooked converted rice
- 1 large carrot, shredded
- 1 medium onion, chopped
- ½ cup each chopped green and sweet red pepper
- ½ cup water
- ½ cup coconut milk
- ⅓ cup lime juice
- ¼ cup flaked coconut
- ¼ cup each raisins and golden raisins
- 8 garlic cloves, minced
- 1 tablespoon grated lime peel
- 1 tablespoon minced fresh gingerroot
- 1 teaspoon salt
- 1 teaspoon each ground coriander and cumin
- ½ teaspoon cayenne pepper
- 1 pound cooked medium shrimp, peeled and deveined
- ½ cup fresh snow peas, cut into thin strips

1. In a 5-qt. slow cooker, combine the broth, rice, vegetables, water, coconut milk, lime juice, coconut, raisins, garlic, lime peel and seasonings. Cover and cook on low for 3 hours or until rice is tender.
2. Stir in shrimp and peas. Cover and cook 15-20 minutes longer or until heated through.

Vegetarian Stuffed Peppers

These filling and flavorful peppers are an updated version of my mom's stuffed peppers, which were a favorite when I was growing up in upstate New York. Whenever I make them, I'm reminded of home.

—MELISSA MCCABE
LONG BEACH, CALIFORNIA

PREP: 30 MIN. **COOK:** 3½ HOURS
MAKES: 6 SERVINGS

- 6 large sweet peppers
- 2 cups cooked brown rice
- 3 small tomatoes, chopped
- 1 cup frozen corn, thawed
- 1 small sweet onion, chopped
- ⅓ cup canned red beans, rinsed and drained
- ⅓ cup canned black beans, rinsed and drained
- ¾ cup cubed Monterey Jack cheese
- 1 can (4¼ ounces) chopped ripe olives
- 4 fresh basil leaves, thinly sliced
- 3 garlic cloves, minced
- 1 teaspoon salt
- ½ teaspoon pepper
- ¾ cup meatless spaghetti sauce
- ½ cup water
- 4 tablespoons grated Parmesan cheese, divided

1. Cut tops off peppers and remove seeds; set aside. In a large bowl, combine the rice, tomatoes, corn, onion and beans. Stir in the Monterey Jack cheese, olives, basil, garlic, salt and pepper. Spoon into peppers.
2. Combine spaghetti sauce and water; pour half into an oval 5-qt. slow cooker. Add the stuffed peppers. Top with remaining sauce. Sprinkle with 2 tablespoons Parmesan cheese.
3. Cover and cook on low for 3½ to 4 hours or until peppers are tender and filling is heated through. Sprinkle with remaining Parmesan cheese.

Stamp-of-Approval Spaghetti Sauce

My father is pretty opinionated...especially about food. This recipe received his nearly unattainable stamp of approval, and I have yet to hear any disagreement from anyone who has tried it!

—MELISSA TAYLOR HIGLEY, ARIZONA

PREP: 30 MIN. **COOK:** 8 HOURS
MAKES: 12 SERVINGS (3 QUARTS)

- 2 **pounds ground beef**
- ¾ **pound bulk Italian sausage**
- 4 **medium onions, finely chopped**
- 8 **garlic cloves, minced**
- 4 **cans (14½ ounces each) diced tomatoes, undrained**
- 4 **cans (6 ounces each) tomato paste**
- ½ **cup water**
- ¼ **cup sugar**
- ¼ **cup Worcestershire sauce**
- 1 **tablespoon canola oil**
- ¼ **cup minced fresh parsley**
- 2 **tablespoons minced fresh basil or 2 teaspoons dried basil**
- 1 **tablespoon minced fresh oregano or 1 teaspoon dried oregano**
- 4 **bay leaves**
- 1 **teaspoon rubbed sage**
- ½ **teaspoon salt**
- ½ **teaspoon dried marjoram**
- ½ **teaspoon pepper**
  Hot cooked spaghetti

1. In a Dutch oven, cook the beef, sausage, onions and garlic over medium heat until meat is no longer pink; drain.

2. Transfer to a 5-qt. slow cooker. Stir in the tomatoes, tomato paste, water, sugar, Worcestershire sauce, oil and seasonings.

3. Cover and cook on low for 8-10 hours. Discard bay leaves. Serve with spaghetti.

Hunter's Delight

We live in the North Woods, so we usually have an ample supply of venison. Our mom made this recipe often when we were growing up, and it was always a family favorite.

—TERRY PAULL
EAGLE RIVER, WISCONSIN

PREP: 15 MIN. **COOK:** 6 HOURS
MAKES: 8 SERVINGS

- ½ **pound sliced bacon, diced**
- 2½ **pounds red potatoes, thinly sliced**
- 2 **medium onions, sliced**
- 1½ **pounds boneless venison steak, cubed**
- 2 **cans (14¾ ounces each) cream-style corn**
- 3 **tablespoons Worcestershire sauce**
- 1 **teaspoon sugar**
- ½ **to 1 teaspoon seasoned salt**

1. In a large skillet, cook bacon over medium heat until crisp; drain. Place potatoes and onions in a 5-qt. slow cooker. Top with venison and bacon.
2. Combine corn, Worcestershire sauce, sugar and seasoned salt; pour over the top. Cover and cook on low for 6-8 hours or until meat and potatoes are tender.

Veggie Lasagna

Here's a veggie-licious alternative to traditional baked lasagna. I suggest using chunky spaghetti sauce.

—LAURA DAVISTER
LITTLE SUAMICO, WISCONSIN

PREP: 25 MIN. **COOK:** 3½ HOURS
MAKES: 2 SERVINGS

- ½ **cup shredded part-skim mozzarella cheese**
- 3 **tablespoons 1% cottage cheese**
- 2 **tablespoons grated Parmesan cheese**
- 2 **tablespoons egg substitute**
- ½ **teaspoon Italian seasoning**
- ⅛ **teaspoon garlic powder**
- ¾ **cup meatless spaghetti sauce**
- ½ **cup sliced zucchini**
- 2 **no-cook lasagna noodles**
- 4 **cups fresh baby spinach**
- ½ **cup sliced fresh mushrooms**

1. In a small bowl, combine the first six ingredients. Spread 1 tablespoon spaghetti sauce on the bottom of a 1½-qt. slow cooker coated with cooking spray. Top with half of the zucchini and a third of the cheese mixture.
2. Break noodles into 1-in. pieces; sprinkle half of the noodles over cheese mixture. Spread with 1 tablespoon sauce. Top with half of the spinach and half of the mushrooms. Repeat layers. Top with remaining cheese mixture and spaghetti sauce.
3. Cover and cook on low for 3½ to 4 hours or until noodles are tender.

Blueberry French Toast

Your slow cooker can be your best friend on a busy morning. Just get this recipe going, run some errands and come back to the aroma of French toast ready to eat.

—ELIZABETH LORENZ PERU, INDIANA

PREP: 30 MIN. + CHILLING
COOK: 3 HOURS
MAKES: 12 SERVINGS (2 CUPS SYRUP)

- 8 **eggs**
- ½ **cup plain yogurt**
- ⅓ **cup sour cream**
- 1 **teaspoon vanilla extract**
- ½ **teaspoon ground cinnamon**
- 1 **cup 2% milk**
- ⅓ **cup maple syrup**
- 1 **loaf (1 pound) French bread, cubed**
- 1½ **cups fresh or frozen blueberries**
- 12 **ounces cream cheese, cubed**

BLUEBERRY SYRUP
- 1 **cup sugar**
- 2 **tablespoons cornstarch**
- 1 **cup cold water**

- ¾ **cup fresh or frozen blueberries, thawed, divided**
- 1 **tablespoon lemon juice**
- 1 **tablespoon butter**

1. In a large bowl, whisk the eggs, yogurt, sour cream, vanilla and cinnamon. Whisk in milk and maple syrup until blended.
2. Place half of the bread in a greased 5- or 6-qt. slow cooker; layer with half of the blueberries, cream cheese and egg mixture. Repeat layers. Cover and refrigerate overnight.
3. Remove from the refrigerator 30 minutes before cooking. Cover and cook on low for 3-4 hours or until a knife inserted in French toast comes out clean.
4. For syrup, in a small saucepan, combine sugar and cornstarch; stir in water until smooth. Add ¼ cup blueberries. Bring to a boil; cook and stir until the berries pop, about 3 minutes. Remove from the heat; stir in the lemon juice, butter and remaining berries. Serve warm with French toast.

FAST FIX ▶ Meatball Tortellini

I combined some favorite staples from our freezer and pantry to come up with this easy, satisfying dish. It uses just a few ingredients and requires little preparation.

—TRACIE BERGERON CHAUVIN, LOUISIANA

PREP: 10 MIN. **COOK:** 3 HOURS
MAKES: 6-8 SERVINGS

- 1 **package (16 ounces) frozen California-blend vegetables, thawed**
- 1 **package frozen fully cooked Italian meatballs (12 ounces) , thawed**
- 2 **cups uncooked dried cheese tortellini**
- 2 **cans (10¾ ounces each) condensed cream of mushroom soup, undiluted**
- 2¼ **cups water**
- 1 **teaspoon Creole seasoning**

1. In a 3-qt. slow cooker, combine the vegetables, meatballs and tortellini. In a large bowl, whisk the soup, water and Creole seasoning. Pour over vegetable mixture; stir well.
2. Cover and cook on low for 3-4 hours or until the tortellini and vegetables are tender.

Editor's Note: *The following spices may be substituted for 1 teaspoon Creole seasoning: ¼ teaspoon each salt, garlic powder and paprika; and a pinch each of dried thyme, ground cumin and cayenne pepper.*

Shredded Venison Sandwiches

My husband hunts deer every November, so I'm always looking for new recipes that use venison. The whole family loves these slow cooker sandwiches flavored with soy sauce, brown sugar, ketchup and hot sauce.
—**RUTH SETTERLUND** FREYBURG, MAINE

PREP: 15 MIN. **COOK:** 8 HOURS
MAKES: 14-18 SERVINGS

- 1 **boneless venison roast (4 pounds)**
- 1½ **cups ketchup**
- 3 **tablespoons brown sugar**
- 1 **tablespoon ground mustard**
- 1 **tablespoon lemon juice**
- 1 **tablespoon soy sauce**
- 1 **tablespoon liquid smoke, optional**
- 2 **teaspoons celery salt**
- 2 **teaspoons pepper**
- 2 **teaspoons Worcestershire sauce**
- 1 **teaspoon onion powder**
- 1 **teaspoon garlic powder**
- ⅛ **teaspoon ground nutmeg**
- 3 **drops hot pepper sauce**
- 14 **to 18 hamburger buns, split**

1. Cut venison roast in half; place in a 5-qt. slow cooker. In a large bowl, combine the ketchup, brown sugar, mustard, lemon juice, soy sauce, liquid smoke if desired and seasonings. Pour over venison. Cover and cook on low for 8-10 hours or until meat is tender.
2. Remove roast; cool slightly. Shred meat with two forks; return to the slow cooker and heat through. Using a slotted spoon, place meat mixture on bun bottoms. Replace tops.

Hash Brown Egg Brunch

Here's a recipe that combines slow cooking with brunch.
It's a wonderful treat to take to a covered-dish event or a
morning get-together.

—**BARB KEITH** EAU CLAIRE, WISCONSIN

PREP: 20 MIN. **COOK:** 4 HOURS **MAKES:** 10 SERVINGS

- 1 **package (32 ounces) frozen shredded hash brown potatoes**
- 1 **pound bacon strips, cooked and crumbled**
- 1 **medium onion, chopped**
- 1 **medium green pepper, chopped**

1½ **cups (6 ounces) shredded cheddar cheese**
12 **eggs**
 1 **cup milk**
 ½ **teaspoon salt**
 ½ **teaspoon pepper**

1. Layer a third of the potatoes, bacon, onion, green
pepper and cheese in a 5-qt. slow cooker coated with
cooking spray. Repeat layers twice. In a large bowl,
whisk eggs, milk, salt and pepper; pour over the top.
2. Cover and cook on high for 30 minutes. Reduce
heat to low; cook for 3½ to 4 hours or until a
thermometer reads 160°.

Slow-Cooked Spaghetti Sauce

PREP: 15 MIN. **COOK:** 7 HOURS
MAKES: 6-8 SERVINGS

- 1 **pound ground beef or bulk Italian sausage**
- 1 **medium onion, chopped**
- 2 **cans (14½ ounces each) diced tomatoes, undrained**
- 1 **can (8 ounces) tomato sauce**
- 1 **can (6 ounces) tomato paste**
- 1 **bay leaf**
- 1 **tablespoon brown sugar**
- 4 **garlic cloves, minced**
- 1 **to 2 teaspoons dried basil**
- 1 **to 2 teaspoons dried oregano**
- 1 **teaspoon salt**
- ½ **to 1 teaspoon dried thyme**
   Hot cooked spaghetti

1. In a large skillet, cook beef and onion over medium heat until meat is no longer pink; drain.

2. Transfer to a 3-qt. slow cooker. Add the next 10 ingredients. Cover and cook on low for 7-8 hours or until heated through. Discard bay leaf. Serve with spaghetti.

❝I like to serve this dish to company. Not only is it delicious and a snap to prepare, but it's economical, too. I'd be lost without my slow cooker!❞

—**SHELLEY MCKINNEY**
NEW CASTLE, INDIANA

Pizza in a Pot

This is one dinner I know my family will always eagerly devour. I like to serve warm breadsticks or garlic toast on the side.

—**DIANNA CLINE**
PHILIPPI, WEST VIRGINIA

PREP: 20 MIN. **COOK:** 3 HOURS
MAKES: 8 SERVINGS

- 1½ **pounds ground beef**
- 1 **medium green pepper, chopped**
- 1 **medium onion, chopped**
- 1 **can (15 ounces) tomato sauce**
- 1 **jar (14 ounces) pizza sauce**
- 2 **tablespoons tomato paste**
- 3 **cups spiral pasta, cooked and drained**
- 2 **packages (3½ ounces each) sliced pepperoni**
- 2 **cups (8 ounces) shredded part-skim mozzarella cheese**

1. In a large skillet, cook the beef, green pepper and onion over medium heat until meat is no longer pink; drain. Stir in the tomato sauce, pizza sauce and tomato paste.

2. In a 5-qt. slow cooker, layer the pasta, beef mixture, pepperoni and cheese. Cover and cook on low for 3-4 hours or until heated through.

Spicy Meatballs with Sauce

Italian sausage makes these meatballs extra flavorful and tender. This recipe rose quickly to the top of my husband's "most-requested" list.

—ROSANNE BERGMAN
ALTA LOMA, CALIFORNIA

PREP: 30 MIN. **COOK:** 5 HOURS
MAKES: 8 SERVINGS

- 1 **egg, lightly beaten**
- ¾ **cup crushed seasoned salad croutons**
- ½ **cup finely chopped onion**
- ¼ **cup finely chopped green pepper**
- 1 **teaspoon garlic powder**
- 1 **teaspoon ground cumin**
- 1 **teaspoon dried oregano**
- 1 **teaspoon pepper**
- 1 **pound bulk Italian sausage**
- 1 **pound ground turkey**

SAUCE
- 3 **tablespoons cornstarch**
- 1 **tablespoon sugar**
- ¾ **cup beef broth**
- 2 **cans (28 ounces each) crushed tomatoes**
- 3 **medium carrots, diced**
- 1 **can (6 ounces) tomato paste**

- 1 **envelope onion soup mix**
- 3 **garlic cloves, minced**
- 1 **teaspoon dried basil**
- ½ **teaspoon crushed red pepper flakes**
     Hot cooked pasta

1. In a large bowl, combine the egg, croutons, onion, green pepper, garlic powder, cumin, oregano and pepper. Crumble sausage and turkey over mixture and mix well. Shape into 1-in. balls. Place in a 5-qt. slow cooker.

2. In a large bowl, combine the cornstarch, sugar and broth until smooth; stir in the tomatoes, carrots, tomato paste, soup mix, garlic, basil and pepper flakes. Pour over meatballs. Cover and cook on low for 5-6 hours or until meatballs are cooked through. Serve with pasta.

3. Serve immediately or cool before placing in a freezer container. Cover and freeze for up to 3 months.

To use frozen meatballs: *Completely thaw in refrigerator. Place meatballs in a large skillet; cover and cook for 10 minutes or until heated through.*

FAST FIX ▶ Slow Cooker Salmon Loaf

I'm always looking for quick, easy dishes that can be prepared ahead of time. I also don't like to heat up my oven during our hot Georgia summers. So I adapted this recipe from one I found in an old slow-cooker book of my grandma's. I serve it with macaroni and cheese and pinto beans.

—KELLY RITTER
DOUGLASVILLE, GEORGIA

PREP: 10 MIN. **COOK:** 4 HOURS
MAKES: 6 SERVINGS

- 2 **eggs, lightly beaten**
- 2 **cups seasoned stuffing croutons**
- 1 **cup chicken broth**
- 1 **cup grated Parmesan cheese**
- ¼ **teaspoon ground mustard**
- 1 **can (14¾ ounces) salmon, drained, bones and skin removed**

1. Cut three 20-in. x 3-in. strips of heavy duty foil; crisscross so they resemble spokes of a wheel. Place strips on the bottom and up the sides of a 3-qt. slow cooker coated with cooking spray.

2. In a large bowl, combine the first five ingredients. Add salmon and mix well. Gently shape mixture into a round loaf. Place in the center of the strips.

3. Cover and cook on low for 4-6 hours or until a thermometer reads 160°. Using foil strips as handles, remove the loaf to a platter.

Burgundy Lamb Shanks

For those who love fall-off-the-bone lamb, this recipe fills the bill. Burgundy wine adds a special depth of flavor to the sauce that's served alongside.

—F. W. CREUTZ SOUTHOLD, NEW YORK

PREP: 10 MIN. **COOK:** 8¼ HOURS **MAKES:** 4 SERVINGS

- 4 lamb shanks (about
     20 ounces each)
     Salt and pepper to taste
- 2 tablespoons dried parsley flakes
- 2 teaspoons minced garlic
- ½ teaspoon dried oregano
- ½ teaspoon grated lemon peel
- ½ cup chopped onion
- 1 medium carrot, chopped
- 1 teaspoon olive oil
- 1 cup Burgundy wine
- 1 teaspoon beef bouillon granules

1. Sprinkle lamb with salt and pepper. Place in a 5-qt. slow cooker. Sprinkle with the parsley, garlic, oregano and lemon peel.

2. In a small saucepan, saute onion and carrot in oil for 3-4 minutes or until tender. Stir in wine and bouillon. Bring to a boil, stirring occasionally. Pour over lamb. Cover and cook on low for 8 hours or until meat is tender.

3. Remove lamb and keep warm. Strain cooking juices and skim fat. In a small saucepan, bring juices to a boil; cook until liquid is reduced by half. Serve with lamb.

178

189

196

Soups, Stews & Chili

Beef 'n' Beans Chili

I took this dish to a church function, and it was such a hit! Several ladies requested the recipe. It's so easy to make. Just put the ingredients in the slow cooker, and dinner's ready before you know it.

—**ANITA HUDSON** SAVOY, TEXAS

PREP: 15 MIN. **COOK:** 6 HOURS **MAKES:** 6-8 SERVINGS

- 3 pounds beef stew meat, cut into 1-inch cubes
- 2 tablespoons brown sugar
- 1½ teaspoons ground mustard
- 1 teaspoon salt
- 1 teaspoon paprika
- ½ teaspoon chili powder
- ¼ teaspoon pepper
- 1 large onion, chopped
- 2 cans (10 ounces each) diced tomatoes and green chilies, undrained
- 1 can (16 ounces) Ranch Style beans (pinto beans in seasoned tomato sauce)
- 1 can (15¼ ounces) whole kernel corn, drained

1. Place the beef in a 3-qt. slow cooker. Combine the brown sugar, mustard, salt, paprika, chili powder and pepper; sprinkle over beef and toss to coat. Top with onion, tomatoes, beans and corn.
2. Cover and cook on low for 6-8 hours or until meat is tender.

Beef Vegetable Soup

Convenient frozen veggies and hash browns make this meaty soup a snap to mix up. Simply brown the ground beef, then stir everything together to simmer all day. It's wonderful served with crusty bread and a salad.

—**CAROL CALHOUN** SIOUX FALLS, SOUTH DAKOTA

PREP: 10 MIN. **COOK:** 8 HOURS
MAKES: 10 SERVINGS (2½ QUARTS)

- 1 pound ground beef
- 1 can (46 ounces) tomato juice
- 1 package (16 ounces) frozen mixed vegetables, thawed
- 2 cups frozen cubed hash brown potatoes, thawed
- 1 envelope onion soup mix

1. In a large skillet, cook beef over medium heat until no longer pink; drain. Transfer to a 5-qt. slow cooker. Stir in the tomato juice, mixed vegetables, potatoes and soup mix.
2. Cover and cook on low for 8-10 hours or until heated through.

Loaded Vegetable Beef Stew

I first had this dish during a trip to Argentina a few years ago and was inspired to re-create it at home. It turned out so well, I wrote "Yum!" on the recipe card!

—KARI CAVEN COEUR D'ALENE, IDAHO

PREP: 40 MIN. **COOK:** 8½ HOURS
MAKES: 12 SERVINGS (1⅓ CUPS EACH)

- 8 **bacon strips, diced**
- 3 **pounds beef stew meat, cut into 1-inch cubes**
- 6 **medium carrots, cut into 1-inch pieces**
- 6 **medium tomatoes, peeled and cut into wedges**
- 4 **medium potatoes, peeled and cubed**
- 3 **cups cubed peeled butternut squash**
- 2 **medium green peppers, chopped**
- 2 **teaspoons dried thyme**
- 2 **garlic cloves, minced**
- 2 **cans (14½ ounces each) beef broth**
- 6 **cups chopped cabbage**
- ½ **teaspoon pepper**

1. In a large skillet, cook bacon over medium heat until crisp. Using a slotted spoon, remove to paper towels to drain. In the drippings, brown beef in batches. Refrigerate the bacon until serving.
2. In a 6-qt. slow cooker, combine the carrots, tomatoes, potatoes, squash, green peppers, thyme and garlic. Top with beef. Pour broth over the top. Cover and cook on low for 8-10 hours.
3. Stir in cabbage and pepper. Cover and cook on high for 30 minutes or until cabbage is tender. Sprinkle each serving with bacon.

Savory Cheese Soup

This small-batch soup is a perfect treat on wintry days. It's so delicious and satisfying, you just might wish there were leftovers!

—ANN HUSEBY
LAKEVILLE, MINNESOTA

PREP: 10 MIN. **COOK:** 5¾ HOURS
MAKES: 2 SERVINGS

- 1 can (14½ ounces) chicken broth
- ¼ cup chopped carrot
- ¼ cup chopped celery
- 1 tablespoon chopped onion
- 1 tablespoon chopped sweet red pepper
- 2 teaspoons butter
- ⅛ to ¼ teaspoon pepper
- 2 tablespoons all-purpose flour
- 2 tablespoons cold water
- 1 package (3 ounces) cream cheese, cubed
- ¾ cup shredded cheddar cheese
- ⅓ cup beer or additional chicken broth
  Croutons, crumbled cooked bacon and sliced green onions, optional

1. In a 1½-qt. slow cooker, combine the first seven ingredients. Cover and cook on low for 5-6 hours or until vegetables are tender.
2. Combine flour and water until smooth; stir into soup. Cover and cook on high for 30 minutes or until thickened.
3. Stir in the cream cheese, cheddar cheese and beer. Cover and cook on low for 15 minutes or until cheeses are melted. Top with croutons, bacon and green onions if desired.

Bacon-Beef Barley Soup

Here's a robust dish that's just the thing for hungry teenage boys! Served over creamy mashed potatoes, this quick, comforting soup will really hit the spot.

—CATHY PETERSON
MENOMINEE, MICHIGAN

PREP: 40 MIN. **COOK:** 7 HOURS
MAKES: 7 SERVINGS

- 4 bacon strips, chopped
- 1½ pounds beef stew meat, cut into ½-inch pieces
- 1 medium onion, chopped
- 4 medium red potatoes, cut into ½-inch cubes
- 1½ cups fresh baby carrots, cut in half lengthwise
- 1 cup frozen corn
- ¼ cup medium pearl barley
- 2 cans (14½ ounces each) beef broth
- 1 can (14½ ounces) diced tomatoes with basil, oregano and garlic, undrained
- 1 jar (12 ounces) home-style beef gravy
- ½ teaspoon pepper
  Mashed potatoes, optional

1. In a large skillet, cook bacon over medium heat until crisp. Using a slotted spoon, remove to paper towels to drain. In the drippings, cook beef and onion until meat is no longer pink; drain.
2. In a 5-qt. slow cooker, layer the potatoes, carrots, corn and barley. Top with beef mixture and bacon. Combine the broth, tomatoes, gravy and pepper; pour over top (do not stir).
3. Cover and cook on low for 7-9 hours or until meat and vegetables are tender. Stir before serving. Serve over mashed potatoes if desired.

Zesty Beef Stew

Preparation couldn't be simpler for this hearty no-fuss stew! I created the recipe when I didn't have some of my usual ingredients for vegetable beef soup. My husband says it's the best I ever made!

—MARGARET TURZA
SOUTH BEND, INDIANA

PREP: 10 MIN. **COOK:** 3½ HOURS
MAKES: 6 SERVINGS

- 1 **pound beef stew meat, cut into 1-inch cubes**
- 1 **package (16 ounces) frozen mixed vegetables, thawed**
- 1 **can (15 ounces) pinto beans, rinsed and drained**
- 1½ **cups water**
- 1 **can (8 ounces) pizza sauce**
- 2 **tablespoons medium pearl barley**
- 1 **tablespoon dried minced onion**
- 2 **teaspoons beef bouillon granules**
- ¼ **teaspoon crushed red pepper flakes**

In a 3-qt. slow cooker, combine all ingredients. Cover and cook on low for 3½ to 4½ hours or until meat is tender.

Forgotten Minestrone

This soup gets its name because the broth simmers for hours, allowing me to work on my freelance writing. But after one taste, you and your family will agree this full-flavored soup is truly unforgettable!

—MARSHA RANSOM
SOUTH HAVEN, MICHIGAN

PREP: 15 MIN. **COOK:** 8½ HOURS
MAKES: 8 SERVINGS (2 QUARTS)

- 1 **pound beef stew meat, cut into ½-inch cubes**
- 1 **can (28 ounces) diced tomatoes, undrained**
- 1 **medium onion, chopped**
- 2 **tablespoons minced dried parsley**
- 2½ **teaspoons salt, optional**
- 1½ **teaspoons ground thyme**
- 1 **beef bouillon cube**
- ½ **teaspoon pepper**
- 6 **cups water**
- 1 **medium zucchini, halved and thinly sliced**
- 2 **cups chopped cabbage**
- 1 **can (15 ounces) garbanzo beans or chickpeas, rinsed and drained**
- 1 **cup uncooked elbow macaroni**
- ¼ **cup grated Parmesan cheese, optional**

1. In a 5-qt. slow cooker, combine the first nine ingredients. Cover and cook on low for 8-10 hours or until meat is tender.
2. Add the zucchini, cabbage, beans and macaroni; cover and cook on high for 30-45 minutes or until macaroni and vegetables are tender. Sprinkle servings with cheese if desired.

Great Northern Bean Chili

My easy version of Southwestern chicken chili uses just a few ingredients. I like to serve it with tortilla chips, sour cream and a dash of hot sauce on top. It's a great alternative to traditional chili.

—**MAMESMOM** TASTE OF HOME ONLINE COMMUNITY

PREP: 20 MIN.   **COOK:** 4 HOURS   **MAKES:** 8 SERVINGS

- 2 **pounds boneless skinless chicken breasts, cut into 1-inch cubes**
- 1 **tablespoon canola oil**
- 1 **jar (48 ounces) great northern beans, rinsed and drained**
- 1 **jar (16 ounces) salsa**
- 1 **can (14½ ounces) chicken broth**
- 1 **teaspoon ground cumin, optional**
- 2 **cups (8 ounces) shredded Monterey Jack cheese**

1. In a large skillet, brown chicken in oil. In a 4- or 5-qt. slow cooker, combine the beans, salsa, broth, cumin if desired and chicken.

2. Cover and cook on low for 4-6 hours or until chicken is tender. Serve with cheese.

Chunky Chicken Soup

I am a stay-at-home mom who relies on my slow cooker for fast, nutritious meals with minimal prep and cleanup time. I knew this recipe was a hit when I didn't have any leftovers and my husband asked me to make it again.

—**NANCY CLOW**
MALLORYTOWN, ONTARIO

PREP: 15 MIN. **COOK:** 4½ HOURS
MAKES: 7 SERVINGS

- 1½ pounds boneless skinless chicken breasts, cut into 2-inch strips
- 2 teaspoons canola oil
- ⅔ cup finely chopped onion
- 2 medium carrots, chopped
- 2 celery ribs, chopped
- 1 cup frozen corn
- 2 cans (10¾ ounces each) condensed cream of potato soup, undiluted
- 1½ cups chicken broth
- 1 teaspoon dill weed
- 1 cup frozen peas
- ½ cup half-and-half cream

1. In a large skillet over medium-high heat, brown chicken in oil. Transfer to a 5-qt. slow cooker; add the onion, carrots, celery and corn.
2. In a large bowl, whisk the soup, broth and dill until blended; stir into slow cooker. Cover and cook on low for 4 hours or until chicken and vegetables are tender.
3. Stir in peas and cream. Cover and cook 30 minutes longer or until heated through.

Creamy Cabbage-Pork Stew

Savory flavors blend beautifully in this easy and filling stew. In a pinch, I sometimes use a ring of cut-up garlic bologna instead of stew meat.

—**RUTH ANN STELFOX**
RAYMOND, ALBERTA

PREP: 20 MIN. **COOK:** 6 HOURS
MAKES: 6 SERVINGS

- 1 pound pork stew meat
- 1 tablespoon canola oil
- 3 cups coarsely chopped cabbage
- 2 cans (10¾ ounces each) condensed cream of celery soup, undiluted
- 1½ cups apple juice
- 2 medium red potatoes, cut into 1-inch pieces
- 3 medium carrots, sliced
- ¼ teaspoon caraway seeds
- ¼ teaspoon pepper
- ½ cup 2% milk

1. In a large skillet over medium-high heat, brown pork in oil on all sides; drain.
2. Transfer pork to a 3-qt. slow cooker; stir in the cabbage, soup, apple juice, potatoes, carrots, caraway and pepper. Cover and cook on low for 6-8 hours or until pork and vegetables are tender. Stir in milk; heat through.

Creamy Ham Chowder

It's wonderful to have this satisfying chowder hot and ready for wintertime guests. They'll think you labored for hours preparing it.

—LEE BREMSON
KANSAS CITY, MISSOURI

PREP: 30 MIN. **COOK:** 3½ HOURS
MAKES: 12 SERVINGS
(ABOUT 3½ QUARTS)

- 4 **cups cubed peeled potatoes**
- 2 **tablespoons chopped onion**
- ½ **cup butter**
- ¾ **cup all-purpose flour**
- ¼ **teaspoon salt**
- ¼ **teaspoon pepper**
  Pinch ground nutmeg
- 4 **cups chicken broth**
- 4 **cups half-and-half cream**
- 2 **cups (8 ounces) shredded cheddar cheese**
- 3 **cups cubed fully cooked ham**
- 1 **package (16 ounces) frozen broccoli cuts, thawed and drained**

1. Place potatoes in a large saucepan and cover with water. Bring to a boil. Reduce heat; cover and cook for 10-15 minutes or until tender.

2. Meanwhile, in another large saucepan, cook onion in butter over medium heat for 4 minutes. Stir in the flour, salt, pepper and nutmeg; gradually add broth. Bring to a boil; cook and stir for 2 minutes or until thickened. Stir in cream and cheese.

3. Transfer to a 5-qt. slow cooker. Drain the potatoes; add to slow cooker. Stir in ham. Cover and cook on low for 3-4 hours.

4. Stir in broccoli. Cover and cook 30 minutes longer or until heated through.

French Onion Soup

It's hard to believe something this delightful came from a slow cooker! Topped with French bread and melted provolone cheese, individual servings are sure to be enjoyed by everyone at your dinner table.

—KRIS RITTER
PITTSBURGH, PENNSYLVANIA

PREP: 15 MIN. **COOK:** 8 HOURS
MAKES: 4 SERVINGS

- 2 **large sweet onions, thinly sliced (about 4 cups)**
- ¼ **cup butter, cubed**
- 2 **cans (14½ ounces each) beef broth**
- 2 **tablespoons sherry or additional beef broth**
- ½ **teaspoon pepper**
- 4 **slices French bread (½ inch thick), toasted**
- 4 **slices provolone cheese**

1. Place onions and butter in a 1½-qt. slow cooker coated with cooking spray. Cover and cook on low for 6 hours or until onions are tender. Stir in the broth, sherry and pepper. Cover and cook 2-3 hours longer or until heated through.

2. Ladle soup into ovenproof bowls. Top each with a slice of toast and cheese. Broil 4-6 in. from the heat for 2-3 minutes or until cheese is melted. Serve immediately.

Hearty Pork Stew

Here's a spicy slow-cooked stew that combines tender chunks of pork with veggies. I garnish bowls of it with chopped green onions and hard-cooked eggs.
—**REBECCA OVERY** EVANSTON, WYOMING

PREP: 10 MIN.   **COOK:** 8½ HOURS   **MAKES:** 8 SERVINGS

- 1½ to 2 pounds boneless pork, cut into 1-inch cubes
- 4 cups water
- 1 can (14½ ounces) stewed tomatoes
- 1 medium onion, chopped
- 1 medium green pepper, chopped
- ⅓ cup reduced-sodium soy sauce
- 1 to 2 tablespoons chili powder
- 1 tablespoon dried celery flakes
- ½ teaspoon garlic powder
- ½ teaspoon pepper
- ⅓ cup cornstarch
- ⅓ cup cold water
  Hot cooked noodles

1. In a 3-qt. slow cooker, combine the first 10 ingredients. Cover and cook on low for 8-10 hours or until meat is tender.

2. Combine cornstarch and water until smooth; gradually stir into slow cooker. Cover and cook on high for 30 minutes or until slightly thickened. Serve in bowls with noodles.

Mexican Beef Stew

Instead of chuck roast, you can also use eye of round for this recipe. Or try serving it with noodles, rice or flour tortillas if you like. Delish!

—PAT DAZIS
CHARLOTTE, NORTH CAROLINA

PREP: 30 MIN. **COOK:** 6 HOURS
MAKES: 8 SERVINGS (4½ QUARTS)

- 4 medium potatoes, peeled and cubed
- 1 can (16 ounces) fat-free refried beans
- 1 can (14½ ounces) reduced-sodium beef broth
- 1 can (10 ounces) enchilada sauce
- 2 cups frozen corn
- 1 large red onion, chopped
- 1 can (4 ounces) chopped green chilies
- 2 tablespoons chopped pickled jalapeno slices
- 1 tablespoon lime juice
- 1 teaspoon ground cumin
  Dash crushed red pepper flakes
- 1 boneless beef chuck roast (3 to 4 pounds)
  Sour cream

1. In a 5-qt. slow cooker, combine the first 11 ingredients. Cut roast in half; transfer to slow cooker.
2. Cover and cook on low for 6-8 hours or until meat and vegetables are tender.
3. Remove meat; cool slightly. Cut meat into bite-sized pieces and return to slow cooker; heat through. Serve with sour cream.

Cauliflower Cheese Soup

Whenever there's a chill in the air, I like to make soup for my family. Cheese adds flavor and creaminess to this one, which is my own recipe.

—RUTH WORDEN
MOSSENA, NEW YORK

PREP: 30 MIN. **COOK:** 3¾ HOURS
MAKES: 8 SERVINGS (2 QUARTS)

- 1 large head cauliflower, broken into florets
- 2 cups chicken broth
- 2 tablespoons reduced-sodium chicken bouillon granules
- 2 cups half-and-half cream
- 2 cups 2% milk
- 1 medium carrot, shredded
- 2 bay leaves
- ¼ teaspoon garlic powder
- ½ cup mashed potato flakes
- 2 cups (8 ounces) shredded cheddar cheese
  Paprika

1. In a large saucepan, combine the cauliflower, broth and bouillon. Bring to a boil. Reduce heat; cover and cook for 20 minutes or until tender. Mash cauliflower.
2. Transfer to a 3-qt. slow cooker. Stir in the cream, milk, carrot, bay leaves and garlic powder. Cover and cook on low for 3 hours. Stir in potato flakes.
3. Cook 30 minutes longer or until thickened. Discard bay leaves. Cool slightly.
4. In a blender, process soup in batches until smooth. Return to the slow cooker; stir in cheese. Cook until soup is heated through and cheese is melted. Garnish with paprika.

Tomato Hamburger Soup

As a full-time teacher, I only have time to prepare meals a few nights each week. This recipe makes a big enough batch to feed my family for two nights.

—JULIE KRUGER
ST. CLOUD, MINNESOTA

PREP: 10 MIN. **COOK:** 4 HOURS
MAKES: 12 SERVINGS (3 QUARTS)

- 1 can (46 ounces) V8 juice
- 2 packages (16 ounces each) frozen mixed vegetables
- 1 pound ground beef, cooked and drained
- 1 can (10¾ ounces) condensed cream of mushroom soup, undiluted
- 2 teaspoons dried minced onion
   Salt and pepper to taste

In a 5-qt. slow cooker, combine the first five ingredients. Cover and cook on high for 4-5 hours or until heated through. Season with salt and pepper.

Beef & Vegetable Soup

I've been making this recipe for more than 20 years. The beer always makes people stop and wonder what the unique flavor is.

—TAMMY LANDRY
SAUCIER, MISSISSIPPI

PREP: 20 MIN. **COOK:** 8 HOURS
MAKES: 6 SERVINGS

- 1 pound lean ground beef (90% lean)
- ½ cup chopped sweet onion
- 1 bottle (12 ounces) beer or nonalcoholic beer
- 1 can (10½ ounces) condensed beef broth, undiluted
- 1½ cups sliced fresh carrots
- 1¼ cups water
- 1 cup chopped peeled turnip
- ½ cup sliced celery
- 1 can (4 ounces) mushroom stems and pieces, drained
- 1 teaspoon salt
- 1 teaspoon pepper
- 1 bay leaf
- ⅛ teaspoon ground allspice

In a large skillet, cook beef and onion over medium heat until meat is no longer pink; drain. Transfer to a 5-qt. slow cooker. Stir in the remaining ingredients. Cover and cook on low for 8-10 hours or until heated through. Discard bay leaf.

Butternut Squash Soup

The golden color, smooth and creamy texture and wonderful taste of this soup is so welcome on a chilly fall day. It has a slightly tangy flavor from the cream cheese, and the cinnamon really comes through.

—**JACKIE CAMPBELL** STANHOPE, NEW JERSEY

PREP: 30 MIN. **COOK:** 6¼ HOURS
MAKES: 14 SERVINGS (2½ QUARTS)

- **1 medium onion, chopped**
- **2 tablespoons butter**
- **1 medium butternut squash (about 4 pounds), peeled and cubed**
- **3 cans (14½ ounces each) vegetable broth**
- **1 tablespoon brown sugar**
- **1 tablespoon minced fresh gingerroot**
- **1 garlic clove, minced**
- **1 cinnamon stick (3 inches)**
- **1 package (8 ounces) cream cheese, softened and cubed**

1. In a small skillet, saute onion in butter until tender. Transfer to a 5-or 6-quart slow cooker; add squash. Combine the broth, brown sugar, ginger, garlic and cinnamon; pour over squash. Cover and cook on low for 6-8 hours or until squash is tender.
2. Cool slightly. Discard cinnamon stick. In a blender, process soup in batches until smooth. Return all to slow cooker. Whisk in cream cheese; cover and cook 15 minutes longer or until cheese is melted.

Texas Stew

As a mother of young children, I rely on family-friendly recipes more and more. Everyone enjoys this stew.

—KIM BALSTAD LEWISVILLE, TEXAS

PREP: 15 MIN. **COOK:** 6 HOURS
MAKES: 10-12 SERVINGS

- 1½ **pounds ground beef**
- 1 **medium onion, chopped**
- 1 **can (15½ ounces) hominy, drained**
- 1 **can (15¼ ounces) whole kernel corn, drained**
- 1 **can (15 ounces) sliced carrots, drained**
- 1 **can (15 ounces) sliced potatoes, drained**
- 1 **can (16 ounces) Ranch Style beans (pinto beans in seasoned tomato sauce)**
- 1 **can (14½ ounces) diced tomatoes, undrained**
- 1 **cup water**
- 1 **teaspoon beef bouillon granules**
- ½ **teaspoon garlic powder**
  Chili powder to taste
  Dash Worcestershire sauce
  Dash hot pepper sauce

1. In a large skillet, cook beef and onion over medium heat until meat is no longer pink; drain. Transfer to a 5-qt. slow cooker. Stir in the remaining ingredients.
2. Cover and cook on low for 6-8 hours or until heated through.

HOMINY

Hominy is made from white or yellow corn that has been treated to remove the hull and inner germ. The puffy kernels have a mild flavor and tender, interesting texture. Grits, the Southern favorite, are made from dried and ground hominy.

Chicken Stew with Gnocchi

My chicken stew fills the house with a wonderful aroma as it bubbles in the slow cooker. Just one whiff and my family heads to the kitchen to see if it's ready!

—MARGE DRAKE JUNIATA, NEBRASKA

PREP: 25 MIN. **COOK:** 6½ HOURS
MAKES: 8 SERVINGS (3 QUARTS)

- 3 **medium parsnips, peeled and cut into ½-inch pieces**
- 2 **large carrots, cut into ½-inch slices**
- 2 **celery ribs, chopped**
- 1 **large sweet potato, peeled and cut into 1-inch cubes**
- 4 **green onions, chopped**
- 3 **pounds bone-in chicken thighs, skin removed**
- ½ **teaspoon dried sage leaves**
- ¼ **teaspoon salt**
- ¼ **teaspoon pepper**
- 4 **cups chicken broth**
- 1 **cup water**
- 3 **tablespoons cornstarch**
- ¼ **cup cold water**
- 1 **package (16 ounces) potato gnocchi**
  Hot pepper sauce, optional

1. Place the parsnips, carrots, celery, sweet potato and onions in a 5-qt. slow cooker. Top with chicken; sprinkle with the sage, salt and pepper. Add the broth and water. Cover and cook on low for 6-8 hours or until the chicken is tender.
2. Remove chicken; when cool enough to handle, remove meat from bones and discard bones. Cut meat into bite-size pieces and return to the slow cooker.
3. Mix cornstarch and cold water until smooth; stir into stew. Add the gnocchi. Cover and cook on high for 30 minutes or until thickened. Season with hot pepper sauce if desired.

Skier's Stew

Assemble this in the morning, put it in the slow cooker and hit the slopes for the whole day! After coming in from the cold, it's so good to have a hot meal waiting when I get home.

—TRACI GANGWER
DENVER, COLORADO

PREP: 20 MIN. **COOK:** 4½ HOURS
MAKES: 8 SERVINGS (3 QUARTS)

- 2 pounds beef stew meat, cut into 1-inch cubes
- 2 tablespoons canola oil
- 8 medium carrots, cut into 1-inch slices
- 6 large potatoes, peeled and cut into 1-inch cubes
- 1 can (15 ounces) tomato sauce
- 1 to 1½ cups water
- 1 envelope onion soup mix

1. In a large skillet, brown meat in batches in oil; drain. Transfer to a 5-qt. slow cooker. Top with vegetables. Combine the tomato sauce, water and soup mix; pour over the top.

2. Cover and cook on low for 4½ to 5 hours or until meat and vegetables are tender.

Zippy Spanish Rice Soup

I created this recipe after ruining a dinner of Spanish rice. I tried to salvage the dish by adding green chiles, cilantro and more water. It was a hit with the whole family! This is hearty enough to be a main dish when served with a garden salad and some corn bread.

—MARILYN SCHETZ
CUYAHOGA FALLS, OHIO

PREP: 20 MIN. **COOK:** 4 HOURS
MAKES: 8 SERVINGS (2 QUARTS)

- 1 pound lean ground beef (90% lean)
- 1 medium onion, chopped
- 3 cups water
- 1 jar (16 ounces) salsa
- 1 can (14½ ounces) diced tomatoes, undrained
- 1 jar (7 ounces) roasted sweet red peppers, drained and chopped
- 1 can (4 ounces) chopped green chilies
- 1 envelope taco seasoning
- 1 tablespoon dried cilantro flakes
- ½ cup uncooked converted rice

1. In a large skillet, cook beef and onion over medium heat until meat is no longer pink; drain.

2. Transfer to a 4- or 5-qt. slow cooker. Add the water, salsa, tomatoes, red peppers, chilies, taco seasoning and cilantro. Stir in rice. Cover and cook on low for 4-5 hours or until rice is tender.

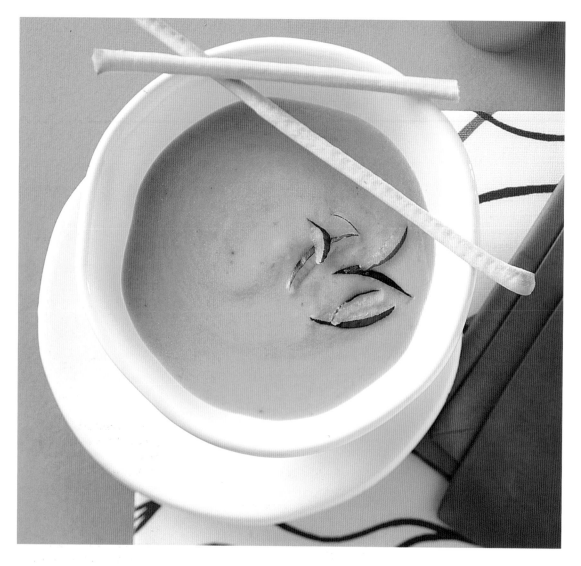

Cheesy Cauliflower Soup

If you prefer chunky soup, skip the blender step and stir
the cheese and cream right into the slow cooker, then
heat on high until the cheese is melted.

—SHERYL PUNTER WOODSTOCK, ONTARIO

PREP: 25 MIN. **COOK:** 5½ HOURS
MAKES: 9 SERVINGS (2¼ QUARTS)

- 1 **large head cauliflower, broken into florets**
- 2 **celery ribs**
- 2 **large carrots**
- 1 **large green pepper**
- 1 **small sweet red pepper**
- 1 **medium red onion**
- 4 **cups chicken broth**
- ½ **teaspoon Worcestershire sauce**
- ¼ **teaspoon salt**
- ⅛ **teaspoon pepper**
- 2 **cups (8 ounces) shredded cheddar cheese**
- 2 **cups half-and-half cream**

1. Place cauliflower in a 4-qt. slow cooker. Chop the
celery, carrots, peppers and onion; add to slow cooker.
Stir in the broth, Worcestershire sauce, salt and
pepper. Cover and cook on low for 5-6 hours or until
vegetables are tender.
2. In a blender, process soup in batches until smooth.
Return all to slow cooker; stir in cheese and cream.
Cover and cook on high for 30 minutes or until cheese
is melted.

Slow-Cooked Potato Soup

I make this healthy potato soup every year for St. Patrick's Day, and we always look forward to it.

—MARY JO O'BRIEN
HASTINGS, MINNESOTA

PREP: 30 MIN. **COOK:** 5 HOURS
MAKES: 2 SERVINGS

- 2¾ cups cubed peeled potatoes, divided
- 1⅓ cups water
- 2 tablespoons butter, cubed
- ⅔ cup cubed fully cooked ham
- 1 celery rib, chopped
- ⅓ cup chopped onion
- ¼ teaspoon garlic powder
- ¼ teaspoon paprika
  Dash pepper
- ¼ pound process cheese (Velveeta), cubed
- ⅓ cup sour cream
  Milk, optional

1. Place 2 cups of potatoes in a saucepan; add water. Bring to a boil. Reduce heat; cover and cook for 10-15 minutes or until tender. Remove from the heat (do not drain). Mash potatoes; stir in butter.
2. In a 1½-qt. slow cooker, combine the ham, celery, onion, garlic powder, paprika, pepper and remaining cubed potatoes. Stir in mashed potatoes; top with cheese. Cover and cook on low for 5-6 hours or until vegetables are tender. Stir in the sour cream until blended. Thin soup with milk if desired.

Chipotle-Black Bean Chili

This thick, slow-cooked chili is really special to me because it cooks itself while I'm at work. My family and friends love it. It's especially nice served with corn bread.

—PATRICIA NIEH
PORTOLA VALLEY, CALIFORNIA

PREP: 15 MIN. **COOK:** 7 HOURS
MAKES: 8 SERVINGS (2½ QUARTS)

- 2 cans (15 ounces each) black beans, rinsed and drained
- 2 cans (14½ ounces each) fire-roasted diced tomatoes, undrained
- 1 large onion, finely chopped
- 1 medium green pepper, finely chopped
- 2 chipotle peppers in adobo sauce, finely chopped
- 2 tablespoons adobo sauce
- 2 garlic cloves, minced
- 1 boneless beef chuck roast (2 pounds), cut into 1-inch cubes
- 1 tablespoon ground cumin
- 1 tablespoon dried oregano
- ½ teaspoon salt
- ½ teaspoon pepper
  Optional toppings: shredded Monterey Jack cheese, reduced-fat sour cream, minced fresh cilantro and lime wedges

1. In a large bowl, combine the beans, tomatoes, onion, green pepper, chipotle peppers, adobo sauce and garlic. In another bowl, combine the beef, cumin, oregano, salt and pepper.
2. Pour half of the tomato mixture into a 4- or 5-qt. slow cooker; add the beef. Top with remaining tomato mixture. Cover and cook on low for 7-9 hours or until meat is tender. Serve with toppings of your choice.

Sausage Pasta Stew

I use my slow cooker to whip up this hearty pasta specialty. It's packed with turkey sausage, beans and veggies. My gang gobbles it up without even realizing that they're eating healthy!

—SARA BOWEN UPLAND, CALIFORNIA

PREP: 20 MIN. **COOK:** 7¼ HOURS
MAKES: 8 SERVINGS

- 1 **pound turkey Italian sausage links, casings removed**
- 4 **cups water**
- 1 **jar (26 ounces) meatless spaghetti sauce**
- 1 **can (16 ounces) kidney beans, rinsed and drained**
- 1 **medium yellow summer squash, halved lengthwise and cut into 1-inch pieces**
- 2 **medium carrots, sliced**
- 1 **medium sweet red or green pepper, diced**
- ⅓ **cup chopped onion**
- 1½ **cups uncooked spiral pasta**
- 1 **cup frozen peas**
- 1 **teaspoon sugar**
- ½ **teaspoon salt**
- ¼ **teaspoon pepper**

1. In a large nonstick skillet, cook the sausage over medium heat until no longer pink; drain and place in a 5-qt. slow cooker. Stir in the water, spaghetti sauce, beans, summer squash, carrots, red pepper and onion.
2. Cover and cook on low for 7-9 hours or until the vegetables are tender.
3. Stir in the pasta, peas, sugar, salt and pepper. Cover and cook on high for 15-20 minutes or until pasta is tender.

Slow-Cooked White Chili

This satisfying, slow-simmered chili features chicken, two kinds of beans and crunchy corn. A family favorite that we enjoy with corn bread, it's quick, easy and tastes great.

—LORI WEBER WENTZVILLE, MISSOURI

PREP: 25 MIN. **COOK:** 5 HOURS
MAKES: 8 SERVINGS (2 QUARTS)

- ¾ **pound boneless skinless chicken breasts, cubed**
- 1 **medium onion, chopped**
- 1 **tablespoon canola oil**
- 1 **garlic clove, minced**
- 1½ **cups water**
- 1 **can (15 ounces) white kidney or cannellini beans, rinsed and drained**
- 1 **can (15 ounces) garbanzo beans or chickpeas, rinsed and drained**
- 1 **can (11 ounces) whole kernel white corn, drained or 1¼ cups frozen shoepeg corn**
- 1 **can (4 ounces) chopped green chilies**
- 1 **to 2 teaspoons chicken bouillon granules**
- 1 **teaspoon ground cumin**

1. In a large skillet, saute chicken and onion in oil until onion is tender. Add garlic; cook 1 minute longer. Transfer to a 3-qt. slow cooker. Stir in the remaining ingredients.
2. Cover and cook on low for 5-6 hours or until the chicken is tender.

Southwest Turkey Stew

I prefer main dishes that let me stay on my diet but still eat what the rest of the family is having. This healthy stew is a hit with both my husband and our young children.

—STEPHANIE HUTCHINSON HELIX, OREGON

PREP: 15 MIN. **COOK:** 5 HOURS **MAKES:** 6 SERVINGS

1½ pounds turkey breast tenderloins, cubed
2 teaspoons canola oil
1 can (15 ounces) turkey chili with beans, undrained
1 can (14½ ounces) diced tomatoes
1 medium sweet red pepper, chopped
1 medium green pepper, chopped
¾ cup chopped onion
¾ cup salsa
3 garlic cloves, minced
1½ teaspoons chili powder
½ teaspoon salt
½ teaspoon ground cumin
1 tablespoon minced fresh cilantro, optional

In a nonstick skillet, brown turkey in oil; transfer to a 3-qt. slow cooker. Stir in the chili, tomatoes, peppers, onion, salsa, garlic, chili powder, salt and cumin. Cover and cook on low for 5-6 hours or until turkey is no longer pink. Garnish with cilantro if desired.

Cabbage Patch Stew

I like to serve steaming helpings of this hearty stew with thick slices of homemade bread. For a quicker prep, substitute coleslaw mix for the chopped cabbage.

—KAREN ANN BLAND GOVE, KANSAS

PREP: 20 MIN. **COOK:** 6 HOURS
MAKES: 8 SERVINGS (2 QUARTS)

- 1 pound lean ground beef (90% lean)
- 1 cup chopped onions
- 2 celery ribs, chopped
- 11 cups coarsely chopped cabbage (about 2 pounds)
- 2 cans (14½ ounces each) stewed tomatoes, undrained
- 1 can (15 ounces) pinto beans, rinsed and drained
- 1 can (10 ounces) diced tomatoes with green chilies, undrained
- ½ cup ketchup
- 1 to 1½ teaspoons chili powder
- ½ teaspoon dried oregano
- ½ teaspoon pepper
- ¼ teaspoon salt
  Sour cream and shredded cheddar cheese, optional

1. In a large skillet, cook the beef, onions and celery over medium heat until meat is no longer pink; drain.
2. Transfer to a 5-qt. slow cooker. Stir in the cabbage, stewed tomatoes, beans, diced tomatoes, ketchup, chili powder, oregano, pepper and salt. Cover and cook on low for 6-8 hours or until cabbage is tender.
3. Serve with sour cream and cheese if desired.

Hearty Split Pea Soup

We started a 39-day soup challenge to eat healthfully after the holidays, figuring if "Survivor" contestants could last for 39 days on little food, surely we could survive on soup! This was our family favorite.

—DEBRA KEIL OWASSO, OKLAHOMA

PREP: 30 MIN. **COOK:** 7 HOURS
MAKES: 6 SERVINGS (2¼ QUARTS)

- 1 large onion, chopped
- 1 cup chopped celery
- 1 cup chopped fresh carrots
- 1 teaspoon dried thyme
- 2 tablespoons olive oil
- 1 package (16 ounces) dried green split peas, rinsed
- 4 cups vegetable broth
- 2 cups water
- 6 ounces Canadian bacon, chopped
- ¼ teaspoon pepper

1. In a large skillet, saute the onion, celery and carrots in oil until tender. Add thyme; cook 1 minute longer.
2. Transfer to a 5-qt. slow cooker. Add the peas, broth and water. Cover and cook on low for 7-8 hours or until peas are tender.
3. Cool slightly. In a blender, process half of the soup until smooth. Return all to the slow cooker. Add bacon and pepper; heat through.

Creamy Bratwurst Stew

I adapted a baked stew recipe from the newspaper to create this hearty slow-cooked version. Rich and creamy, it is so comforting on cold winter nights!

—SUSAN HOLMES
GERMANTOWN, WISCONSIN

PREP: 20 MIN. **COOK:** 6½ HOURS
MAKES: 8 SERVINGS

- 4 medium potatoes, cubed
- 2 medium carrots, coarsely chopped
- 2 celery ribs, chopped
- 1 cup chopped onion
- ¾ cup chopped green pepper
- 2 pounds fresh bratwurst links, cut into 1-inch slices
- ½ cup chicken broth
- 1 teaspoon salt
- 1 teaspoon dried basil
- ½ teaspoon pepper
- 2 cups half-and-half cream
- 3 tablespoons cornstarch
- 3 tablespoons cold water

1. In a 5-qt. slow cooker, combine the potatoes, carrots, celery, onion and green pepper. Top with bratwurst slices. Combine the broth, salt, basil and pepper; pour over top. Cover and cook on low for 6-7 hours or until a thermometer reads 160° and vegetables are tender.

2. Stir in cream. Combine cornstarch and water until smooth; stir into stew. Cover and cook on high for 30 minutes or until thickened.

Veggie Potato Soup

Chock-full of potatoes, my vegetarian soup is as filling as it is flavorful. I love using my slow cooker. It makes mealtime during the week s much less stressful.

—HANNAH THOMPSON
SCOTTS VALLEY, CALIFORNIA

PREP: 20 MIN. **COOK:** 5½ HOURS
MAKES: 11 SERVINGS (2¾ QUARTS)

- 3 cans (14½ ounces each) vegetable broth
- 6 medium potatoes, cubed
- 1 medium carrot, thinly sliced
- 1 large leek (white portion only), chopped
- ¼ cup butter, cubed
- 1 garlic clove, minced
- 1 teaspoon dried thyme
- ¾ teaspoon salt
- ¼ teaspoon dried marjoram
- ¼ teaspoon pepper
- ¼ cup all-purpose flour
- 1½ cups half-and-half cream
- 1 cup frozen peas, thawed

1. In a 5-qt. slow cooker, combine the first 10 ingredients. Cover and cook on low for 5-6 hours or until vegetables are tender.

2. In a small bowl, combine flour and cream until smooth; add to slow cooker. Stir in peas. Cover and cook on high for 30 minutes or until slightly thickened.

LEEKS

Leeks resemble large green onions and have a mild flavor. To prepare, cut off the root end and tough green tops. Split the white portion in half and swish the pieces in a bowl of water to rinse away any sand between the layers. Then chop or slice. While leek tops aren't typically used in recipes, well-rinsed tops can be used to flavor homemade stock. Cut them into large pieces so they'll be easy to discard.

Hungarian Stew

As the owner of a fitness center, I rely on my slow cooker often to create nutritious meals for my family. This hearty stew brings back comforting memories.
—**SUSAN KAIN** WOODBINE, MARYLAND

PREP: 30 MIN. **COOK:** 7 HOURS **MAKES:** 6 SERVINGS

- 4 **medium potatoes, cut into 1-inch cubes**
- 2 **medium onions, chopped**
- 1 **pound beef stew meat, cut into 1-inch cubes**
- 2 **tablespoons canola oil**
- 1½ **cups water**
- 3 **teaspoons paprika**
- 1 **teaspoon salt**
- 1 **teaspoon caraway seeds**
- 1 **teaspoon tomato paste**
- 1 **garlic clove, minced**
- 2 **medium green peppers, cut into 1-inch pieces**
- 2 **medium tomatoes, peeled, seeded and chopped**
- 3 **tablespoons all-purpose flour**
- 3 **tablespoons cold water**
- ½ **cup sour cream**

1. Place potatoes and onions in a 3-qt. slow cooker. In a large skillet, brown meat in oil on all sides. Place over potato mixture.

2. Pour off excess fat from skillet. Add water to the drippings, stirring to loosen browned bits from pan; heat through. Stir in the paprika, salt, caraway seeds, tomato paste and garlic. Pour into the slow cooker. Cover and cook on low for 6-8 hours.

3. Add green peppers and tomatoes; cover and cook 1 hour longer or until meat and vegetables are tender. With a slotted spoon, transfer meat and vegetables to a large serving bowl; cover and keep warm.

4. Pour cooking juices into a small saucepan. Combine flour and cold water until smooth; gradually whisk into the pan. Bring to a boil; cook and stir for 2 minutes or until thickened. Remove from the heat; whisk in sour cream. Stir into meat mixture.

Slow Cooker Chili

PREP: 15 MIN.   **COOK:** 6 HOURS
MAKES: 12 SERVINGS (3 QUARTS)

- 2 **pounds ground beef**
- 4 **cans (16 ounces each) kidney beans, rinsed and drained**
- 1 **can (28 ounces) stewed tomatoes, undrained**
- 1 **can (15 ounces) pizza sauce**
- 1 **can (4 ounces) chopped green chilies**
- ¼ **cup chopped onion**
- 4 **to 5 teaspoons chili powder**
- 2 **garlic cloves, minced**
- 1 **teaspoon dried basil**
- ½ **teaspoon salt**
- ⅛ **teaspoon pepper**

1. In a large skillet, cook beef over medium heat until no longer pink; drain. Transfer to a 5-qt. slow cooker. Stir in the remaining ingredients.

2. Cover and cook on low for 6 hours or until heated through.

❝For chili with the classic flavor you crave but little fuss, this slow cooker recipe is hard to beat. You'll want to make it regularly for your family.❞

—SANDY MCKENZIE
BRAHAM, MINNESOTA

Southwestern Stew

Green chilies, spices and tender meat blend beautifully in this slow-cooked favorite. Over the years it has become our traditional Super-Bowl-Sunday meal.

—VIRGINIA PRICE
CHEYENNE, WYOMING

PREP: 20 MIN.   **COOK:** 6 HOURS
MAKES: 6 SERVINGS

- 1½ **pounds boneless pork, cut into ½-inch cubes**
- 2 **tablespoons canola oil**
- 1 **medium onion, chopped**
- 1 **can (15½ ounces) yellow hominy, drained**
- 1 **can (14½ ounces) diced tomatoes, undrained**
- 1 **can (4 ounces) chopped green chilies**
- ½ **cup water**
- ½ **teaspoon chili powder**
- ¼ **teaspoon garlic powder**
- ¼ **teaspoon salt**
- ¼ **teaspoon ground cumin**
- ¼ **teaspoon pepper**

1. In a large skillet over medium-high heat, brown pork in oil. Add onion; cook and stir until tender.

2. Transfer to a 3-qt. slow cooker; add remaining ingredients. Cover and cook on low for 6-7 hours or until meat is tender.

White Bean Chicken Chili

My sister shared this chili recipe with me. I usually double it and add one extra can of beans. The jalapeno adds just enough heat to notice but not too much for my children!

—KRISTINE BOWLES RIO RANCHO, NEW MEXICO

PREP: 35 MIN. **COOK:** 3 HOURS
MAKES: 6 SERVINGS

- ¾ **pound boneless skinless chicken breasts, cubed**
- ½ **teaspoon salt**
- ¼ **teaspoon pepper**
- 1 **medium onion, chopped**
- 4 **garlic cloves, minced**
- 1 **jalapeno pepper, seeded and chopped**
- 2 **teaspoons dried oregano**
- 1 **teaspoon ground cumin**
- 2 **tablespoons olive oil**
- 2 **cans (15 ounces each) white kidney or cannellini beans, rinsed and drained, divided**
- 3 **cups chicken broth, divided**
- 1½ **cups (6 ounces) shredded cheddar cheese**
  Sour cream and minced fresh cilantro, optional

1. Sprinkle chicken with salt and pepper. In a large skillet over medium heat, brown the chicken in oil.
2. Stir in the onion, garlic and jalapeno; cook 2 minutes longer. Sprinkle with oregano and cumin; cook 1 minute longer or until chicken is browned and vegetables are tender. Transfer to a 3-qt. slow cooker.
3. In a small bowl, mash 1 cup of beans; add ½ cup broth and stir until blended. Add to the slow cooker with the remaining beans and broth.
4. Cover and cook on low for 3 to 3½ hours or until chicken is tender. Stir before serving. Sprinkle with cheese. Garnish with sour cream and cilantro if desired.

Editor's Note: *Wear disposable gloves when cutting hot peppers; the oils can burn skin. Avoid touching your face.*

Spinach White Bean Soup

This meatless soup is great for a busy weeknight supper when I get home from my job as a college nursing professor. It's filling and provides plenty of nutrients to keep me healthy.

—BRENDA JEFFERS OTTUMWA, IOWA

PREP: 20 MIN. **COOK:** 6¼ HOURS
MAKES: 8 SERVINGS (2 QUARTS)

- 3 **cans (14½ ounces each) vegetable broth**
- 1 **can (15½ ounces) great northern beans, rinsed and drained**
- 1 **can (15 ounces) tomato puree**
- ½ **cup finely chopped onion**
- ½ **cup uncooked converted long grain rice**
- 2 **garlic cloves, minced**
- 1 **teaspoon dried basil**
- ½ **teaspoon salt**
- ¼ **teaspoon pepper**
- 1 **package (6 ounces) fresh baby spinach, coarsely chopped**
- ¼ **cup shredded Parmesan cheese**

In a 4-qt. slow cooker, combine the first nine ingredients. Cover and cook on low for 6-7 hours or until heated through. Stir in spinach. Cover and cook for 15 minutes or until spinach is wilted. Sprinkle with cheese.

Zesty Italian Soup

While visiting my sister-in-law, we had a delicious Italian soup at a local restaurant. We decided to duplicate it at home and came up with this recipe. You can vary the seasonings and types of canned tomatoes you use to suit your own family's tastes—and make it your own!

—**MYRNA SIPPEL** THOMPSON, ILLINOIS

PREP: 15 MIN. **COOK:** 7 HOURS
MAKES: 10 SERVINGS (3½ QUARTS)

- 1 **pound bulk Italian sausage**
- 3 **cans (14½ ounces each) reduced-sodium chicken broth**
- 1 **can (15 ounces) black beans, rinsed and drained**
- 1 **can (15 ounces) pinto beans, rinsed and drained**
- 1 **can (14½ ounces) diced tomatoes and green chilies, undrained**
- 1 **can (14½ ounces) Italian diced tomatoes**
- 1 **large carrot, chopped**
- 1 **jalapeno pepper, seeded and chopped**
- 1½ **teaspoons Italian seasoning**
- 1 **teaspoon dried minced garlic**
- 1½ **cups cooked elbow macaroni**

1. In a large skillet, cook sausage over medium heat until no longer pink; drain.

2. Transfer to a 5-qt. slow cooker. Stir in the broth, beans, tomatoes, carrot, jalapeno, Italian seasoning and garlic.

3. Cover and cook on low for 7-8 hours or until heated through. Just before serving, stir in macaroni.

Editor's Note: *Wear disposable gloves when cutting hot peppers; the oils can burn skin. Avoid touching your face.*

Simple Chicken Stew

This hefty stew was an experiment of my husband's. It turned out to be our favorite Sunday dinner!

—**AMY DULLING** ROCKWOOD, TENNESSEE

PREP: 20 MIN. **COOK:** 6 HOURS **MAKES:** 2 SERVINGS

- 1 can (10¾ ounces) condensed cream of chicken soup, undiluted
- 1 cup water
- ½ pound boneless skinless chicken breast, cubed
- 1 large potato, peeled and cubed
- 2 medium carrots, sliced
- ½ cup sliced fresh mushrooms
- ¼ cup chopped onion
- 1 teaspoon chicken bouillon granules
- ¼ teaspoon poultry seasoning

1. In a 1½-qt. slow cooker, combine all ingredients.
2. Cover and cook on low for 6-7 hours or until chicken and vegetables are tender.

Slow-Cooked Meatball Stew

I came up with this hearty meal as another way to use frozen meatballs. It's quick to put together in the morning and ready when my husband gets home in the evening.

—IRIS SCHULTZ MIAMISBURG, OHIO

PREP: 15 MIN. **COOK:** 9 HOURS
MAKES: 6 SERVINGS

- 3 medium potatoes, peeled and cut into ½-inch cubes
- 1 pound fresh baby carrots, quartered
- 1 large onion, chopped
- 3 celery ribs, sliced
- 1 package (12 ounces) frozen fully cooked home-style meatballs
- 1 can (10¾ ounces) condensed tomato soup, undiluted
- 1 can (10½ ounces) beef gravy
- 1 cup water
- 1 envelope onion soup mix
- 2 teaspoons beef bouillon granules

1. Place the potatoes, carrots, onion, celery and meatballs in a 5-qt. slow cooker. Combine the remaining ingredients; pour over meatball mixture.

2. Cover and cook on low for 9-10 hours or until the vegetables are crisp-tender.

No-Fuss Potato Soup

For a busy-day supper, my family loves to have big steaming bowls of this delicious soup, along with fresh bread from our bread machine.

—DOTTY EGGE
PELICAN RAPIDS, MINNESOTA

PREP: 15 MIN. **COOK:** 7½ HOURS
MAKES: 8-10 SERVINGS
(ABOUT 3 QUARTS)

- 6 cups cubed peeled potatoes
- 5 cups water
- 2 cups chopped onions
- ½ cup chopped celery
- ½ cup thinly sliced carrots
- ¼ cup butter, cubed
- 4 teaspoons chicken bouillon granules or 2 vegetable bouillon cubes
- 2 teaspoons salt
- ¼ teaspoon pepper
- 1 can (12 ounces) evaporated milk
- 3 tablespoons minced fresh parsley
  Minced chives, optional

1. In a 5-qt. slow cooker, combine the first nine ingredients. Cover and cook on low for 7-8 hours or until the vegetables are tender.

2. Add milk and parsley. Cover and cook 30 minutes longer or until heated through. Garnish with chives if desired.

Red Bean Vegetable Soup

Cajun spices boost the flavor of this nutritious soup loaded with veggies.

—RONNIE LAPPE
BROWNWOOD, TEXAS

PREP: 15 MIN. **COOK:** 6 HOURS
MAKES: 12 SERVINGS (3 QUARTS)

- 3 **large sweet red peppers, chopped**
- 3 **celery ribs, chopped**
- 2 **medium onions, chopped**
- 4 **cans (16 ounces each) kidney beans, rinsed and drained**
- 4 **cups chicken broth**
- 2 **bay leaves**
- ½ **to 1 teaspoon salt**
- ½ **to 1 teaspoon Cajun seasoning**
- ½ **teaspoon pepper**
- ¼ **teaspoon hot pepper sauce**

In a 5-qt. slow cooker, combine all ingredients. Cover and cook on low for 6 hours or until vegetables are tender. Discard bay leaves.

Hamburger Stew

It's great to come home after work knowing that I have this delicious meal waiting in the slow cooker.

—MARY JO WALKER
JASPER, TENNESSEE

PREP: 15 MIN. **COOK:** 6 HOURS
MAKES: 6 SERVINGS

- 2 **large potatoes, sliced**
- 2 **medium carrots, sliced**
- 1 **can (15 ounces) peas, drained**
- 3 **medium onions, sliced**
- 2 **celery ribs, sliced**
- 1½ **pounds ground beef, cooked and drained**
- 1 **can (10¾ ounces) condensed tomato soup, undiluted**
- 1⅓ **cups water**

In a 5-qt. slow cooker, layer the first six ingredients. Combine soup and water; pour over beef. Cover and cook on low for 6-8 hours or until vegetables are tender.

Sausage Rice Chili

I'd call this zesty meat-and-rice chili an easy meal in a bowl. The seasonings add irresistible flavor!

—MARIETTA SLATER JUSTIN, TEXAS

PREP: 15 MIN. **COOK:** 7 HOURS
MAKES: 6 SERVINGS

- 1 **pound bulk pork sausage**
- 2 **cups water**
- 1 **can (16 ounces) chili beans, undrained**
- 1 **can (14½ ounces) diced tomatoes, undrained**
- ¾ **cup uncooked long grain rice**
- ¼ **cup chopped onion**
- 1 **tablespoon chili powder**
- 1 **teaspoon Worcestershire sauce**
- 1 **teaspoon prepared mustard**
- ¾ **teaspoon salt**
- ⅛ **teaspoon garlic powder**
- 1 **cup (4 ounces) shredded cheddar cheese**

1. In a large skillet, cook sausage over medium heat until no longer pink; drain.

2. Transfer to a 3-qt. slow cooker. Add the next 10 ingredients; stir well. Cover and cook on low for 7 hours or until rice is tender. Stir in cheese during the last 10 minutes of cooking time.

Home-Style Chicken Soup

PREP: 15 MIN. **COOK:** 6¼ HOURS
MAKES: 4 SERVINGS

- 1 can (14½ ounces) chicken broth
- 1 can (14½ ounces) diced tomatoes, undrained
- 1 cup cubed cooked chicken
- 1 can (8 ounces) mushroom stems and pieces, drained
- ¼ cup sliced fresh carrot
- ¼ cup sliced celery
- 1 bay leaf
- ⅛ teaspoon dried thyme
- ¾ cup cooked egg noodles

In a 1½-qt. slow cooker, combine the first eight ingredients. Cover and cook on low for 6 hours. Stir in noodles; cover and cook on high for 15 minutes. Discard bay leaf.

❝I've relied on this easily prepared broth on many occasions. Mom gave me the recipe, and we love it.❞

—**KATHY RAIRIGH**
MILFORD, INDIANA

French Beef Stew

When it comes to making a thick and hearty, classic beef stew, I let my slow cooker do the work. I simply toss a green salad, and dinner is served!

—**IOLA EGLE** BELLA VISTA, ARKANSAS

PREP: 20 MIN. **COOK:** 9 HOURS
MAKES: 8-10 SERVINGS

- 3 medium potatoes, peeled and cubed
- 2 pounds beef stew meat
- 4 medium carrots, sliced
- 2 medium onions, sliced
- 3 celery ribs, sliced
- 2 cups tomato juice
- 1 cup water
- ⅓ cup quick-cooking tapioca
- 1 tablespoon sugar
- 1 tablespoon salt
- 1 teaspoon dried basil
- ½ teaspoon pepper

1. Place potatoes in a greased 5-qt. slow cooker. Top with beef, carrots, onions and celery. In a large bowl, combine the remaining ingredients. Pour over the vegetables.
2. Cover and cook on low for 9-10 hours or until the meat and vegetables are tender.

Hobo Stew

I got this recipe from my husband's family in Missouri. And I've yet to meet anyone who doesn't rave about this easy stew.

—**DICK BRAZEAL** CARLIN, NEVADA

PREP: 15 MIN. **COOK:** 6 HOURS
MAKES: 8 SERVINGS

- 1½ pounds ground beef
- 1 medium onion, diced
- 3 cans (10¾ ounces each) condensed minestrone soup, undiluted
- 2 cans (15 ounces each) Ranch Style beans (pinto beans in seasoned tomato sauce)
- 1 can (10 ounces) diced tomatoes and green chilies, undrained

1. In a large skillet, cook beef and onion over medium heat until the meat is no longer pink; drain. Transfer to a 3-qt. slow cooker. Add the remaining ingredients.
2. Cover and cook on low for 6 hours or until heated through.

Chicken Soup with Beans

I place lime-flavored tortilla chips into the serving bowls before ladling in this Southwestern soup. Loaded with chicken, beans, corn, tomatoes and green chilies, it's so satisfying!

—PENNY PERONIA
WEST MEMPHIS, ARKANSAS

PREP: 20 MIN. **COOK:** 6 HOURS
MAKES: 12 SERVINGS (3 QUARTS)

- 1 large onion, chopped
- 1 tablespoon canola oil
- 2 garlic cloves, minced
- 1¼ pounds boneless skinless chicken breasts, cooked and cubed
- 2 cans (15½ ounces each) great northern beans, rinsed and drained
- 3 cans (7 ounces each) white or shoepeg corn, drained
- 1 can (10 ounces) diced tomatoes and green chilies, undrained
- 3 cups water
- 1 can (4 ounces) chopped green chilies
- 2 tablespoons lime juice
- 1 teaspoon lemon-pepper seasoning
- 1 teaspoon ground cumin
- ¼ teaspoon salt
- ¼ teaspoon pepper

1. In a small skillet, saute onion in oil until tender. Add garlic; cook 1 minute longer.
2. Transfer to a 5-qt. slow cooker. Stir in the chicken, beans, corn, tomatoes, water, chopped green chilies, lime juice and seasonings. Cover and cook on low for 6-7 hours or until heated through.

Zippy Steak Chili

Looking for a thick, chunky chili with a little extra kick for your game-day party? Try my recipe. It was given to me by a co-worker originally from Texas.

—DENISE HABIB
POOLESVILLE, MARYLAND

PREP: 15 MIN. **COOK:** 6 HOURS
MAKES: 5 SERVINGS

- 1 pound beef top sirloin steak, cut into ½-inch cubes
- ½ cup chopped onion
- 2 tablespoons canola oil
- 2 tablespoons chili powder
- 1 teaspoon garlic powder
- 1 teaspoon ground cumin
- 1 teaspoon dried oregano
- 1 teaspoon pepper
- 2 cans (10 ounces each) diced tomatoes and green chilies, undrained
- 1 can (15½ ounces) chili starter
  Shredded cheddar cheese, chopped onion and sour cream, optional

1. In a large skillet, cook steak and onion in oil over medium heat until meat is browned. Sprinkle with seasonings.
2. In a 3-qt. slow cooker, combine tomatoes and chili starter. Stir in beef mixture. Cover and cook on low for 6-8 hours or until meat is tender. Serve with cheese, onion and sour cream if desired.
Editor's Note: *This recipe was tested with Bush's Traditional Chili Starter.*

Sweet Potato Lentil Stew

Years ago, I fell in love with the spicy flavor and wonderful aroma of this hearty slow-cooker recipe. You can serve the stew alone—or as a topper for meat or poultry. It's great either way!

—**HEATHER GRAY** LITTLE ROCK, ARKANSAS

PREP: 5 MIN. **COOK:** 5 HOURS **MAKES:** 6 SERVINGS

- **4 cups vegetable broth**
- **1¼ pounds sweet potatoes, peeled and cubed (about 3 cups)**
- **1½ cups dried lentils, rinsed**
- **3 medium carrots, cut into chunks**
- **1 medium onion, chopped**
- **4 garlic cloves, minced**
- **½ teaspoon ground cumin**
- **¼ teaspoon ground ginger**
- **¼ teaspoon cayenne pepper**
- **¼ cup minced fresh cilantro**
- **¼ teaspoon salt**

In a 3-qt. slow cooker, combine the first nine ingredients. Cover and cook on low for 5-6 hours or until vegetables are tender. Stir in cilantro and salt.

207

210

218

Side Dishes

||||||||||||||||||||||||||||||||||||||||||||||||||||||||||||||||||||||||||||||||||||||||||||||||||||||||||||||||||||||||||||||||||||||

Potluck Macaroni and Cheese

Here's a great way to make America's most popular comfort food. The dish turns out cheesy, rich and extra-creamy.

—JENNIFER BABCOCK CHICOPEE, MASSACHUSETTS

PREP: 25 MIN. **COOK:** 2 HOURS
MAKES: 16 SERVINGS (¾ CUP EACH)

- 3 cups uncooked elbow macaroni
- 1 pound process cheese (Velveeta), cubed
- 2 cups (8 ounces) shredded Mexican cheese blend
- 2 cups (8 ounces) shredded white cheddar cheese
- 1¾ cups milk
- 1 can (12 ounces) evaporated milk
- 3 eggs, lightly beaten
- ¾ cup butter, melted

1. Cook macaroni according to package directions; drain. Place in a greased 5-qt. slow cooker. Stir in the remaining ingredients.
2. Cover and cook on low for 2-3 hours or until a thermometer reads 160°, stirring once.

FAST FIX Lazy-Day Cranberry Relish

This no-fuss condiment simmers away while I take on other holiday preparations. It's especially delicious with turkey.

—JUNE FORMANEK BELLE PLAINE, IOWA

PREP: 5 MIN. **COOK:** 6 HOURS + CHILLING **MAKES:** 3 CUPS

- 2 cups sugar
- 1 cup orange juice
- 1 teaspoon grated orange peel
- 4 cups fresh or frozen cranberries

1. In a 1½ qt. slow cooker, combine sugar, orange juice and peel; stir until sugar is dissolved. Add the cranberries.
2. Cover and cook on low for 6 hours. Mash the mixture. Transfer to a small bowl; cool. Refrigerate until chilled.

FAST FIX Warm Fruit Salad

I use canned goods and my slow cooker to whip up an old-fashioned side dish that's loaded with sweet fruits. It makes a heartwarming accompaniment to many menus.

—MARY ANN JONNS MIDLOTHIAN, ILLINOIS

PREP: 10 MIN. **COOK:** 2 HOURS
MAKES: 14-18 SERVINGS

- 2 cans (29 ounces each) sliced peaches, drained
- 2 cans (29 ounces each) pear halves, drained and sliced
- 1 can (20 ounces) pineapple chunks, drained
- 1 can (15¼ ounces) apricot halves, drained and sliced
- 1 can (21 ounces) cherry pie filling

In a 5-qt. slow cooker, combine the peaches, pears, pineapple and apricots. Top with pie filling. Cover and cook on high for 2 hours or until heated through. Serve with a slotted spoon.

Brown Rice and Vegetables

This nutritious rice dish, full of big chunks of butternut squash and sweet potatoes, is a good combination of sweet and savory flavors.

—TASTE OF HOME TEST KITCHEN

PREP: 20 MIN. **COOK:** 5 HOURS **MAKES:** 12 SERVINGS

- 1 **cup uncooked brown rice**
- 1 **medium butternut squash (about 3 pounds), cubed**
- 2 **medium apples, coarsely chopped**
- 1 **medium sweet potato, peeled and cubed**
- 1 **medium onion, chopped**
- 1 **teaspoon salt**
- ½ **teaspoon pepper**
- 1 **can (14½ ounces) reduced-sodium chicken broth**
- ½ **cup raisins**
- 1 **tablespoon minced fresh tarragon or 1 teaspoon dried tarragon**

1. Place rice in a greased 4- or 5-qt. slow cooker. In a large bowl, combine the squash, apples, sweet potato, onion, salt and pepper; add to slow cooker. Pour broth over vegetables.

2. Cover and cook on low for 5-6 hours or until vegetables are tender. Stir in raisins and tarragon.

Make-Ahead Mashed Potatoes

Sour cream and cream cheese add richness to tasty make-ahead potatoes. They're wonderful when time is tight because they don't require any last-minute mashing.

—TRUDY VINCENT
VALLES MINES, MISSOURI

PREP: 20 MIN. **COOK:** 2 HOURS
MAKES: 8-10 SERVINGS

- 1 package (3 ounces) cream cheese, softened
- ½ cup sour cream
- ¼ cup butter, softened
- 1 envelope ranch salad dressing mix
- 1 teaspoon dried parsley flakes
- 6 cups warm mashed potatoes (without added milk and butter)

In a large bowl, combine the cream cheese, sour cream, butter, salad dressing mix and parsley; stir in potatoes. Transfer to a 3-qt. slow cooker. Cover and cook on low for 2-3 hours.

Editor's Note: *This recipe was tested with fresh potatoes (not instant) in a slow cooker with heating elements surrounding the unit, not only in the base.*

Slow Cooker Ratatouille

Not only does this classic recipe make a phenomenal side dish, but you can also serve it with sliced French bread for a warm and easy appetizer. Try it in the summer with your garden-fresh vegetables.

—JOLENE WALTERS
NORTH MIAMI, FLORIDA

PREP: 20 MIN. + STANDING
COOK: 3 HOURS
MAKES: 10 SERVINGS

- 1 large eggplant, peeled and cut into 1-inch cubes
- 2 teaspoons salt, divided
- 3 medium tomatoes, chopped
- 3 medium zucchini, halved lengthwise and sliced
- 2 medium onions, chopped
- 1 large green pepper, chopped
- 1 large sweet yellow pepper, chopped
- 1 can (6 ounces) pitted ripe olives, drained and chopped
- 1 can (6 ounces) tomato paste
- ½ cup minced fresh basil
- 2 garlic cloves, minced
- ½ teaspoon pepper
- 2 tablespoons olive oil

1. Place eggplant in a colander over a plate; sprinkle with 1 teaspoon salt and toss. Let stand for 30 minutes. Rinse and drain well. Transfer to a 5-qt. slow cooker coated with cooking spray.
2. Stir in the tomatoes, zucchini, onions, green and yellow peppers, olives, tomato paste, basil, garlic, pepper and remaining salt. Drizzle with oil. Cover and cook on high for 3-4 hours or until vegetables are tender.

Hearty Wild Rice

PREP: 15 MIN. **COOK:** 5 HOURS
MAKES: 10-12 SERVINGS

- 1 **pound ground beef**
- ½ **pound bulk pork sausage**
- 6 **celery ribs, diced**
- 2 **cans (10½ ounces each) condensed beef broth, undiluted**
- 1¼ **cups water**
- 1 **medium onion, chopped**
- 1 **cup uncooked wild rice**
- 1 **can (4 ounces) mushroom stems and pieces, drained**
- ¼ **cup reduced-sodium soy sauce**

1. In a large skillet, cook beef and sausage over medium heat until no longer pink; drain.
2. Transfer to a 5-qt. slow cooker. Stir in the celery, broth, water, onion, rice, mushrooms and soy sauce. Cover and cook on high for 1 hour. Reduce heat to low; cover and cook for 4 hours or until the rice is tender.

❝My father-in-law used to make this casserole in the oven. I switched to the slow cooker so I wouldn't need to keep an eye on it. It's great alongside beef or pork.❞
—**GARNET PETTIGREW**
COLUMBIA CITY, INDIANA

Boston Baked Beans

Simmered in molasses, these beans are perfect for your next potluck. The sauce is sweet, dark and rich. And the beans will complement anything you serve with them.
—**DARLENE DUNCAN**
LANGHORNE, PENNSYLVANIA

PREP: 20 MIN. + SOAKING
COOK: 10 HOURS
MAKES: 10 SERVINGS

- 1 **pound dried navy beans**
- 6 **cups water, divided**
- ¼ **pound diced salt pork or 6 bacon strips, cooked and crumbled**
- 1 **large onion, chopped**
- ½ **cup packed brown sugar**
- ½ **cup molasses**
- ¼ **cup sugar**
- 1 **teaspoon ground mustard**
- 1 **teaspoon salt**
- ½ **teaspoon ground cloves**
- ½ **teaspoon pepper**

1. Sort beans and rinse in cold water. Place beans in a 3- or 4-qt. slow cooker; add 4 cups water. Cover and let stand overnight.
2. Drain and rinse beans, discarding liquid. Return beans to slow cooker; add salt pork.
3. In a small bowl, combine the onion, brown sugar, molasses, sugar, mustard, salt, cloves, pepper and remaining water. Pour mixture over beans; stir to combine.
4. Cover and cook on low for 10-12 hours or until beans are tender.

FAST FIX Italian Mushrooms

Just four ingredients create a rich and flavorful side dish that's wonderful with beef. Try these mushrooms with grilled steak in the summer or a savory roast in winter.

—**KIM REICHERT** ST. PAUL, MINNESOTA

PREP: 10 MIN. **COOK:** 4 HOURS **MAKES:** 6 SERVINGS

1 **pound medium fresh mushrooms**
1 **large onion, sliced**
½ **cup butter, melted**
1 **envelope Italian salad dressing mix**

In a 3-qt. slow cooker, layer mushrooms and onion. Combine butter and salad dressing mix; pour over vegetables. Cover and cook on low for 4-5 hours or until vegetables are tender. Serve with a slotted spoon.

Slow-Cooked Mac 'n' Cheese

Slow-Cooked Mac 'n' Cheese: the words alone are enough to make mouths water. This is comfort food at its best: rich and extra-cheesy. Best of all, because it's made in the slow cooker, it's easy!

—SHELBY MOLINA
WHITEWATER, WISCONSIN

PREP: 25 MIN. **COOK:** 2 HOURS
MAKES: 9 SERVINGS

- 2 **cups uncooked elbow macaroni**
- 1 **can (12 ounces) evaporated milk**
- 1½ **cups milk**
- 2 **eggs**
- ¼ **cup butter, melted**
- 1 **teaspoon salt**
- 2½ **cups (10 ounces) shredded cheddar cheese**
- 2½ **cups (10 ounces) shredded sharp cheddar cheese, divided**

1. Cook macaroni according to package directions; drain and rinse in cold water. In a large bowl, combine the evaporated milk, milk, eggs, butter and salt. Stir in the cheddar cheese, 2 cups sharp cheddar cheese and macaroni.
2. Transfer to a greased 3-qt. slow cooker. Cover and cook on low for 2-3 hours or until center is set, stirring once. Sprinkle with remaining sharp cheddar cheese.

SHARP CHEDDAR

Sharp cheddar cheese has been aged longer than regular cheddar. As cheese ages, its flavor becomes more pronounced. Using aged cheese in a recipe can add complexity and rich flavor, even to humble favorites like mac 'n' cheese.

Glazed Spiced Carrots

Glazed carrots make a classic side dish for special occasions. This recipe is easy to put together, leaving your oven and stovetop free for other cooking creations.

—TASTE OF HOME TEST KITCHEN

PREP: 10 MIN. **COOK:** 6 HOURS
MAKES: 6 SERVINGS

- 2 **pounds fresh baby carrots**
- ½ **cup peach preserves**
- ¼ **cup packed brown sugar**
- ½ **cup butter, melted**
- 1 **teaspoon vanilla extract**
- ½ **teaspoon ground cinnamon**
- ¼ **teaspoon salt**
- ⅛ **teaspoon ground nutmeg**
- 2 **tablespoons cornstarch**
- 2 **tablespoons water**
  Toasted chopped pecans, optional

1. Place carrots in a 3-qt. slow cooker. Combine the preserves, brown sugar, butter, vanilla, cinnamon, salt and nutmeg. Combine cornstarch and water until smooth; stir into preserve mixture. Pour over carrots.
2. Cover and cook on low for 6-8 hours or until tender. Stir carrots; sprinkle with pecans if desired.

Jalapeno Creamed Corn

PREP: 15 MIN. **COOK:** 4 HOURS
MAKES: 8 SERVINGS

- 2 packages (16 ounces each) frozen corn
- 1 package (8 ounces) cream cheese, softened and cubed
- 4 jalapeno peppers, seeded and finely chopped
- ¼ cup butter, cubed
- 2 tablespoons water
- ½ teaspoon salt
- ¼ teaspoon pepper

In a 3-qt. slow cooker, combine all ingredients. Cover and cook on low for 4-5 hours or until corn is tender, stirring occasionally.

Editor's Note: *Wear disposable gloves when cutting hot peppers; the oils can burn skin. Avoid touching your face.*

❝My version of creamed corn gets its spicy kick from jalapeno peppers. Try a chopped poblano or small red bell pepper for a more mild side dish.❞

—**JUDY CARTY** WICHITA, KANSAS

Easy Squash Stuffing

My friends rave about this creamy side dish. It jazzes up stuffing mix with fresh summer squash, carrots and onion.

—**PAMELA THORSON**
HOT SPRINGS, ARKANSAS

PREP: 15 MIN. **COOK:** 4 HOURS
MAKES: 8 SERVINGS

- ¼ cup all-purpose flour
- 1 can (10¾ ounces) condensed cream of chicken soup, undiluted
- 1 cup (8 ounces) sour cream
- 2 medium yellow summer squash, cut into ½-inch slices
- 1 small onion, chopped
- 1 cup shredded carrots
- 1 package (8 ounces) stuffing mix
- ½ cup butter, melted

1. In a large bowl, combine the flour, soup and sour cream. Add the vegetables and gently stir to coat.

2. Combine stuffing mix and butter; sprinkle half into a 3-qt. slow cooker. Top with vegetable mixture and remaining stuffing mixture. Cover and cook on low for 4-5 hours or until vegetables are tender.

Slow-Cooked Bean Medley

I often change the variety of beans in this classic recipe, using whatever I have on hand to total five 15- to 16-ounce cans. The sweet and tangy sauce makes any combination delicious!

—**PEGGY GWILLIM** STRASBOURG, SASKATCHEWAN

PREP: 25 MIN. **COOK:** 5 HOURS
MAKES: 12 SERVINGS (¾ CUP EACH)

- 1½ cups ketchup
- 2 celery ribs, chopped
- 1 medium onion, chopped
- 1 medium green pepper, chopped
- 1 medium sweet red pepper, chopped
- ½ cup packed brown sugar
- ½ cup water
- ½ cup Italian salad dressing
- 2 bay leaves
- 1 tablespoon cider vinegar
- 1 teaspoon ground mustard
- ⅛ teaspoon pepper
- 1 can (16 ounces) kidney beans, rinsed and drained
- 1 can (15½ ounces) black-eyed peas, rinsed and drained
- 1 can (15½ ounces) great northern beans, rinsed and drained
- 1 can (15¼ ounces) whole kernel corn, drained
- 1 can (15¼ ounces) lima beans, rinsed and drained
- 1 can (15 ounces) black beans, rinsed and drained

1. In a 5-qt. slow cooker, combine the first 12 ingredients. Stir in the remaining ingredients.
2. Cover and cook on low for 5-6 hours or until onion and peppers are tender. Discard bay leaves.

Creamy Red Potatoes

I like using my slow cooker to make these tasty potatoes in a rich and creamy sauce. Be sure to stir them well before serving to help the cheese mixture thicken.

—ELAINE RYAN HOLLEY, NEW YORK

PREP: 15 MIN. **COOK:** 5 HOURS
MAKES: 8 SERVINGS

- 7 **cups cubed uncooked red potatoes**
- 1 **cup (8 ounces) 4% cottage cheese**
- ½ **cup sour cream**
- ½ **cup cubed process cheese (Velveeta)**
- 1 **tablespoon dried minced onion**
- 2 **garlic cloves, minced**
- ½ **teaspoon salt**
  Paprika and minced chives, optional

1. Place the potatoes in a 3-qt. slow cooker. In a blender, puree cottage cheese and sour cream until smooth. Transfer to a large bowl; stir in the process cheese, onion, garlic and salt. Pour over potatoes and mix well.
2. Cover and cook on low for 5-6 hours or until potatoes are tender. Stir well before serving. Garnish with paprika and chives if desired.

Old-Fashioned Dressing

Remember Grandma's wonderful turkey dressing? Savor it again, combined with flavorful herbs and crisp veggies, in this family-favorite recipe. You'll love that you can make it in your slow cooker.

—SHERRY VINK LACOMBE, ALBERTA

PREP: 35 MIN. **COOK:** 3 HOURS
MAKES: 8 SERVINGS

- ½ **cup butter, cubed**
- 2 **celery ribs, chopped**
- 1 **cup sliced fresh mushrooms**
- 1 **medium onion, chopped**
- ½ **cup minced fresh parsley**
- 2 **teaspoons rubbed sage**
- 2 **teaspoons dried marjoram**
- 1 **teaspoon dried thyme**
- 1 **teaspoon poultry seasoning**
- ½ **teaspoon pepper**
- ¼ **teaspoon salt**
- 6 **cups cubed day-old white bread**
- 6 **cups cubed day-old whole wheat bread**
- 1 **can (14½ ounces) chicken broth**

1. In a large skillet, melt butter. Add the celery, mushrooms and onion; saute until tender. Stir in the seasonings. Place bread cubes in a large bowl. Stir in vegetable mixture. Add broth; toss to coat.
2. Transfer to a 3-qt. slow cooker coated with cooking spray. Cover and cook on low for 3-4 hours or until heated through.

Jazzed-Up Green Bean Casserole

After trying many variations of this old standby, I decide to give it a little extra kick. With its crunchy texture, cheesy goodness and bacon, it'll make any dinner holiday-special!

—SCOTT RUGH PORTLAND, OREGON

PREP: 20 MIN. **COOK:** 5½ HOURS
MAKES: 10 SERVINGS

- 2 packages (16 ounces each) frozen cut green beans, thawed
- 2 cans (10¾ ounces each) condensed cream of mushroom soup, undiluted
- 1 can (8 ounces) sliced water chestnuts, drained
- 1 cup 2% milk
- 6 bacon strips, cooked and crumbled
- 1 teaspoon pepper
- ⅛ teaspoon paprika
- 4 ounces process cheese (Velveeta), cubed
- 1 can (2.8 ounces) French-fried onions

In a 4-qt. slow cooker, combine the green beans, soup, water chestnuts, milk, bacon, pepper and paprika. Cover and cook on low for 5-6 hours or until beans are tender; stir in cheese. Cover and cook for 30 minutes or until cheese is melted. Sprinkle with French-fried onions.

FAST FIX Easy Sweet Potato Casserole

It takes only five ingredients to create this sweet potato side dish, and what a handy way to free up the oven for other dishes. A granola topping adds a nice crunch.

—TASTE OF HOME TEST KITCHEN

PREP: 20 MIN. **COOK:** 5 HOURS
MAKES: 6 SERVINGS

- 2¼ pounds sweet potatoes, peeled and cubed
- ¾ teaspoon salt
- ⅛ teaspoon pepper
- 1 cup peach pie filling
- 2 tablespoons butter, melted
- ¼ teaspoon ground cinnamon
- ½ cup granola without raisins, optional

Place potatoes in a 3-qt. slow cooker coated with cooking spray. Toss with salt and pepper. Top with pie filling and drizzle with butter. Sprinkle with cinnamon. Cover and cook on low for 5-7 hours or until potatoes are tender. Sprinkle with granola if desired.

FAST FIX Creamy Hash Brown Potatoes

I like fixing a batch of these cheesy slow-cooker potatoes for potlucks and other big gatherings. Frozen hash browns, canned soup and flavored cream cheese make it so quick and easy to put together.

—JULIANNE HENSON
STREAMWOOD, ILLINOIS

PREP: 5 MIN. **COOK:** 3½ HOURS
MAKES: 12-14 SERVINGS

- 1 package (32 ounces) frozen cubed hash brown potatoes
- 1 can (10¾ ounces) condensed cream of potato soup, undiluted
- 2 cups (8 ounces) shredded Colby-Monterey Jack cheese
- 1 cup (8 ounces) sour cream
- ¼ teaspoon pepper
- ⅛ teaspoon salt
- 1 carton (8 ounces) spreadable chive and onion cream cheese

1. Place potatoes in a lightly greased 3-qt. slow cooker. In a large bowl, combine soup, cheese, sour cream, pepper and salt. Pour over potatoes and mix well.

2. Cover and cook on low for 3½ to 4 hours or until potatoes are tender. Stir in cream cheese.

Scalloped Potatoes & Ham

Here's a rich oven favorite that I adapted to cook by itself while I'm away. Now, it's all ready to serve when I get home, making it a real winner in my book!

—JONI HILTON ROCKLIN, CALIFORNIA

PREP: 25 MIN. **COOK:** 8 HOURS
MAKES: 16 SERVINGS (¾ CUP EACH)

- 1 **can (10¾ ounces) condensed cheddar cheese soup, undiluted**
- 1 **can (10¾ ounces) condensed cream of mushroom soup, undiluted**
- 1 **cup 2% milk**
- 10 **medium potatoes, peeled and thinly sliced**
- 3 **cups cubed fully cooked ham**
- 2 **medium onions, chopped**
- 1 **teaspoon paprika**
- 1 **teaspoon pepper**

1. In a small bowl, combine the soups and milk. In a greased 5-qt. slow cooker, layer half of the potatoes, ham, onions and soup mixture. Repeat layers. Sprinkle with paprika and pepper.
2. Cover and cook on low for 8-10 hours or until the potatoes are tender.

FAST FIX Italian Spaghetti Squash

You'll want to try this unique and easy way to cook spaghetti squash. Be sure the squash is on the small or medium side so it fits in the slow cooker when cut in half.

—MELISSA BROOKS SPARTA, WISCONSIN

PREP: 15 MIN. **COOK:** 6¼ HOURS **MAKES:** 4 SERVINGS

- 1 **medium spaghetti squash**
- 1 **cup sliced fresh mushrooms**
- 1 **can (14½ ounces) diced tomatoes, undrained**
- 1 **teaspoon dried oregano**
- 1 **teaspoon salt**
- ¼ **teaspoon pepper**
- ¾ **cup shredded part-skim mozzarella cheese**

1. Cut squash in half lengthwise; discard seeds. Place squash, cut side up, in a 6- or 7-qt. slow cooker. Layer with mushrooms, tomatoes, oregano, salt and pepper. Cover and cook on low for 6-8 hours or until squash is tender.
2. Sprinkle with cheese. Cover and cook another 15 minutes or until cheese is melted. When squash is cool enough to handle, use a fork to separate spaghetti squash strands.

Everything Stuffing

Both my husband and father go crazy for this stuffing! It also freezes well, so we're able to enjoy it long after Thanksgiving has passed.

—BETTE VOTRAL
BETHLEHEM, PENNSYLVANIA

PREP: 30 MIN. **COOK:** 3 HOURS
MAKES: 9 SERVINGS

- ½ pound bulk Italian sausage
- 4 cups seasoned stuffing cubes
- 1½ cups crushed corn bread stuffing
- ½ cup chopped toasted chestnuts or pecans
- ½ cup minced fresh parsley
- 1 tablespoon minced fresh sage or 1 teaspoon rubbed sage
- ⅛ teaspoon salt
- ⅛ teaspoon pepper
- 1¾ cups sliced baby portobello mushrooms
- 1 package (5 ounces) sliced fresh shiitake mushrooms
- 1 large onion, chopped
- 1 medium apple, peeled and chopped
- 1 celery rib, chopped
- 3 tablespoons butter
- 1 can (14½ ounces) chicken broth

1. In a large skillet, cook sausage over medium heat until no longer pink; drain. Transfer to a large bowl. Stir in the stuffing cubes, corn bread stuffing, chestnuts, parsley, sage, salt and pepper.

2. In the same skillet, saute the mushrooms, onion, apple and celery in butter until tender. Stir into stuffing mixture. Add enough broth to reach desired moistness. Transfer to a 4-qt. slow cooker. Cover and cook on low for 3 hours, stirring once.

Harvard Beets

Fresh beets can be delicious when combined with aromatic spice and a sweet hint of orange. These boast a perfect balance of sweet and sour flavors.

—TASTE OF HOME TEST KITCHEN

PREP: 15 MIN. **COOK:** 7 HOURS
MAKES: 6 SERVINGS

- 2 pounds small fresh beets, peeled and halved
- ½ cup sugar
- ¼ cup packed brown sugar
- 2 tablespoons cornstarch
- ½ teaspoon salt
- ¼ cup orange juice
- ¼ cup cider vinegar
- 2 tablespoons butter
- 1½ teaspoons whole cloves

1. Place beets in a 3-qt. slow cooker. In a small bowl, combine sugar, brown sugar, cornstarch and salt. Stir in the orange juice and vinegar. Pour over beets; dot with butter. Place cloves on a double thickness of cheesecloth; bring up corners of cloth and tie with string to form a bag. Place bag in slow cooker.

2. Cover and cook on low for 7-8 hours or until tender. Discard the spice bag.

Vegetable Medley

Bring out the best in all those garden-fresh veggies with this nutritious side dish. It's a great complement to any entree.

—TERRY MALY OLATHE, KANSAS

PREP: 15 MIN. **COOK:** 5 HOURS
MAKES: 8 SERVINGS

- 4 cups diced peeled potatoes
- 1½ cups frozen whole kernel corn or 1 can (15¼ ounces) whole kernel corn, drained
- 4 medium tomatoes, seeded and diced
- 1 cup sliced carrots
- ½ cup chopped onion
- ¾ teaspoon salt
- ½ teaspoon sugar
- ½ teaspoon dill weed
- ⅛ teaspoon pepper

In a 3-qt. slow cooker, combine all ingredients. Cover and cook on low for 5-6 hours or until vegetables are tender.

Corn Spoon Bread

My spoon bread is moister then corn pudding made in the oven, plus the cream cheese is a nice addition. It goes great with Thanksgiving turkey or Christmas ham.

—TAMARA ELLEFSON
FREDERIC, WISCONSIN

PREP: 15 MIN. **COOK:** 3 HOURS
MAKES: 8 SERVINGS

- 1 package (8 ounces) cream cheese, softened
- ⅓ cup sugar
- 1 cup 2% milk
- 2 eggs
- 2 tablespoons butter, melted
- 1 teaspoon salt
- ¼ teaspoon ground nutmeg
  Dash pepper
- 2⅓ cups frozen corn, thawed
- 1 can (14¾ ounces) cream-style corn
- 1 package (8½ ounces) corn bread/muffin mix

1. In a large bowl, beat cream cheese and sugar until smooth. Gradually beat in milk. Beat in the eggs, butter, salt, nutmeg and pepper until blended. Stir in corn and cream-style corn. Stir in corn bread mix just until moistened.
2. Pour into a greased 3-qt. slow cooker. Cover and cook on high for 3-4 hours or until center is almost set.

FAST FIX Nacho Hash Brown Casserole

This tasty slow cooker recipe produces the best hash browns ever! Soft and super cheesy, they make a comforting side dish for meats and poultry.

—PAT HABIGER SPEARVILLE, KANSAS

PREP: 15 MIN. **COOK:** 3¼ HOURS
MAKES: 8 SERVINGS

- 1 package (32 ounces) frozen cubed hash brown potatoes, thawed
- 1 can (10¾ ounces) condensed cream of celery soup, undiluted
- 1 can (10¾ ounces) condensed nacho cheese soup, undiluted
- 1 large onion, finely chopped
- ⅓ cup butter, melted
- 1 cup (8 ounces) reduced-fat sour cream

In a greased 3-qt. slow cooker, combine the first five ingredients. Cover and cook on low for 3-4 hours or until potatoes are tender. Stir in sour cream. Cover and cook 15-30 minutes longer or until heated through.

Winter Fruit Compote

You can make this colorful fruit relish up to a week in advance. It makes a nice accompaniment to turkey, chicken or pork throughout the year— or during the holidays.

—ESTHER CHESNEY
CARTHAGE, MISSOURI

PREP: 10 MIN.
COOK: 1¼ HOURS + COOLING
MAKES: 2½ CUPS

- 1 package (12 ounces) fresh or frozen cranberries, thawed
- ⅔ cup packed brown sugar
- ¼ cup orange juice concentrate
- 2 tablespoons raspberry vinegar
- ½ cup chopped dried apricots
- ½ cup golden raisins
- ½ cup chopped walnuts, toasted

1. In a 1½-qt. slow cooker, combine the cranberries, brown sugar, orange juice concentrate and vinegar. Cover and cook on low for 1¼ to 1¾ hours or until cranberries pop and mixture is thickened.
2. Turn off the heat; stir in the apricots, raisins and walnuts. Cool to room temperature. Refrigerate leftovers.

Cheddar Spirals

Our kids just love this cheesy pasta and will sample a spoonful right from the slow cooker when they walk by. Sometimes I add cocktail sausages, sliced Polish sausage or cubed ham to make it into a hearty dinner.

—HEIDI FERKOVICH
PARK FALLS, WISCONSIN

PREP: 20 MIN. **COOK:** 2½ HOURS
MAKES: 15 SERVINGS (¾ CUP EACH)

- 1 **package (16 ounces) spiral pasta**
- 2 **cups half-and-half cream**
- 1 **can (10¾ ounces) condensed cheddar cheese soup, undiluted**
- ½ **cup butter, melted**
- 4 **cups (16 ounces) shredded cheddar cheese**

1. Cook pasta according to the package directions; drain. In a greased 5-qt. slow cooker, combine the cream, soup and butter until smooth; stir in the cheese and pasta.
2. Cover and cook on low for 2½ hours or until cheese is melted.

Hearty Beans with Beef

My husband raved about this sweet bean dish after tasting it at a party, so I knew I had to get the recipe. It's perfect for get-togethers because you can mix it up a day early and toss it in the slow cooker a few hours before guests arrive.

—JAN BIEHL LEESBURG, INDIANA

PREP: 15 MIN. **COOK:** 3 HOURS
MAKES: 8-10 SERVINGS

- 1 **pound ground beef**
- 1 **medium onion, chopped**
- 1 **can (16 ounces) baked beans, undrained**
- 1 **can (15½ ounces) butter beans, rinsed and drained**
- ½ **cup ketchup**
- ⅓ **cup packed brown sugar**
- 1 **tablespoon barbecue sauce**
- ¼ **teaspoon Worcestershire sauce**

1. In a large skillet, cook beef and onion over medium heat until meat is no longer pink; drain. Transfer to a 5-qt. slow cooker. Stir in the remaining ingredients.
2. Cover and cook on high for 3-4 hours or until heated through.

Slow-Cooked Bacon & Beans

Bacon adds subtle smokiness to this hearty side dish
that's loaded with flavor. Brown sugar, vinegar and a hint
of molasses make the sauce irresistible!

—SUE LIVERMORE DETROIT LAKES, MINNESOTA

PREP: 25 MIN. **COOK:** 6 HOURS
MAKES: 12 SERVINGS (¾ CUP EACH)

- 1 **package (1 pound) sliced bacon, chopped**
- 1 **cup chopped onion**
- 2 **cans (15 ounces each) pork and beans, undrained**
- 1 **can (16 ounces) kidney beans, rinsed and drained**
- 1 **can (16 ounces) butter beans, rinsed and drained**
- 1 **can (15¼ ounces) lima beans, rinsed and drained**
- 1 **can (15 ounces) black beans, rinsed and drained**
- 1 **cup packed brown sugar**
- ½ **cup cider vinegar**
- 1 **tablespoon molasses**
- 2 **teaspoons garlic powder**
- ½ **teaspoon ground mustard**

1. In a large skillet, cook bacon and onion over
medium heat until bacon is crisp. Remove to paper
towels to drain.
2. In a 4-qt. slow cooker, combine the remaining
ingredients; stir in bacon mixture. Cover and cook
on low for 6-8 hours or until heated through.

223

222

229

Sweets, Snacks & Drinks

Apple Betty with Almond Cream

I love to make this treat for friends during the peak of apple season. I plan a quick meal of soup and bread, so we can get right to the dessert!

—**LIBBY WALP** CHICAGO, ILLINOIS

PREP: 15 MIN. **COOK:** 3 HOURS **MAKES:** 8 SERVINGS

- 3 **pounds tart apples, peeled and sliced**
- 10 **slices cinnamon-raisin bread, cubed**
- ¾ **cup packed brown sugar**
- ½ **cup butter, melted**
- 1 **teaspoon almond extract**
- ½ **teaspoon ground cinnamon**
- ¼ **teaspoon ground cardamom**
- ⅛ **teaspoon salt**

WHIPPED CREAM
- 1 **cup heavy whipping cream**
- 2 **tablespoons sugar**
- 1 **teaspoon grated lemon peel**
- ½ **teaspoon almond extract**

1. Place apples in an ungreased 4- or 5-qt. slow cooker. In a large bowl, combine the bread, brown sugar, butter, extract, cinnamon, cardamom and salt; spoon over apples. Cover and cook on low for 3-4 hours or until apples are tender.

2. In a small bowl, beat cream until it begins to thicken. Add the sugar, lemon peel and extract; beat until soft peaks form. Serve with apple mixture.

Cheese-Trio Artichoke & Spinach Dip

No appetizer spread is complete without at least one amazing dip, and this is it! Creamy, cheesy and chock-full of veggies, it will quickly become your new go-to appetizer.

—**DIANE SPEARE** KISSIMMEE, FLORIDA

PREP: 20 MIN. **COOK:** 2 HOURS **MAKES:** 4 CUPS

- 1 **cup chopped fresh mushrooms**
- 1 **tablespoon butter**
- 2 **garlic cloves, minced**
- 1½ **cups mayonnaise**
- 1 **package (8 ounces) cream cheese, softened**
- 1 **cup plus 2 tablespoons grated Parmesan cheese, divided**
- 1 **cup (4 ounces) shredded part-skim mozzarella cheese, divided**
- 1 **can (14 ounces) water-packed artichoke hearts, rinsed, drained and chopped**
- 1 **package (10 ounces) frozen chopped spinach, thawed and squeezed dry**
- ¼ **cup chopped sweet red pepper**
  Toasted French bread baguette slices

1. In a large skillet, saute mushrooms in butter until tender. Add garlic; cook 1 minute longer.

2. In a large bowl, combine the mayonnaise, cream cheese, 1 cup Parmesan cheese and ¾ cup mozzarella cheese. Add the mushroom mixture, artichokes, spinach and red pepper.

3. Transfer to a 3-qt. slow cooker. Sprinkle with remaining cheeses. Cover and cook on low for 2-3 hours or until heated through. Serve with baguette slices.

Sweet 'n' Tangy Chicken Wings

Here's a festive recipe that's perfect for parties. Put the wings in before you prepare for the party, and in a few hours, you'll have wonderful appetizers!

—IDA TUEY SOUTH LYON, MICHIGAN

PREP: 20 MIN. **COOK:** 3¼ HOURS
MAKES: ABOUT 2½ DOZEN

- **3 pounds chicken wingettes (about 30)**
- **½ teaspoon salt, divided**
-    **Dash pepper**
- **1½ cups ketchup**
- **¼ cup packed brown sugar**
- **¼ cup red wine vinegar**
- **2 tablespoons Worcestershire sauce**
- **1 tablespoon Dijon mustard**
- **1 teaspoon minced garlic**
- **1 teaspoon liquid smoke, optional**
-    **Sesame seeds, optional**

1. Sprinkle chicken wings with a dash of salt and pepper. Broil 4-6 in. from the heat for 5-10 minutes on each side or until golden brown. Transfer to a greased 5-qt. slow cooker.

2. Combine the ketchup, brown sugar, vinegar, Worcestershire sauce, mustard, garlic, liquid smoke if desired and remaining salt; pour over wings. Toss to coat.

3. Cover and cook on low for 3¼ to 3¾ hours or until chicken juices run clear. Sprinkle with sesame seeds if desired.

FAST FIX ▶ Sweet & Spicy Peanuts

With a caramel-like coating, these crunchy peanuts have a touch of heat from the hot sauce. They make a tasty snack any time of day.

—TASTE OF HOME TEST KITCHEN

PREP: 10 MIN.
COOK: 1½ HOURS + COOLING
MAKES: 4 CUPS

- 3 cups salted peanuts
- ½ cup sugar
- ⅓ cup packed brown sugar
- 2 tablespoons hot water
- 2 tablespoons butter, melted
- 1 tablespoon Sriracha Asian hot chili sauce or hot pepper sauce
- 1 teaspoon chili powder

1. Place the peanuts in a greased 1½-qt. slow cooker. In a small bowl, combine the sugars, water, butter, hot sauce and chili powder. Pour over peanuts. Cover and cook on high for 45 minutes; stir. Cover and cook 45 minutes longer.
2. Spread on waxed paper to cool. Store in an airtight container.

Fudgy Peanut Butter Cake

I clipped this recipe from the paper years ago. My husband and son enjoy the warm cake with ice cream and nuts on top. It fills the house with a great aroma while cooking.

—BONNIE EVANS
NORCROSS, GEORGIA

PREP: 10 MIN.   **COOK:** 1½ HOURS
MAKES: 4 SERVINGS

- ⅓ cup milk
- ¼ cup peanut butter
- 1 tablespoon canola oil
- ½ teaspoon vanilla extract
- ¾ cup sugar, divided
- ½ cup all-purpose flour
- ¾ teaspoon baking powder
- 2 tablespoons baking cocoa
- 1 cup boiling water
  Vanilla ice cream

1. In a large bowl, beat the milk, peanut butter, oil and vanilla until well blended. In a small bowl, combine ¼ cup sugar, flour and baking powder; gradually beat into milk mixture until blended. Spread into a 1½-qt. slow cooker coated with cooking spray.
2. In a small bowl, combine cocoa and remaining sugar; stir in boiling water. Pour into slow cooker (do not stir).
3. Cover and cook on high for 1½ to 2 hours or until a toothpick inserted near the center comes out clean. Serve warm with ice cream.

Editor's Note: *Reduced-fat peanut butter is not recommended for this recipe.*

Bacon Cheese Dip

I've tried several appetizer recipes before, but this one is a surefire people-pleaser. The thick dip has lots of bacon flavor and keeps friends happily munching.

—SUZANNE WHITAKER
KNOXVILLE, TENNESSEE

PREP: 15 MIN. **COOK:** 2 HOURS
MAKES: 4 CUPS

- 2 packages (8 ounces each) cream cheese, cubed
- 4 cups (16 ounces) shredded cheddar cheese
- 1 cup half-and-half cream
- 2 teaspoons Worcestershire sauce
- 1 teaspoon dried minced onion
- 1 teaspoon prepared mustard
- 16 bacon strips, cooked and crumbled
  Tortilla chips or French bread slices

1. In a 1½-qt. slow cooker, combine the first six ingredients. Cover and cook on low for 2-3 hours or until cheeses are melted, stirring occasionally.
2. Just before serving, stir in bacon. Serve warm with tortilla chips or bread.

Granola Apple Crisp

Tender apples are tucked beneath a sweet granola topping in this classic crisp. For variety, replace the apples with your favorite fruit.

—BARBARA SCHINDLER
NAPOLEON, OHIO

PREP: 20 MIN. **COOK:** 5 HOURS
MAKES: 6-8 SERVINGS

- 8 medium tart apples, peeled and sliced
- ¼ cup lemon juice
- 1½ teaspoons grated lemon peel
- 2½ cups granola with fruit and nuts
- 1 cup sugar
- 1 teaspoon ground cinnamon
- ½ cup butter, melted

1. In a large bowl, toss the apples, lemon juice and peel. Transfer to a greased 3-qt. slow cooker. Combine the granola, sugar and cinnamon; sprinkle over apples. Drizzle with butter.
2. Cover and cook on low for 5-6 hours or until the apples are tender. Serve warm.

Blueberry Grunt

If you love blueberries, then you can't go wrong with this easy slow-cooked dessert. For a special treat, serve it warm with vanilla ice cream.

—CLEO GONSKE REDDING, CALIFORNIA

PREP: 20 MIN. **COOK:** 2½ HOURS **MAKES:** 6 SERVINGS

- 4 **cups fresh or frozen blueberries**
- ¾ **cup sugar**
- ½ **cup water**
- 1 **teaspoon almond extract**

DUMPLINGS

- 2 **cups all-purpose flour**
- 4 **teaspoons baking powder**
- 1 **teaspoon sugar**
- ½ **teaspoon salt**
- 1 **tablespoon cold butter**
- 1 **tablespoon shortening**
- ¾ **cup 2% milk**
     Vanilla ice cream, optional

1. In a 3-qt. slow cooker, combine the blueberries, sugar, water and extract. Cover and cook on high for 2-3 hours or until bubbly.

2. For dumplings, in a small bowl, combine the flour, baking powder, sugar and salt. Cut in the butter and shortening until crumbly. Stir in milk just until moistened.

3. Drop by tablespoonfuls onto hot blueberry mixture. Cover and cook 30 minutes longer or until a toothpick inserted in a dumpling comes out clean. Serve warm with ice cream if desired.

Cocktail Franks

Don't want to deal with leftovers from your party? Serve these tempting sausages in a sweet and savory sauce. I've never had even one piece go uneaten!

—JO ANN RENNER XENIA, OHIO

PREP: 15 MIN. **COOK:** 1 HOUR
MAKES: 16 SERVINGS

- 2 **pounds smoked sausage links**
- 1 **bottle (8 ounces) Catalina salad dressing**
- 1 **bottle (8 ounces) Russian salad dressing**
- ½ **cup packed brown sugar**
- ½ **cup pineapple juice**

1. Cut sausages diagonally into ½-in. slices; cook in a skillet over medium heat until lightly browned. Transfer sausages to a 3-qt. slow cooker; discard drippings.
2. Add dressings, brown sugar and juice to skillet; cook and stir over medium-low heat until sugar is dissolved. Pour over sausages. Cover and cook on low for 1-2 hours or until heated through.
Editor's Note: *French salad dressing may be substituted for one or both dressings.*

Mulled Merlot

Our delightful recipe is sure to warm up your holiday guests! Keeping it ready to serve in the slow cooker means that you'll have time to enjoy the party.

—TASTE OF HOME TEST KITCHEN

PREP: 10 MIN. **COOK:** 1 HOUR
MAKES: 9 SERVINGS

- 4 **cinnamon sticks (3 inches)**
- 4 **whole cloves**
- 2 **bottles (750 milliliters each) merlot**
- ½ **cup sugar**
- ½ **cup orange juice**
- ½ **cup brandy**
- 1 **medium orange, thinly sliced**

1. Place cinnamon sticks and cloves on a double thickness of cheesecloth; bring up the corners of the cloth and tie with string to form a bag.
2. In a 3-qt. slow cooker, combine the merlot, sugar, orange juice, brandy and orange slices. Add spice bag. Cover and cook on high for 1 hour or until heated through. Discard spice bag and orange slices. Serve warm.

Barbecue Chicken Wings

I got this recipe from a friend but altered the spices a bit to suit my family's tastes. Be sure you have plenty of extra napkins on hand. These wings are messy to eat but oh, so good!

—JEAN ANN HERRITT CANTON, OHIO

PREP: 45 MIN. **COOK:** 1 HOUR
MAKES: ABOUT 2½ DOZEN

- 3 **pounds whole chicken wings**
- 2 **cups ketchup**
- ½ **cup honey**
- 2 **tablespoons lemon juice**
- 2 **tablespoons canola oil**
- 2 **tablespoons soy sauce**
- 2 **tablespoons Worcestershire sauce**
- 1 **tablespoon paprika**
- 4 **garlic cloves, minced**
- 1½ **teaspoons curry powder**
- ½ **teaspoon pepper**
- ⅛ **teaspoon hot pepper sauce**

1. Cut chicken wings into three sections; discard wing tips. Place wings in a greased 15-in. x 10-in. x 1-in. baking pan. Bake at 350° for 35-40 minutes or until the juices run clear.
2. In a large bowl, combine the remaining ingredients. Pour ½ cup into a 3-qt. slow cooker. Drain chicken wings; add to slow cooker. Drizzle with remaining sauce.
3. Cover and cook on low for 1 hour, stirring occasionally.
Editor's Note: *Uncooked chicken wing sections (wingettes) may be substituted for whole chicken wings.*

MEASURING HONEY

For easy cleanup, spritz the measuring cup with cooking spray before measuring sticky ingredients like honey.

Hot Crab Dip

One batch of this slow cooker appetizer isn't enough for my family, so I often double the recipe. Bits of sweet onion give the creamy dip just the right amount of crunch.

—TERRI PERRIER SIMONTON, TEXAS

PREP: 10 MIN. **COOK:** 2 HOURS
MAKES: 2 CUPS

- 1 **package (8 ounces) cream cheese, softened**
- ½ **cup finely chopped sweet onion**
- ¼ **cup grated Parmesan cheese**
- ¼ **cup mayonnaise**
- 2 **garlic cloves, minced**
- 2 **teaspoons sugar**
- 1 **can (6 ounces) crabmeat, drained, flaked and cartilage removed**
   Assorted crackers

In a 1½-qt. slow cooker, combine the first six ingredients; stir in crab. Cover and cook on low for 2-3 hours or until heated through. Serve with crackers.

FAST FIX Mini Hot Dogs 'n' Meatballs

PREP: 5 MIN. **COOK:** 3 HOURS **MAKES:** 8 CUPS

- 1 package (12 ounces) frozen fully cooked Italian meatballs
- 1 package (16 ounces) miniature hot dogs or smoked sausages
- 1 package (3½ ounces) sliced pepperoni
- 1 jar (24 ounces) meatless spaghetti sauce
- 1 bottle (18 ounces) barbecue sauce
- 1 bottle (12 ounces) chili sauce

In a 5-qt. slow cooker, combine all ingredients. Cover and cook on low for 3-4 hours or until heated through.

“Hot appetizers don't come much easier than this. Since it's so popular, I usually double the recipe. Try increasing the heat factor by using a spicier barbecue or spaghetti sauce. Make it your own!”

—ANDREA CHAMBERLAIN MACEDON, NEW YORK

Slow Cooker Mexican Dip

My husband, Jamie, and I love to entertain, and we make this hearty seven-ingredient dip often. Using our slow cooker leaves us free to share quality time with our guests. And isn't that the purpose of a party?

—HEATHER COURTNEY AMES, IOWA

PREP: 15 MIN. **COOK:** 1½ HOURS
MAKES: 8 CUPS

- 1½ **pounds ground beef**
- 1 **pound bulk hot Italian sausage**
- 1 **cup chopped onion**
- 1 **package (8.8 ounces) ready-to-serve Spanish rice**
- 1 **can (16 ounces) refried beans**
- 1 **can (10 ounces) enchilada sauce**
- 1 **pound process cheese (Velveeta), cubed**
- 1 **package tortilla chip scoops**

1. In a Dutch oven, cook the beef, sausage and onion over medium heat until meat is no longer pink; drain. Heat rice according to package directions.

2. In a 3-qt. slow cooker, combine the meat mixture, rice, beans, enchilada sauce and cheese. Cover and cook on low for 1½ to 2 hours or until cheese is melted. Serve with tortilla scoops.

FAST FIX Ginger Tea Drink

Looking for something new and special to serve to guests? Let a soothing green tea simmer while you concentrate on preparing other dishes for your gathering. Everyone is sure to ask for the recipe.

—ALEXANDRA MARCOTTY CLEVELAND HEIGHTS, OHIO

PREP: 15 MIN. **COOK:** 2 HOURS
MAKES: 8 SERVINGS (2 QUARTS)

- 4 **cups boiling water**
- 15 **individual green tea bags**
- 4 **cups white grape juice**
- 1 **to 2 tablespoons honey**
- 1 **tablespoon minced fresh gingerroot**
  Crystallized ginger, optional

1. In a 3-qt. slow cooker, combine boiling water and tea bags. Cover and let stand for 10 minutes. Discard tea bags. Stir in the remaining ingredients. Cover and cook on low for 2-3 hours or until heated through.

2. Strain if desired before serving warm. Garnish with crystallized ginger if desired.

Chipotle Ham 'n' Cheese Dip

If you like throwing dinner parties for friends, you just can't beat a convenient slow cooker recipe like this one. Who wants to be stuck in the kitchen? Just set the cooker on low and enjoy visiting with guests.

—**LISA RENSHAW** KANSAS CITY, MISSOURI

PREP: 15 MIN. **COOK:** 1 HOUR
MAKES: 7 CUPS

- 2 **packages (8 ounces each) cream cheese, cubed**
- 1 **can (12 ounces) evaporated milk**
- 2 **cups (8 ounces) shredded Gouda cheese**
- 1 **cup (4 ounces) shredded cheddar cheese**
- 2 **tablespoons chopped chipotle pepper in adobo sauce**
- 1 **teaspoon ground cumin**
- 2 **cups diced fully cooked ham Fresh vegetables or tortilla chips**

1. In a 3-qt. slow cooker, combine the first six ingredients. Cover and cook on low for 40 minutes.
2. Stir in ham; cook 20 minutes longer or until heated through. Serve the dip warm with fresh vegetables or chips.

FAST FIX ▶ Cranberry Sauerkraut Meatballs

I tried these meatballs at a friend's birthday party, and now I make them all the time. Super-easy to prepare, they're ideal for potlucks or those Sunday afternoon football games.

—**LISA CASTELLI** PLEASANT PRAIRIE, WISCONSIN

PREP: 15 MIN. **COOK:** 4 HOURS
MAKES: ABOUT 5 DOZEN

- 1 **can (14 ounces) whole-berry cranberry sauce**
- 1 **can (14 ounces) sauerkraut, rinsed and well drained**
- 1 **bottle (12 ounces) chili sauce**
- ¾ **cup packed brown sugar**
- 1 **package (32 ounces) frozen fully cooked homestyle meatballs, thawed**

In a 4-qt. slow cooker, combine the cranberry sauce, sauerkraut, chili sauce and brown sugar. Stir in meatballs. Cover and cook on low for 4-5 hours or until heated through.

Slow Cooker Party Mix

A nicely seasoned snack mix is always a party-time favorite. It's so simple but so satisfying. For variety, try substituting cashews for the peanuts.

—**DANA HUGHES** GRESHAM, OREGON

PREP: 5 MIN. **COOK:** 1 HOUR
MAKES: ABOUT 3 QUARTS

- 4 **cups Wheat Chex**
- 4 **cups Cheerios**
- 3 **cups pretzel sticks**
- 1 **can (12 ounces) salted peanuts**
- ¼ **cup butter, melted**
- 2 **to 3 tablespoons grated Parmesan cheese**
- 1 **teaspoon celery salt**
- ½ **to ¾ teaspoon seasoned salt**

In a 5-qt. slow cooker, combine cereals, pretzels and peanuts. Combine the butter, cheese, celery salt and seasoned salt; drizzle over cereal mixture and mix well. Cover and cook on low for 1 to 1½ hours, stirring every 20 minutes. Serve warm or at room temperature.

Slow-Cooked Salsa

I love the fresh taste of homemade salsa, but as a working mother, I don't have much time to make it. So I came up with this slow-cooked version that practically makes itself!

—TONI MENARD LOMPOC, CALIFORNIA

PREP: 15 MIN. **COOK:** 2½ HOURS + COOLING
MAKES: ABOUT 2 CUPS

- 10 **plum tomatoes**
- 2 **garlic cloves**
- 1 **small onion, cut into wedges**
- 2 **jalapeno peppers**
- ¼ **cup cilantro leaves**
- ½ **teaspoon salt, optional**

1. Core tomatoes. Cut a small slit in two tomatoes; insert a garlic clove into each slit. Place tomatoes and onion in a 3-qt. slow cooker.

2. Cut stems off jalapenos; remove seeds if a milder salsa is desired. Place jalapenos in the slow cooker.

3. Cover and cook on high for 2½ to 3 hours or until vegetables are softened (some may brown slightly); cool.

4. In a blender, combine the tomato mixture, cilantro and salt if desired; cover and process until blended. Refrigerate leftovers.

Editor's Note: *Wear disposable gloves when cutting hot peppers; the oils can burn skin. Avoid touching your face.*

Italian Appetizer Meatballs

Store-bought spaghetti sauce speeds up the preparation of tasty homemade meatballs. The leftovers make terrific sub sandwiches with mozzarella or provolone cheese.

—RENE MCCRORY
INDIANAPOLIS, INDIANA

PREP: 40 MIN. **COOK:** 2 HOURS
MAKES: 4 DOZEN

- 2 eggs, lightly beaten
- ½ cup dry bread crumbs
- ¼ cup 2% milk
- 2 teaspoons grated Parmesan cheese
- 1 teaspoon salt
- ¼ teaspoon pepper
- ⅛ teaspoon garlic powder
- 1 pound ground beef
- 1 pound bulk Italian sausage
- 2 jars (24 ounces each) spaghetti sauce

1. In a large bowl, combine the first seven ingredients. Crumble beef and sausage over mixture and mix well. Shape into 1-in. balls.
2. Place meatballs on a greased rack in a shallow baking pan. Bake at 400° for 15-20 minutes or until no longer pink.
3. Transfer meatballs to a 4-qt. slow cooker; add spaghetti sauce. Cover and cook on high for 2-3 hours or until heated through.

Green Olive Dip

Olive fans will love this dip. It's cheesy and full of beef and beans. I also like to use it as a festive filling for taco shells.

—BETH DUNAHAY LIMA, OHIO

PREP: 30 MIN. **COOK:** 3 HOURS
MAKES: 8 CUPS

- 1 pound ground beef
- 1 medium sweet red pepper, chopped
- 1 small onion, chopped
- 1 can (16 ounces) refried beans
- 1 jar (16 ounces) mild salsa
- 2 cups (8 ounces) shredded part-skim mozzarella cheese
- 2 cups (8 ounces) shredded cheddar cheese
- 1 jar (5¾ ounces) sliced green olives with pimientos, drained Tortilla chips

1. In a large skillet, cook the beef, pepper and onion over medium heat until meat is no longer pink; drain.
2. Transfer to a greased 3-qt. slow cooker. Add the beans, salsa, cheeses and olives. Cover and cook on low for 3-4 hours or until cheese is melted, stirring occasionally. Serve with chips.

WORK AHEAD

Consider preparing meatballs in bulk to save on prep time. You can make several batches of meatballs, bake them and then freeze until needed. Simply thaw the frozen meatballs in the refrigerator overnight and you'll be ready to go.

Warm Pomegranate Punch

If you're looking for something special to serve on a chilly evening, try a lightly spiced hot punch. It has a subtle tea flavor, and the juices create just the right balance of sweet and tart.

—TASTE OF HOME TEST KITCHEN

PREP: 10 MIN. **COOK:** 2 HOURS
MAKES: 10 SERVINGS (2½ QUARTS)

- 4 **cups pomegranate juice**
- 4 **cups unsweetened apple juice**
- 2 **cups brewed tea**
- ½ **cup sugar**
- ⅓ **cup lemon juice**
- 3 **cinnamon sticks (3 inches)**
- 12 **whole cloves**

1. In a 4- or 5-qt. slow cooker, combine the first five ingredients. Place cinnamon sticks and cloves on a double thickness of cheesecloth; bring up corners of cloth and tie with string to form a bag. Add to slow cooker.

2. Cover and cook on low for 2-3 hours or until heated through. Discard spice bag. Serve warm.

Barbecued Party Starters

These sweet and tangy bites are sure to tide everyone over until dinner. Set out some fun toothpicks or cocktail picks on the buffet to make for easy nibbling.

—ANASTASIA WEISS
PUNXSUTAWNEY, PENNSYLVANIA

PREP: 30 MIN. **COOK:** 2 HOURS
MAKES: 18 SERVINGS (⅓ CUP EACH)

- 1 **pound ground beef**
- ¼ **cup finely chopped onion**
- 1 **package (16 ounces) miniature hot dogs, drained**
- 1 **jar (12 ounces) apricot preserves**
- 1 **cup barbecue sauce**
- 1 **can (20 ounces) pineapple chunks, drained**

1. In a small bowl, combine beef and onion. Shape into 1-in. balls. In a large skillet, cook meatballs in batches until no longer pink; drain.

2. Transfer to a 3-qt. slow cooker; add the hot dogs, preserves and barbecue sauce. Cover and cook on high for 2-3 hours or until heated through. Stir in pineapple; heat through.

Gingerbread Pudding Cake

Sweet spices and a half cup of molasses give my dessert a delightful old-fashioned flavor. It's pretty topped with a dollop of whipped cream.

—BARBARA COOK YUMA, ARIZONA

PREP: 20 MIN. **COOK:** 2 HOURS + STANDING
MAKES: 6-8 SERVINGS

¼ cup butter, softened
¼ cup sugar
1 egg white
1 teaspoon vanilla extract
½ cup molasses
1 cup water
1¼ cups all-purpose flour
¾ teaspoon baking soda
½ teaspoon ground cinnamon
½ teaspoon ground ginger
¼ teaspoon salt
¼ teaspoon ground allspice
⅛ teaspoon ground nutmeg
½ cup chopped pecans
TOPPING
6 tablespoons brown sugar
¾ cup hot water
⅔ cup butter, melted

1. In a large bowl, cream butter and sugar until light and fluffy. Beat in egg white and vanilla. Combine molasses and water. Combine the flour, baking soda, cinnamon, ginger, salt, allspice and nutmeg; gradually add to creamed mixture alternately with molasses mixture, beating well after each addition. Fold in pecans.
2. Pour into a greased 3-qt. slow cooker. Sprinkle with brown sugar. Combine hot water and butter; pour over batter (do not stir).
3. Cover and cook on high for 2 to 2½ hours or until a toothpick inserted near center of cake comes out clean. Turn off the heat. Let stand for 15 minutes. Serve warm.

Christmas Punch

I got the recipe for this rosy red punch from a co-worker at our office Christmas party.

—PATRICIA DICK ANDERSON, INDIANA

PREP: 15 MIN. **COOK:** 3 HOURS
MAKES: 22 SERVINGS (¾ CUP EACH)

- 1 **quart brewed tea**
- 1 **quart unsweetened apple juice**
- 1 **quart orange juice**
- 1 **quart unsweetened pineapple juice**
- 1 **package (9 ounces) red-hot candies**

In a 6-qt. slow cooker, combine all ingredients. Cover and cook on low for 3-4 hours or until candies are melted, stirring occasionally.

Butterscotch Cider

You'll love the taste of butterscotch and cinnamon in this party-perfect hot apple cider.

—KAREN MACK WEBSTER, NEW YORK

PREP: 5 MIN. **COOK:** 3 HOURS
MAKES: 18 SERVINGS (1 CUP EACH)

- 1 **gallon apple cider or juice**
- 2 **cups butterscotch schnapps liqueur**
- 8 **cinnamon sticks (3 inches)**

In a 6-qt. slow cooker, combine all ingredients. Cover and cook on low for 3-4 hours or until heated through.

Sweet-and-Sour Chicken Wings

These wings are a fun appetizer for gatherings. I also like to serve them over rice as a main dish. Any way you do it, these will be a hit!

—JUNE EBERHARDT
MARYSVILLE, CALIFORNIA

PREP: 15 MIN. **COOK:** 3 HOURS
MAKES: 32 APPETIZERS

- 1 **cup sugar**
- 1 **cup cider vinegar**
- ½ **cup ketchup**
- 2 **tablespoons reduced-sodium soy sauce**
- 1 **teaspoon chicken bouillon granules**
- 16 **chicken wings**
- 6 **tablespoons cornstarch**
- ½ **cup cold water**

1. In a small saucepan, combine the first five ingredients. Bring to a boil; cook and stir until sugar is dissolved. Cut wings into three sections; discard wing tip sections.
2. Transfer to a 3-qt. slow cooker; add vinegar mixture. Cover and cook on low for 3-4 hours or until chicken juices run clear.
3. Transfer wings to a serving dish and keep warm. Skim fat from cooking juices; transfer to a small saucepan. Bring liquid to a boil.
4. Combine cornstarch and water until smooth. Gradually stir into pan. Bring to a boil; cook and stir for 2 minutes or until thickened. Spoon over chicken. Serve with a slotted spoon.
Editor's Note: *Uncooked chicken wing sections (wingettes) may be substituted for whole chicken wings.*

Crispy Snack Mix

This recipe proves that you can make just about anything in the slow cooker, even a delightfully crispy snack mix!

—**JANE PAIR SIMS** DE LEON, TEXAS

PREP: 10 MIN. **COOK:** 2½ HOURS
MAKES: ABOUT 2½ QUARTS

- 4½ cups crispy chow mein noodles
- 4 cups Rice Chex
- 1 can (9¾ ounces) salted cashews
- 1 cup flaked coconut, toasted
- ½ cup butter, melted
- 2 tablespoons reduced-sodium soy sauce
- 2¼ teaspoons curry powder
- ¾ teaspoon ground ginger

1. In a 5-qt. slow cooker, combine the noodles, cereal, cashews and coconut. In a small bowl, whisk the butter, soy sauce, curry powder and ginger; drizzle over cereal mixture and mix well.
2. Cover and cook on low for 2½ hours, stirring every 30 minutes. Serve warm or at room temperature.

FAST FIX ▶ Hot Wing Dip

Since I usually have the ingredients on hand, this reliable go-to recipe is one that I serve often.

—**COLEEN CORNER** GROVE CITY, PENNSYLVANIA

PREP: 10 MIN. **COOK:** 1 HOUR
MAKES: 4½ CUPS

- 2 cups shredded cooked chicken
- 1 package (8 ounces) cream cheese, cubed
- 2 cups (8 ounces) shredded cheddar cheese
- 1 cup ranch salad dressing
- ½ cup Louisiana-style hot sauce
  Tortilla chips and/or celery sticks
  Minced fresh parsley, optional

1. In a 3-qt. slow cooker, combine the chicken, cream cheese, cheddar cheese, salad dressing and hot sauce.
2. Cover and cook on low for 1-2 hours or until cheese is melted. Serve with chips and/or celery. Sprinkle with the parsley if desired.

FAST FIX ▶ Reuben Spread

I love Reuben anything, and this appetizer is a favorite. It's a warm and yummy crowd-pleaser, perfect for rallying your Super Bowl crowd!

—**JUNE HERKE** WATERTOWN, SOUTH DAKOTA

PREP: 10 MIN. **COOK:** 4 HOURS
MAKES: 3¾ CUPS

- 2 packages (8 ounces each) cream cheese, cubed
- 4 cups (16 ounces) shredded Swiss cheese
- 1 can (14 ounces) sauerkraut, rinsed and well drained
- 4 packages (2 ounces each) thinly sliced deli corned beef, chopped
- ½ cup Thousand Island salad dressing
  Snack rye bread

In a 1½-qt. slow cooker, combine the first five ingredients. Cover and cook on low for 4 hours; stir to blend. Serve with snack rye bread.

Spinach Artichoke Dip

Here's a creamy, delicious appetizer that's just the thing for special occasions. It's especially good served with Asiago cheese bread for dipping.

—JAN HABERSTICH WATERLOO, IOWA

PREP: 15 MIN.   **COOK:** 2 HOURS   **MAKES:** 3 CUPS

- 1 **can (14 ounces) water-packed artichoke hearts, rinsed, drained and chopped**
- 1 **cup fresh baby spinach, chopped**
- ½ **cup sour cream**
- ½ **cup mayonnaise**
- ½ **cup shredded part-skim mozzarella cheese**
- ½ **cup shredded Parmesan cheese**
- ⅓ **cup chopped red onion**
- ¼ **teaspoon garlic powder**
  Assorted crackers or breads

In a 1½-qt. slow cooker, combine the first eight ingredients. Cover and cook on low for 2-3 hours or until heated through. Serve with crackers or breads.

FAST FIX Minister's Delight

A friend gave me the recipe for this wonderful dessert, saying that a minister's wife fixed it every Sunday so she named it accordingly.

—MARY ANN POTTER
BLUE SPRINGS, MISSOURI

PREP: 5 MIN. **COOK:** 2 HOURS
MAKES: 10-12 SERVINGS

- 1 can (21 ounces) cherry or apple pie filling
- 1 package yellow cake mix (regular size)
- ½ cup butter, melted
- ⅓ cup chopped walnuts, optional

Place pie filling in a 1½-qt. slow cooker. Combine cake mix and butter (mixture will be crumbly); sprinkle over filling. Sprinkle with walnuts if desired. Cover and cook on low for 2-3 hours.

FAST FIX Seafood Cheese Dip

Here's a change of pace from many slow cooker dips. Shrimp and crab make it special.

—MICHELLE DOMM
ATLANTA, NEW YORK

PREP: 15 MIN. **COOK:** 1½ HOURS
MAKES: 5 CUPS

- 1 package (32 ounces) process cheese (Velveeta), cubed
- 2 cans (6 ounces each) lump crabmeat, drained
- 1 can (10 ounces) diced tomatoes and green chilies, undrained
- 1 cup frozen cooked salad shrimp, thawed
  French bread baguettes, sliced and toasted

In a greased 3-qt. slow cooker, combine the cheese, crab, tomatoes and shrimp. Cover and cook on low for 1½ to 2 hours or until cheese is melted, stirring occasionally. Serve with baguettes.

FAST FIX Hot Spiced Cherry Cider

This heartwarming cider is great to have simmering in the slow cooker after being out in the cold.

—MARLENE WICZEK
LITTLE FALLS, MINNESOTA

PREP: 5 MIN. **COOK:** 4 HOURS
MAKES: 4 QUARTS

- 1 gallon apple cider or juice
- 2 cinnamon sticks (3 inches)
- 2 packages (3 ounces each) cherry gelatin

Place cider in a 6-qt. slow cooker; add cinnamon sticks. Cover and cook on high for 3 hours. Stir in gelatin; cook 1 hour longer. Discard cinnamon sticks before serving.

Mulled Dr Pepper

When neighbors or friends visit us on a chilly evening, I'll serve this warm beverage with ham sandwiches and deviled eggs.

—BERNICE MORRIS
MARSHFIELD, MISSOURI

PREP: 10 MIN. **COOK:** 2 HOURS
MAKES: 8-10 SERVINGS

- 8 cups Dr Pepper
- ¼ cup packed brown sugar
- ¼ cup lemon juice
- ½ teaspoon ground allspice
- ½ teaspoon whole cloves
- ¼ teaspoon salt
- ¼ teaspoon ground nutmeg
- 3 cinnamon sticks (3 inches)

1. In a 3-qt. slow cooker, combine all ingredients.
2. Cover and cook on low for 2 hours or until heated through. Discard the cloves and the cinnamon sticks.

FAST FIX ▶ Marmalade Meatballs

When I brought this snappy recipe to work for a potluck, I started cooking the meatballs in the morning, and by lunch time they were ready. They disappeared fast!

—JEANNE KISS
GREENSBURG, PENNSYLVANIA

PREP: 10 MIN. **COOK:** 4 HOURS
MAKES: ABOUT 5 DOZEN

- 1 bottle (16 ounces) Catalina salad dressing
- 1 cup orange marmalade
- 3 tablespoons Worcestershire sauce
- ½ teaspoon crushed red pepper flakes
- 1 package (32 ounces) frozen fully cooked homestyle meatballs, thawed

In a 3-qt. slow cooker, combine the salad dressing, marmalade, Worcestershire sauce and pepper flakes. Stir in meatballs. Cover and cook on low for 4-5 hours or until heated through.

Cranberry Stuffed Apples

Cinnamon, nutmeg and walnuts add a homey autumn flavor to stuffed apples. The recipe makes a great dessert or after-school snack.

—GRACIELA SANDVIGEN
ROCHESTER, NEW YORK

PREP: 10 MIN. **COOK:** 4 HOURS
MAKES: 5 SERVINGS

- 5 medium apples
- ⅓ cup fresh or frozen cranberries, thawed and chopped
- ¼ cup packed brown sugar
- 2 tablespoons chopped walnuts
- ¼ teaspoon ground cinnamon
- ⅛ teaspoon ground nutmeg
  Whipped cream or vanilla ice cream, optional

1. Core apples, leaving bottoms intact. Peel top third of each apple; place in a 5-qt. slow cooker. Combine the cranberries, brown sugar, walnuts, cinnamon and nutmeg; spoon into apples.
2. Cover and cook on low for 4-5 hours or until apples are tender. Serve with whipped cream or ice cream if desired.

APPLE CORING TIPS

Use an apple corer or small sharp knife to core the apples. Be sure to leave the bottom whole so that the filling stays inside. To easily remove small bits of seed or core, try a melon baller.

Hot Chili Cheese Dip

To simplify party preparation, I use my slow cooker to create this thick, cheesy dip. Your guests won't believe how good it is!

—JEANIE CARRIGAN MADERA, CALIFORNIA

PREP: 20 MIN. **COOK:** 4 HOURS **MAKES:** 6 CUPS

- 1 medium onion, finely chopped
- 2 teaspoons canola oil
- 2 garlic cloves, minced
- 2 cans (15 ounces each) chili without beans
- 2 cups salsa
- 2 packages (3 ounces each) cream cheese, cubed
- 2 cans (2¼ ounces each) sliced ripe olives, drained
  Tortilla chips

1. In a small skillet, saute onion in oil until tender. Add garlic; cook 1 minute longer.

2. Transfer to a 3-qt. slow cooker. Stir in the chili, salsa, cream cheese and olives. Cover and cook on low for 4 hours or until heated through, stirring occasionally. Stir before serving with tortilla chips.

Gingered Pears

Thanks to my slow cooker, I can serve a special dessert without much effort at all. These tender pears feature a surprise filling of candied ginger and pecans.

—CATHERINE MUELLER ST. PAUL, MINNESOTA

PREP: 35 MIN. **COOK:** 4 HOURS **MAKES:** 6 SERVINGS

- ½ cup finely chopped crystallized ginger
- ¼ cup packed brown sugar
- ¼ cup chopped pecans
- 1½ teaspoons grated lemon peel
- 6 medium Bartlett or D'Anjou pears
- 2 tablespoons butter, cubed
  Vanilla ice cream and caramel ice cream topping, optional

1. In a small bowl, combine the ginger, brown sugar, pecans and lemon peel. Using a melon baller or long-handled spoon, core pears to within ¼-in. of bottom. Spoon ginger mixture into the center of each.

2. Place pears upright in a 5-qt. slow cooker. Top each with butter. Cover and cook on low for 4-5 hours or until tender. Serve with ice cream and caramel topping if desired.

Strawberry Rhubarb Sauce

My colorful fruit sauce features a delightful combination of rhubarb and strawberry flavors. It's the perfect addition to vanilla ice cream. I also like to serve this delicious sauce over pancakes.

—NANCY COWLISHAW BOISE, IDAHO

PREP: 15 MIN. **COOK:** 4¼ HOURS
MAKES: 4½ CUPS

- 6 **cups sliced fresh or frozen rhubarb, thawed**
- 1 **cup sugar**
- ½ **cup unsweetened apple juice**
- 3 **cinnamon sticks (3 inches)**
- ½ **teaspoon grated orange peel**
- ¼ **teaspoon ground ginger**
- 1 **pint fresh strawberries, halved**
  Vanilla ice cream

1. Place the rhubarb, sugar, juice, cinnamon sticks, orange peel and ginger in a 3-qt. slow cooker. Cover and cook on low for 4-5 hours or until rhubarb is tender.

2. Stir in the strawberries; cover and cook 15 minutes longer or until heated through. Discard the cinnamon sticks. Serve with ice cream.

Wassail Bowl Punch

All ages will enjoy this warming punch. The blend of spice, fruit and hot tea is scrumptious. You can assemble it before heading out for a winter activity and sip away the chill when you return. It's ready whenever you are.

—MARGARET HARMS
JENKINS, KENTUCKY

PREP: 10 MIN. **COOK:** 1 HOUR
MAKES: 3½ QUARTS

- 4 **cups hot brewed tea**
- 4 **cups cranberry juice**
- 4 **cups unsweetened apple juice**
- 2 **cups orange juice**
- 1 **cup sugar**
- ¾ **cup lemon juice**
- 3 **cinnamon sticks (3 inches)**
- 12 **whole cloves**

1. In a 5-qt. slow cooker, combine the first six ingredients. Place the cinnamon sticks and cloves on a double thickness of cheesecloth; bring up corners of cloth and tie with string to form a bag. Add to slow cooker.

2. Cover and cook on high 1 hour or until punch begins to boil. Discard spice bag. Serve warm.

Sweet Kahlua Coffee

PREP: 10 MIN. **COOK:** 3 HOURS
MAKES: 9 SERVINGS (2¼ QUARTS)

- 2 **quarts hot water**
- ½ **cup Kahlua (coffee liqueur)**
- ¼ **cup creme de cacao**
- 3 **tablespoons instant coffee granules**
- 2 **cups heavy whipping cream**
- ¼ **cup sugar**
- 1 **teaspoon vanilla extract**
- 2 **tablespoons grated chocolate**

1. In a 4-qt. slow cooker, combine the water, Kahlua, creme de cacao and coffee granules. Cover and cook on low for 3-4 hours or until heated through.
2. In a large bowl, beat cream until it begins to thicken. Add sugar and vanilla; beat until stiff peaks form.
3. Ladle coffee into mugs. Garnish with whipped cream and grated chocolate.

FAST FIX ▶ Party Meatballs

Meatballs are always great for parties. This is an easy twist on the usual recipe, and it's very fast to make.

—DEBBIE PAULSEN
APOLLO BEACH, FLORIDA

PREP: 10 MIN. **COOK:** 3 HOURS
MAKES: ABOUT 5 DOZEN

- 1 **package (32 ounces) frozen fully cooked homestyle meatballs, thawed**
- 1 **bottle (14 ounces) ketchup**
- ¼ **cup A.1. steak sauce**
- 1 **tablespoon minced garlic**
- 1 **teaspoon Dijon mustard**

Place meatballs in a 3-qt. slow cooker. In a small bowl, combine the ketchup, steak sauce, garlic and mustard. Pour over meatballs. Cover and cook on low for 3-4 hours or until meatballs are heated through.

Slow-Cooked Applesauce

My sweet and chunky applesauce is perfect as a snack or served alongside roasted turkey or pork.

—SUSAN WASSON
MONTGOMERY, NEW YORK

PREP: 20 MIN. **COOK:** 6 HOURS
MAKES: 12 CUPS

- 6 **pounds apples (about 18 medium), peeled and sliced**
- 1 **cup sugar**
- 1 **cup water**
- 1 **teaspoon salt**
- 1 **teaspoon ground cinnamon**
- ¼ **cup butter, cubed**
- 2 **teaspoons vanilla extract**

In a 5-qt. slow cooker, combine the apples, sugar, water, salt and cinnamon. Cover and cook on low for 6-8 hours or until tender. Stir in butter and vanilla. Mash if desired. Serve warm or cold.

"I always have this drink ready in the slow cooker at my annual holiday open house. I set out the whipped cream and grated chocolate in festive dishes so guests can help themselves."

—RUTH GRUCHOW
YORBA LINDA, CALIFORNIA

FAST FIX ▶ Nacho Salsa Dip

Here's a zesty dip that's an easy solution for almost any get-together and allows me to spend more time with my guests. I always have requests to bring it when my husband and I attend parties or potlucks.
—**SALLY HULL** HOMESTEAD, FLORIDA

PREP: 15 MIN. **COOK:** 3 HOURS **MAKES:** 7 CUPS

- 1 **pound ground beef**
- ⅓ **cup chopped onion**
- 2 **pounds process cheese (Velveeta), cubed**
- 1 **jar (16 ounces) chunky salsa**
- ¼ **teaspoon garlic powder**
  Tortilla chips or cubed French bread

1. In a large skillet, cook beef and onion over medium heat until meat is no longer pink; drain well.
2. Transfer to a greased 3-qt. slow cooker; stir in the cheese, salsa and garlic powder. Cover and cook on low for 3-4 hours or until heated through. Stir; serve warm with tortilla chips or cubed bread.

Hot Holiday Cider

This slightly tart apple cider is so nice for a holiday open house. It fills the room with a wonderful aroma.
—**CINDY TOBIN** WEST BEND, WISCONSIN

PREP: 10 MIN. **COOK:** 3 HOURS
MAKES: 14 SERVINGS (3½ QUARTS)

- 2 **quarts apple cider or juice**
- 1 **quart cranberry juice**
- 2 **cups orange juice**
- ½ **cup sugar**
- 3 **cinnamon sticks (3 inches)**
- 1 **teaspoon whole allspice**
- 1 **teaspoon whole cloves**

1. In a 5- or 6-qt. slow cooker, combine the cider, juices and sugar. Place the cinnamon sticks, allspice and cloves on a double thickness of cheesecloth; bring up corners of cloth and tie with string to form a bag. Place in slow cooker.
2. Cover and cook on low for 3-4 hours or until heated through. Discard spice bag. Serve warm.

Rice Pudding

For an old-fashioned sweet treat just like Grandma made, try my rich and delicious rice pudding. It's made wonderfully light with whipped cream folded in at the end.

—JENNIFER BENNETT
SALEM, INDIANA

PREP: 15 MIN.
COOK: 3 HOURS + CHILLING
MAKES: 4 SERVINGS

- 1¼ cups 2% milk
- ½ cup sugar
- ½ cup uncooked converted rice
- ½ cup raisins
- 2 eggs, lightly beaten
- 1 teaspoon ground cinnamon
- 1 teaspoon butter, melted
- 1 teaspoon vanilla extract
- ¾ teaspoon lemon extract
- 1 cup heavy whipping cream, whipped
  Additional whipped cream and ground cinnamon, optional

1. In a 1½-qt. slow cooker, combine the first nine ingredients. Cover and cook on low for 2 hours; stir. Cover and cook 1-2 hours longer or until rice is tender. Transfer to a small bowl; cool. Refrigerate until chilled.
2. Just before serving, fold in whipped cream. Garnish each serving with additional cream and cinnamon if desired.

FAST FIX Cheddar-Swiss Reuben Spread

You'll need only five ingredients to stir up this hearty dip that tastes like a Reuben sandwich. It's requested at all the gatherings we attend.

—PAM ROHR TROY, OHIO

PREP: 5 MIN. **COOK:** 3 HOURS
MAKES: ABOUT 5 CUPS

- 2½ cups cubed cooked corned beef
- 1 can (14 ounces) sauerkraut, rinsed and well drained
- 2 cups (8 ounces) shredded Swiss cheese
- 2 cups (8 ounces) shredded cheddar cheese
- 1 cup mayonnaise
  Snack rye bread

In a 3-qt. slow cooker, combine the first five ingredients. Cover and cook on low for 3-4 hours or until heated through and cheese is melted, stirring occasionally. Serve warm with rye bread.

FAST FIX Tropical Tea

Try simmering up a batch of fragrant, flavorful tea for your next family gathering. It's sure to chase away winter's chill.

—IRENE HELEN ZUNDEL
CARMICHAELS, PENNSYLVANIA

PREP: 15 MIN. **COOK:** 2 HOURS
MAKES: 10 SERVINGS (2½ QUARTS)

- 6 cups boiling water
- 6 individual tea bags
- 1½ cups orange juice
- 1½ cups unsweetened pineapple juice
- ⅓ cup sugar
- 1 medium navel orange, halved and sliced
- 2 tablespoons honey

1. In a 5-qt. slow cooker, combine boiling water and tea bags. Cover and let stand for 5 minutes. Discard tea bags. Stir in remaining ingredients.
2. Cover and cook on low for 2-4 hours or until heated through. Serve warm.

Tangy Barbecue Wings

When I took these savory chicken wings to work, they were gone before I even got a bite! Spicy ketchup, vinegar, molasses and honey create a tangy sauce that's lip-smacking good.
—**SHERRY PITZER** TROY, MISSOURI

PREP: 1½ HOURS **COOK:** 3 HOURS
MAKES: ABOUT 4 DOZEN

- 5 **pounds chicken wings**
- 2½ **cups hot and spicy ketchup**
- ⅔ **cup white vinegar**
- ½ **cup plus 2 tablespoons honey**
- ½ **cup molasses**
- 1 **teaspoon salt**
- 1 **teaspoon Worcestershire sauce**
- ½ **teaspoon onion powder**
- ½ **teaspoon chili powder**
- ½ **to 1 teaspoon liquid smoke, optional**

1. Cut chicken wings into three sections; discard wing tip sections. Place chicken wings in two greased 15-in. x 10-in. x 1-in. baking pans. Bake, uncovered, at 375° for 30 minutes; drain. Turn wings; bake 20-25 minutes longer or until juices run clear.
2. Meanwhile, in a large saucepan, combine the ketchup, vinegar, honey, molasses, salt, Worcestershire sauce, onion powder and chili powder. Add liquid smoke if desired. Bring to a boil. Reduce heat; simmer, uncovered, for 25-30 minutes.
3. Drain wings; place a third of them in a 5-qt. slow cooker. Top with about 1 cup sauce. Repeat layers twice. Cover and cook on low for 3-4 hours. Stir before serving.

Editor's Note: *Uncooked chicken wing sections (wingettes) may be substituted for whole chicken wings.*

Hot Fudge Cake

A cake baked in a slow cooker may seem unusual. But smiles around the dinner table will prove just how tasty it is. Sometimes, for a change of pace, I substitute butterscotch chips for chocolate.

—**MARLEEN ADKINS**
PLACENTIA, CALIFORNIA

PREP: 20 MIN. **COOK:** 4 HOURS
MAKES: 8 SERVINGS

- 1¾ **cups packed brown sugar, divided**
- 1 **cup all-purpose flour**
- 6 **tablespoons baking cocoa, divided**
- 2 **teaspoons baking powder**
- ½ **teaspoon salt**
- ½ **cup 2% milk**
- 2 **tablespoons butter, melted**
- ½ **teaspoon vanilla extract**
- 1½ **cups semisweet chocolate chips**
- 1¾ **cups boiling water**
  Vanilla ice cream

1. In a small bowl, combine 1 cup brown sugar, flour, 3 tablespoons cocoa, baking powder and salt. Combine the milk, butter and vanilla; stir into dry ingredients just until combined.
2. Spread into a 3-qt. slow cooker coated with cooking spray. Sprinkle with chocolate chips. In another bowl, combine the remaining brown sugar and cocoa; stir in boiling water. Pour over batter (do not stir).
3. Cover and cook on high for 4 to 4½ hours or until a toothpick inserted near center of cake comes out clean. Serve warm with ice cream.

Editor's Note: *This recipe does not use eggs.*

General Recipe Index

Alphabetical Recipe Index